AF480110

'PUG,'
'FIREBALL,'
AND COMPANY:

116 YEARS OF PROFESSIONAL BASEBALL
IN DES MOINES, IOWA

Steve Dunn

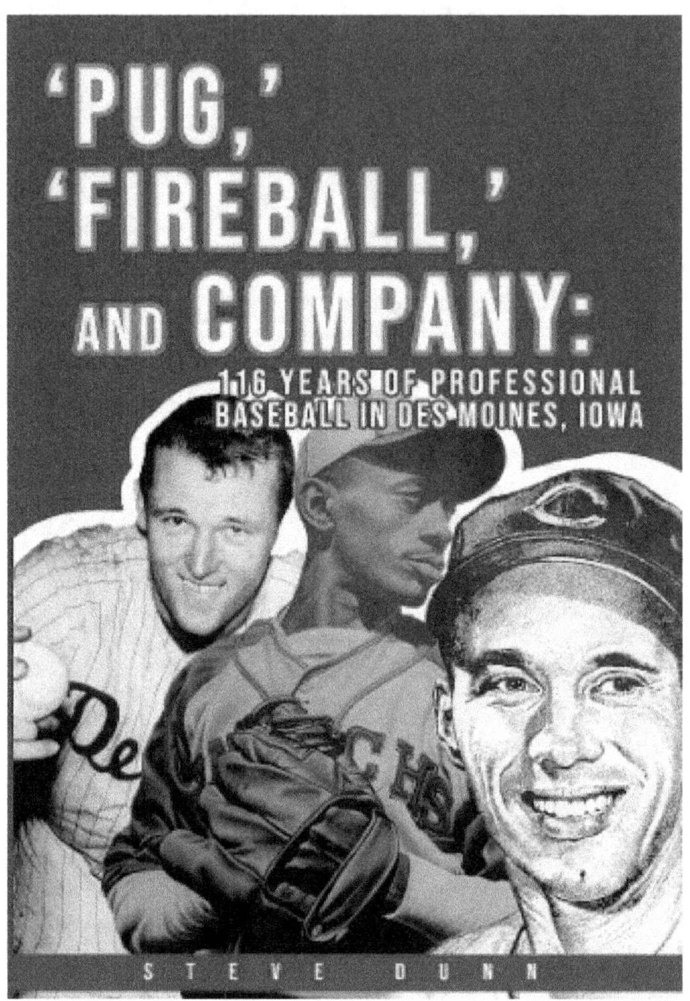

From left
Jack Kerrigan (Courtesy of Scott Sailor/Iowa Cubs),
Satchel Paige (Courtesy of NoirTech Research, Inc.),
Bob Feller (Courtesy of Steve Dunn)

Dedication

This labor of love is dedicated to my parents, Lloyd and Eloise, who watched my Little League games; took me to Chicago Cubs games at Wrigley Field in Chicago, Crosley Field in Cincinnati, and Forbes Field in Pittsburgh; and allowed me to listen to the Cubs on the car radio when we were driving across Illinois and Iowa to visit relatives.

Table of Contents

Foreword

I have been part of professional baseball in central Iowa for forty years. I have been an intern, an operations manager, a general manager, a team president, and an owner in that time frame.

I've seen countless stars of the game play in my park. I've created crazy promotions to market the team. I've been tied to the Chicago Cubs as my major league affiliate all forty of those years. I've knocked down an old stadium and built a new stadium on top of it. The Iowa Cubs and the many other events that I've held at the stadium have drawn over 18 million fans in those forty years.

The irony of all of that history is that it is a small percentage of professional baseball that central Iowa has experienced. Steve Dunn has presented a very detailed accounting of that long baseball history in this book. The history of professional baseball includes a long list of Hall of Famers who have played in Des Moines. It includes Des Moines' role in Negro League baseball.

This book also chronicles all the different locations of stadiums throughout the Des Moines area and lists all the different teams that have been based in Des Moines. I think you will be very surprised to learn about all the significant professional baseball events that have occurred in central Iowa. Steve gives a great accounting of all things professional baseball In Des Moines. I'm glad that I've been a small part of it.

Sam Bernabe
President/general manager
Iowa Cubs

Chapter 1

*Hawkeyes open play
near Raccoon River in 1887;
Prohibitionists win pennant in 1888*

With a few exceptions, professional baseball has been played in Des Moines since 1887. That's not counting the amateur clubs, such as the Capital City Club, which dates back to 1866, one year after the Civil War. A year later, Des Moines had nine baseball clubs.

Des Moines' professional clubs have had such names as the Boosters, Bruins, Oaks, Prohibitionists, Undertakers and currently, Iowa Cubs, or I-Cubs for short.

Des Moines Demons Courtesy: Scott Sailor/Iowa Cubs

Whatever the name, Des Moines' professional baseball teams have entertained millions of fans at nine venues throughout the city. Since the I-Cubs became a triple-A affiliate in 1969, the club has drawn 18,712,768 fans under five ownership groups. During twelve of those seasons, the I-Cubs attracted at least 500,000 spectators, the gold standard of minor league baseball.

So how have the city's ties to professional baseball evolved?

In September 1886, prominent Des Moines attorney William Park and a group of businessmen invited organizer and manager Will Bryan of Charleston, South Carolina, to establish a team in Des Moines. "He is a gentleman who has devoted himself for years to base ball [sic] matters, and is eminently fitted for the work," the *Iowa State Register* claimed a day before Bryan arrived in Des Moines.[1]

1888 DSM team (Courtesy: John Liepa)

Park, the treasurer, and club secretary Charles Sherman, son of Des Moines businessman Hoyt Sherman and nephew of Civil War general William Tecumseh Sherman, were the most active officers.[2] W.R. Warfield, a well-known grocer, was president, and A.M. Wright, the manager of the Continental Clothing House, served as vice president. The other directors and stockholders were James Berryhill, Dr. E.F. Cruttenden, Walter McCain, and John Chase. "The men who are interested in this are solid business men, who see the importance and advantage a professional club would give to Des Moines," the *Iowa State Register* wrote. "It would be the means of bringing to the city from many new sources money and people. The city now has a chance which seldom comes to any place of securing admission to a good league, and the opportunity should not be lost."[3]

On October 13, Des Moines was admitted to the Northwestern League along with Milwaukee, Minneapolis, and St. Paul. Soon afterwards, Bryan started to obtain players for the 1887 season, "picking the best that could be secured from the several leagues."[4] The new franchise was organized as a stock company with $5,000 of paid up capital stock and plans to increase the amount to $20,000. Ten businessmen took $500 each in stock. A total of $2,000 was put aside for player contracts. Another $2,000 was invested in the new ballpark and other buildings on SW Seventh Street. A total of $1,000 was earmarked for general expenses.[5]

By the end of 1886, the new Des Moines franchise had signed Bryan and ten players as fans eagerly looked forward to professional baseball. In fact, Bryan observed that "the people here are all worked up over ball, and even the awful cold weather does not keep the fever down."[6] The thirty-two-year-old Bryan managed first in 1882 at Council Bluffs, where he built the ballpark and organized the team. After managing the Leadville Blues, he played for Omaha and Evansville, Indiana. Then he organized the Southern League and the Nashville, Tennessee, ballclub in the same league in 1885. When he left to go to Macon, Georgia, Nashville was in second place. Under his guidance, Macon climbed from seventh to fourth place in the Southern League in 1885. After the season, Charleston, South Carolina, hired him to organize a team in that city.[7]

Born on July 26, 1851, in Howard County, Indiana, William Park and his family moved soon afterward to the Indianola area where his father Andrew farmed. After graduating from Simpson College in Indianola, he enrolled in the College of Law at the University of Michigan at Ann Arbor, Michigan. One source says Park graduated from the Michigan law school.[8] Another source claims a severe illness prevented him from completing his law course after eight months of study.[9]

Park was appointed deputy clerk of the U.S. Circuit Court in Des Moines in 1873, a post he held for seven years. After he was admitted to the bar in July 1880, Park was associated with attorney W.S. Clark for a short time, and then he formed a partnership with Fred Lehman in 1882. The association with Lehman lasted for nine years until Lehman moved to St. Louis to become an attorney for the Wabash Railroad Company. Park's next partnership with W.E. Odell ended in January 1897; then he and attorney C.A. Ballerich joined forces.

Park served as attorney for the State Traveling Men's Association, Northwestern Railroad, and Iowa Savings & Loan Association among other organizations. He also was president of the Polk County Bar Association and Commercial Exchange. In addition, Park belonged to the Independent Order of Odd Fellows, Benevolent Protective Order of Elks, and Knights of Pythias of Iowa.

He and his wife, Sophia, had seven children: Ernest, Bessie, Howard, William, Helen, Andrew, and Philip, who died at age three-and-a-half.

The new team called the Hawkeyes had enough money to hold spring training in mid-February 1887 in New Orleans. Their exhibition schedule included games against Marshalltown-native Adrian "Cap" Anson's Chicago White Stockings in Little Rock and Hot Springs, Arkansas, and Chris Van Der Ahe's St. Louis Browns in St. Louis.[10]

A publication called *Persinger's Saturday Times* that catered to the city's elite featured a four-column, front-page story about the Hawkeyes on March 26, 1887. The spread also included portraits and short bios of each of the twelve players on the team.[11] "What made this article unusual is that it appeared in a society paper read primarily by Des Moines' elite and with a large female readership that usually ignored sports," Iowa baseball historian John Liepa noted.[12]

Captain and second baseman Tim Brosnan played with Bryan at Charleston in 1886. He finished the season at Brockton in the New England League where he hit .315 to lead all second basemen. *Persinger's Saturday Times* described the five-foot-eight-inch, 160-pound infielder as "a quick, sharp hitter, and a fine baserunner."[13]

Charles Faatz, a five-foot-ten-inch, 180-pound catcher, had previously played with Oswego, Milwaukee, and Minneapolis. "He is a fine catcher and hard hitter," *Persinger's* said.[14] Another catcher, six-foot-two-inch, 170-pound Elmer Sutcliffe, played for the Chicago White Stockings when they won the National League pennant in 1885. "He is a great catcher and fielder, a hard hitter and a fine base runner," the newspaper said.[15]

Sam Larocque, a five-foot-eight-inch, 190-pound fielder, was called "the hardest hitter in the league."[16] From May 1 to July 24 last season, Larocque collected seventy-eight hits, including five home runs, eight triples, and eighteen doubles. "For a man weighing 190 pounds, he is a wonderful base runner, for he has twenty-four stolen bases to his credit in fifty-one games," *Persinger's* said.[17]

Another fielder, five-foot-eleven-inch, 190-pound Guerdon Whitely, had played for the Chicago Reserves, Boston of the National League, and Lynn in the New England League. He was described as "the longest and surest thrower from the out field [sic] in the country, and is the longest thrower in the Northwestern League."[18]

First baseman M.J. Bresnahan, six-feet-two and 199 pounds, hit .285 for Haverhill, which finished four and a half games behind first place Portland in the New England League in 1886. *Persinger's* described Bresnahan as "a terrific hitter, two- and three-base hits being his favorites."[19]

Another fielder, five-foot-eight-inch, 170-pound Bill Van Dyke, played for Oshkosh and Lincoln in 1886. The newspaper called Van Dyke "one of the best base runners in the profession, and a good batter."[20] "He is a fine thrower and a wonderfully quick fielder and will fill right field to a nicety."[21]

Meanwhile, third baseman Billy Alvord, five-feet-ten inches, 187 pounds, played for Bridgeport in the New England League in 1886. "He is a fine fielder, hard hitter, and the finest thrower across the diamond from third to first there is in the profession," *Persinger's* wrote.[22] Catcher Harry Sage caught fifty-five out of sixty games for St. Paul in 1886. "He is a terror to base runners, as his throwing to bases is perfect," the newspaper said.[23]

Pitcher Frank Wells, five-foot-seven inches, 145 pounds, played for Southern League champion Atlanta in 1886. "He is remarkable for his nerve and staying qualities, which won him seven, fourteen and fifteen inning games last season," *Persinger's* said. "He is a prize, and much is looked for from him this season."[24] Less was known about pitcher Samuel Bittle, who was discovered by Faatz. "He is [sic] terrific speed and good control of the ball, is young and ambitious, with nerves to back it—all good qualities for a successful pitcher," *Persinger's* concluded.[25] Another hurler, J.H. Campbell, five-feet- seven inches, 155 pounds, played with Staten Island in the Eastern League and Plattsburg in the New York State League the previous season. "He is practicing daily and says he will be in good shape when the season opens," *Persinger's* noted.[26]

Season tickets cost twelve dollars for sixty home games. The price of single-game tickets was twenty-five cents and fifty cents for reserved seats behind the batter.

On Thursday, April 14, 1887, the Des Moines Hawkeyes defeated the Omaha Omahogs, 20-3, in the first game played at Athletic Park on Southwest Seventh Street near the Raccoon River. The Hawkeyes outhit the visitors from the Western League twenty-one to three. Five Des Moines players had three hits apiece: third baseman Larocque, catcher Sutcliffe, shortstop Alvord, center fielder Whiteley, and second baseman/captain Brosnan.

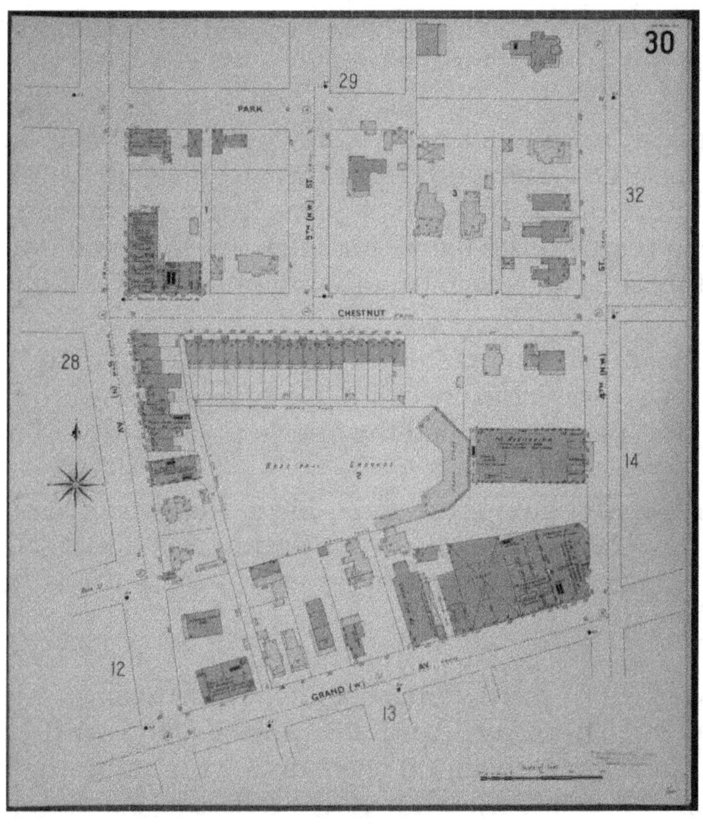

DSM ballpark 1901 (Courtesy: Sanborn Fire Insurance Map)

Whitely hit the first home run in Hawkeyes history with a two-run shot in the six-run second inning. Des Moines also put up crooked numbers in the fourth inning (three runs), sixth inning (four runs), and eighth inning (five runs). Whitely, Larocque, Alvord, and Brosnan also collected doubles in the Hawkeyes' opener.

About 2,000 people turned out for the historic occasion, which lasted two hours and ten minutes. The game had only one umpire, which was not unusual for the times.

That night, a banquet with a six-course meal was held for the team at the White Elephant. After the meal, cigars were distributed and a male quartet "furnished some excellent music."[27] A local doctor also thanked the team "for the work they had done while on their [preseason] Southern trip, their gentlemanly conduct, etc."[28]

The Hawkeyes completed their season opening three-game sweep with a 9-5 victory over the Omahogs on Saturday, April 16. Nearly 2,000 people watched the one-hour-and-fifty-minute game.

Before the first game, the *Iowa State Register* dispelled rumors that the Des Moines Base Ball Association was dissatisfied with the team's manager and that there were "dissentions among the players."[29]

Rain washed out two games against Cap Anson's Chicago White Stockings on Thursday, April 28, and Friday, April 29, in Des Moines. Approximately 2,500 spectators with umbrellas and rubber coats were on hand the first day when the game was called in Chicago's half of the fourth inning with the White Stockings ahead, 1-0. "It was the first time many of our people had seen the Chicagos and they thought it was worth the time and money spent to see Anson and his young bloods, along with [Ed] Williamson, [Fred] Pfeffer and [Tom] Burns the old standbys," a special correspondent for *The Sporting News* said.[30] The next day, about 3,000 people attended the abbreviated game that was called in the bottom of the second inning with Chicago ahead, 6-5. "The grounds were so slippery that it was impossible to do anything at all," *The Sporting*

News reported. "Several errors were made on both sides, which accounts for the runs more than the heavy hitting."[31]

The Hawkeyes needed ten innings to defeat St. Paul, 6-4, in the first Northwestern League game at Athletic Park on April 30, 1887. "Fully two thousand people were present at Athletic Park yesterday afternoon, and they witnessed one of the finest exhibitions of ball playing they will have the pleasure of seeing this year," the *Iowa State Register* reported. "The audience was very enthusiastic and applauded every good play, whether made by the home team or visitors, and when the eighth inning showed the score a tie, the people were fairly insane."[32]

Batting first, the Hawkeyes scored twice in the tenth inning to break the 4-4 tie. The first batter Sage singled, stole second, and advanced to third on a slow roller. Four batters later, he scored when the St. Paul center fielder mishandled Alvord's fly ball. Alvord then reached second on the St. Paul pitcher's balk and scored on Whitely's double. In the bottom of the tenth, St. Paul got a runner to second but could not score.

Hawkeye hurler Frank Wells and St. Paul pitcher Lee Viau each went the distance and allowed nine hits in the two-hour-and-fifteen-minute contest. Wells struck out eight, walked four, and gave up only one earned run. St. Paul's nine hits included a triple by shortstop Jack Crooks, and doubles by right fielder Clarence Murphy and catcher Len Stockwell.

Des Moines' nine hits included a three-base hit by Whitely and doubles by Whitely, Brosnan, and Van Dyke. St. Paul mounds man Viau, who hit fifth in the order, struck out six, walked two, and gave up only two earned runs.

By June, the injury-riddled Hawkeyes had dropped to third place. Despite adding William "Wild Bill" Hutchison, Australian-born Joe Quinn, William "Bug" Holliday, and Danny Stearns to the roster and replacing Bryan, the club continued to struggle. [33]

The Hawkeyes finished fourth at 73-47, four-and-half games behind first-place Oshkosh, in their first season under managers Bryan and Charlie Morton. Van Dyke led the Northwestern League that year in stolen bases with 108.[34]

Des Moines and nine other clubs formed the Western Association on Wednesday, October 26, 1887, in Chicago.[35] "The association is a sort of catchpenny affair, which will depend on Sunday games for sustenance and it is doubtful if it will merit or receive sufficient patronage to keep it alive," the *Chicago Tribune* predicted.[36]

In 1888, the team was renamed the Prohibitionists and was expected to win the Western Association title. In January, the *Iowa State Register* predicted the ballclub would come out on top because it was "the strongest and best balanced" in terms of batting, fielding, and baserunning.[37] A correspondent for *The Sporting News* said a month later that "Des Moines rather has the call for first place from all appearances."[38] Perhaps expressing a bit of self-doubt, the correspondent added, "It is rather a small town for so expensive a team, unless they turn out phenomenal audiences to witness the games, which they should with such a team."[39]

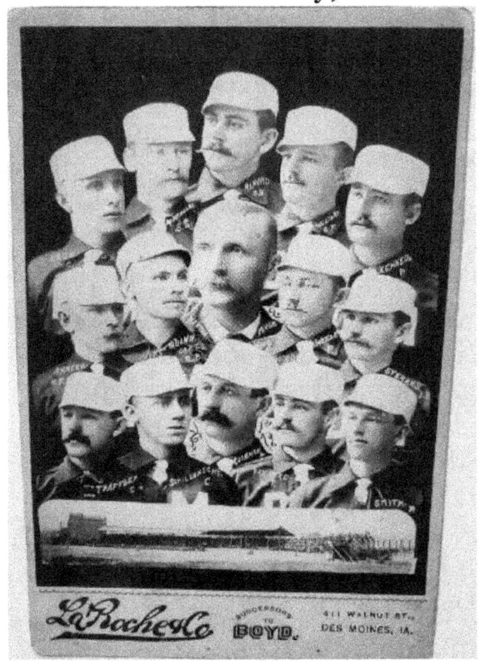

1889 Prohibitionists
(Courtesy: John Liepa)

About three weeks before the season opener, the *Iowa State Register* reported the Western Association board of directors had hired four umpires who could not be removed "except for drunkenness and dishonesty."[40] The four arbiters were W.

Fessenden, Charles Powers, Steve Hagan, and John Brennan. This year, the newspaper noted, the rest of the Western Association would copy Des Moines' practice of showing the complete score by innings of all games on the scoreboard.

On Saturday, April 7, 1888, the Prohibitionists swamped the Cigar-makers, 53-3, in a preseason tune-up. The pitchers and catchers for Des Moines played only two innings apiece.

An afternoon parade featuring the Des Moines and St. Paul teams in carriages kicked off Opening Day festivities that season. The entourage was led by a platoon of police officers and the twenty-piece First Regiment band. "The parade . . . was quite a showy affair and attracted a great deal of notice along the line of march," the *Iowa State Register* observed. "The band was stationed in the grandstand during the game and discoursed some very sweet music."[41]

Approximately two thousand people—seventy-six more than the previous year— were on hand at 3:30 p.m. to see the Prohibitionists beat their northern opponents, 6-2. Des Moines scored twice in the first and second innings, once in the fourth, and once in the fifth inning. St. Paul scored once in the first and fourth innings. "There was very little kicking on the part of either club at the umpire's decisions," the *Iowa State Register* noted.[42]

On June 2, *The Sporting News* in St. Louis published short bios with sketches of the players and manager Charlie Morton. Morton, thirty-three, had managed several clubs in the East, West, and South before coming to Des Moines. "Besides being a good manager, he is a good ball player and a thorough gentleman," the publication wrote.[43] Left-handed pitcher Ed Cushman, thirty-six, had previously played for Milwaukee, Toledo, Ohio, and Erie, Pennsylvania. "His greatest feat was when he made two two-baggers off a pitcher and every night for a week after that a telegraph boy could be seen running up the steps of his boarding house with telegrams of congratulations," *The Sporting News* said, "and he hardly had time to pitch a game of ball so many telegrams did he receive."[44]

Pitcher Ted Kennedy, twenty-three, had started his pro career with Keokuk. In 1887, he played for La Crosse, Wisconsin, but was released near the end of the season. "He is very heavy on his feet," the St. Louis publication reported. "Some say he weighs a ton when he starts to run the bases."[45] Catcher Bill Traffley, twenty-eight, played for International League champion Toronto in 1887. He was described as "a good batter" who "will no doubt prove a tower of strength to the club."[46]

Catcher Harry Sage, twenty-four, played for St. Paul and Rock Island, Illinois, before coming to the Prohibitionists. *The Sporting News* praised him profusely: "Harry is one of the greatest backstops in the minor leagues and would sooner catch a man running to second than eat a good dinner."[47] Shortstop Jimmy Macullar, thirty-three, played for Topeka in 1887 after stints with Cincinnati and Baltimore. "He will lend great help to Des Moines in securing the pennant," *The Sporting News* predicted.[48]

Left fielder Bill Van Dyke, twenty-four, was described as "one of the greatest of fielders" and "the second best base runner to [Bug] Holliday."[49] Holliday, the Prohibitionists' twenty-one-year-old center fielder, was a "great fielder, batter and base runner."[50] His moustache also caught the attention of the publication known eventually as "the Bible of baseball." "Bug has a moustache of which he is very proud and he never gets tired of twirling it to the great amusement of the other players," *The Sporting News* wrote.[51]

George "Orator" Shafer, thirty-six, was so upset after Des Moines was shut out in the last game of the season in 1887 that "he refused to ride down the elevator with other members of the team and slowly wended his way home in a baggage wagon."[52] Third baseman Billy Alvord, a St. Louis native, started his baseball career in Vincennes, Indiana, and was sought by Chicago and New York in the National League after the 1887 season. Dan Stearns, twenty-six, "a heavy hitter and fine fielder," played for Macon, Georgia, in 1886, and Topeka in 1887.[53] Another St. Louis native, twenty-five-year-old second baseman Joe Quinn, was described as "a good batter, a fine fielder and a very fast base runner."[54] The team also had a mascot in the form of a large pelican. Before a game, he "spreads his enormous wings and shows himself a fitting emblem of the strength and character of the team," *The Sporting News* wrote.[55]

The Prohibitionists captured the Western Association pennant by beating the Kansas City Blues 4-1 and 5-3 in early October after finishing first with a 73-40 mark during the regular season. On October 11, 1888, two parades and a banquet were held to honor the team. Holliday batted .309, stole a team-high sixty-five bases, and tied Shafer for the league lead with 147 hits that season. Quinn hit .309 and stole forty bags. Shafer batted .307 and pilfered thirty-one bases.

Four Des Moines pitchers won at least twelve games. Bill Hutchison compiled a 23-10 record and 1.48 earned run average, completed thirty-two games, and struck out 204 hitters. Ed Cushman finished 20-12 with a 1.34 earned run average and thirty-one complete games. Ted Kennedy sported a 12-4 mark with fifteen complete games. Fred Smith won fourteen of twenty-seven decisions, had a 2.07 earned run average, and finished twenty-six games. By year's end, however, only two players remained on the roster of the championship team after the sale of its best players, such as Hutchison and Holliday.[56]

After reaching the pinnacle of success in 1888, the Prohibitionists finished in the Western Association cellar the next season with a 41-77 record, forty-and-a-half games out of first place. "Professional baseball had come to Iowa's capital city," Iowa baseball historian John Liepa concluded. "However, the first three seasons showed inconsistency at both the player and managerial level as well as a need for closer professional oversight of finances. Despite Des Moines' problems, the popularity of baseball throughout Iowa flourished."[57]

The team got off to a fast start in 1890, splitting a two-game series with the Cleveland Spiders, winners of the 1889 Temple Cup, the equivalent of today's World Series trophy.[58]

Despite a number of promotions, however, the club's financial situation worsened as the season wore on. On August 10, 1890, the

Des Moines franchise and players were sold to a group in Lincoln, Nebraska, where the team finished the season. For the second straight season, the team finished in the Western Association cellar, thirty-two games out of first place.

A new Western Association franchise for Des Moines was awarded to Sidney Frick in January 1894. A second ballpark was built in Valley Junction (now known as West Des Moines) for the Prohibitionists' Sunday games. Under managers Hugh Nicol and Bill Traffley, the Prohibitionists finished second to last with a 55-73 record. They improved to 71-55 the next season, finishing in third place in the Western Association.

In February 1896, Sidney Frick sold the franchise to real estate mogul William Bennett, who retained Traffley as the team's manager. "Base ball (sic) enthusiasts as a general rule are pleased with the change," the *Des Moines Leader* said. "No one has reason to complain of the class of ball Frick has furnished, for it has been good, but they have complained that at critical times when the expenditure of a little money might have brought the pennant to Des Moines, he has refused to stand by Traffley and spend the necessary amount to secure the services of additional players to land the rag."[59]

Frick had come to Des Moines approximately three years earlier as a relative unknown "with hardly enough means to engage in the real estate business," the *Leader* added. "He succeeded in a measure, and when the organization of the Western Association was talked of he decided to go into the base ball [sic] business."[60]

Confessing he did not know a foul tip from an out at second base, Frick let Traffley run the Prohibitionists the first season and made at least $5,000.[61] However, Traffley did not have as much control of the club in 1895, and as a result, the players said, "Des Moines lost the pennant after it had been won."[62]

A Polk County native, Bennett grew up on a farm four miles west of the capital. After making a "neat fortune" farming himself, he moved to Des Moines and acquired valuable property between Des

Moines and Valley Junction and immediately west of Greenwood Park in Des Moines.[63]

Despite having little baseball experience, Bennett became interested in the game and very popular with the players. "It is the general opinion he [Bennett] will make a careful, painstaking and liberal manager who will become popular with the base ball [sic] going public and do much to create a growth of base ball [sic] sentiment and popularity in the city," the *Des Moines Leader* said.[64]

The team announced a twelve-game exhibition schedule starting April 2, 3, and 4 against Pittsburgh and ending May 4 and 5 against the Minneapolis Millers of the Western League. The only road games on the preseason schedule were at St. Joseph on April 13 and at St. Paul on April 18 and 19.

By mid-March 1896, the Prohibitionists' new uniforms and bats had arrived in Des Moines. The uniforms were described as "by far the prettiest Des Moines players have worn on the field."[65] The *Des Moines Leader* noted the club's new made-to-order bats were "of all sizes, weights, and shapes."[66]

President Bennett was also upgrading the Prohibitionists' Sunday ballpark in Valley Junction. A long cinder path was built along the railroad tracks where special trains stopped. A wire fence was removed so that fans could get to and from the ballpark without walking back to the gate. Bennett also had another entrance built so crowds could get in and out of the ballpark faster. Seats were widened, and a water-tight roof was added.

A parade preceded the Prohibitionists' first game of the 1896 season against the Minneapolis Millers on Saturday, April 4. Led by police and the Des Moines Union band, the parade also included carriages with Governor Drake, state officers, Des Moines mayor John MacVicar, city council members, city officials, the players, and firefighters. When they arrived at the ballpark, the governor and city officials gave short speeches, followed by the governor's ceremonial first pitch.

Traffley's team knocked off the Millers, 5-2, with approximately two thousand people on hand. "Des Moines . . . demonstrated beyond doubt that the team is much stronger than last year," the *Des Moines Leader* said.[67] The Prohibitionists jumped out to a 2-0 lead in the first inning when Pete Lohman's two-out triple drove in Judge McCredie and Lohman scored on Byron McKibben's double. Des Moines added two runs in the fourth when McKibben walked, Eddie Hickey tripled, and Traffley drove in Hickey with a single. Minneapolis scored once in the sixth and once in the eighth inning to cut the deficit to two at 4-2. The Prohibitionists padded their lead in the ninth when Tom Letcher singled with two outs and drove in Hickey from second base. The *Des Moines Leader* described McCredie as "a prime favorite" of the crowd, "a swift player" at shortstop, a "hard hitter," and "a phenomenal thrower."[68]

Despite the team's winning ways, attendance failed to meet expectations, causing Traffley to tell the *Des Moines Leader* on June 22 that he and president Bennett were close to giving up the franchise. "When we were down in fifth place last year, we were getting better patronage and still the crowds were complaining because we did not play better ball," Traffley told reporters. "People said if we would get together a paying team, our patronage would increase."[69]

Admitting that the threat to move the team was in part an attempt to increase fan support, Traffley added, "I can place the team in another town on twenty-four hours' notice."[70] If attendance did not improve, the team would be moved immediately or some players would be sold so that the level of the team's performance matched the attendance, the *Des Moines Leader* indicated.

After the Quincy Bluebirds' franchise disbanded on July 16 and the St. Joseph Saints shut down four days later, the league disbanded on August 1. Quincy finished in seventh place with a 31-37 record; St. Joseph came in last at 31-44.

On August 10, Traffley resigned as manager and decided to try to put a team in the Class B Virginia State League. In addition, Tom Letcher, who jumped the ballclub and went to the Grand Rapids Yellow Jackets in the Class A Western League, and Kid Mohler, who moved to the Columbus Buckeyes in the same circuit, refused to return to the Prohibitionists. The team was told that as long as the players were paid and the ballclub remained intact, Letcher and Mohler were bound by their contracts with Des Moines.[71]

Despite the uncertainty, the Prohibitionists captured the Western Association title in 1896 with a 56-22 mark, ten-and-a-half games ahead of second-place Dubuque. At one point, the Des Moines team won twenty-six straight games.[72] Letcher scored a league-high eighty-eight runs and Frank Figgemeier led all pitchers with seventeen wins and an .850 winning percentage.[73]

Fourteen years later, the *Des Moines Register and Leader* noted that "the team that was managed by the late 'Bill' Traffley . . . was so good that it broke up the league and ended professional baseball for a while in Des Moines."[74]

Five players—McKibben, Hickey, Mohler, Letcher, and Lohman—were training daily at the Drake University gym by March 7 of the next season.

On Friday, April 2, 1897, William Park died at his home at 1125 Pleasant Street in Des Moines after a six-month-long illness associated with "liver and bowel troubles."[75] His wife, Sophia, and six children were at his bedside at the time of his death. Son Ernest and daughter Bessie, who were attending the University of Wisconsin at Madison, Wisconsin, were called home the previous day to be with their father. The *Iowa State Register's* obituary said Park's law practice "was as extensive and lucrative as that of any attorney in the city or state."[76] Park was also described as "one of the most popular men of the city."[77]

The funeral was held the following Sunday afternoon at Park's home with presiding elder Emory Miller and Dr. E.L. Eaton officiating. "The floral offerings were abundant and beautiful," the *Iowa State Register* reported.[78] The newspaper described the funeral as "one of the largest ever seen in the city."[79] Park's law partner, Charles Ballerich, conducted the Knights of Pythias rite, which was "most beautiful and impressive," at the gravesite.[80]

On Monday, April 12, the Iowa Senate voted twenty-three to seven to ban playing baseball and football on Sundays. It took only twenty minutes to approve the measure, which also banned fishing on those days. The *Iowa State Register* predicted the Iowa House would probably concur, and the bill would become law.[81] By August 7, however, it appeared the law was being ignored. "The local authorities have seen fit to wink at it and allow the management of the local team to violate the Sunday laws," the *Des Moines Leader* said. "Under former city administrations base ball [sic] was prohibited within the city limits. But the 'reform administration' is evidently seeking the patronage of the law breaking element, judging by the direct violation of various laws that are being countenanced by the city officials."[82]

Before the Prohibitionists beat Cedar Rapids, 7-4, in June, the ballclub's president, Sidney Frick, called out his team for its halfhearted play up to that point. "Mr. Frick told them [the players] that he believed it was for their interest as well as his own that they play ball," the *Iowa State Register* reported the next day. "He said he believed he had the best team in the league, and if they would take hold and work as they should, Des Moines could be in first place within a short time."[83] At that point, the Prohibitionists were in third place with a 40-22 record.

On Monday, August 9, 1897, Frick reiterated that the Prohibitionists would fold if the team did not get better support. "We cannot pay salaries and keep a team here that will play first class ball when our crowds rarely number two hundred people," Frick told a reporter. "If the people will support me, I will yet show them the best ball they have ever seen."[84]

Although Des Moines had a 67-57 record in 1897, the public viewed the Western Association as an inferior league. In turn, real estate speculator Frick tried several promotions to boost attendance, including a series of boxing exhibitions.[85] The franchise was moved to Quincy, Illinois, in mid-February 1898, and the league disbanded on June 26 of that year.

On December 22, 1897, the *Des Moines Register* and *Leader* reported that Des Moines had been awarded a franchise in Ban

Johnson's Western League. The club's owner, Sidney Frick, had hoped to own a Western League franchise in Des Moines and Western Association teams in Omaha and Sioux City.[86]

A week after the Des Moines newspaper article, Johnson, Charles Comiskey, and Tom Loftus came to Des Moines to meet with Frick and other local residents. However, the deal fell apart because Frick did not raise enough cash and he refused to share control of the franchise with large investors.[87]

The *Des Moines Leader* reported on Friday, January 28, 1898, that Johnson had told Frick a day earlier that Des Moines would not get a Western League franchise. The Western League's president added that the league planned to add an eighth team in another city, probably Omaha.

In a written statement, Johnson said, "The Western League is not so anxious to secure a city for the franchise as it is for a good man. We are satisfied Des Moines is a good city and would support a team, but we are not satisfied that Frick is the man for the place.

"In fact," Johnson added, "we are satisfied he is not the man. He is persistent, but that does not make a base ball [sic] manager. With the right kind of a man, a team would win in Des Moines, but it would take a man willing to risk a little and engage players."[88]

Referring to his visit to Des Moines in December, Johnson said, "We were favorably impressed with Des Moines when we visited there, and were convinced that it is a city the league ought to keep an eye on, but the feeling there seemed be one of distrust toward Frick. [A] complaint was made that he was not liberal in his management, so we concluded to give him up."[89]

The newspaper also reported on January 28 that Johnson and two others had been in Omaha the previous day and had looked at sites for baseball. "Last evening," the *Leader* said, "they said that the city [Omaha] appeared to be ripe for baseball; that they were pleased with the prospects, and that the franchise might be transferred there."[90]

The paper also claimed that Frick put his experience up against Johnson's and planned to use players from the Grand Rapids, Michigan, team's list of reserves.

Chapter 2

New ballpark, name changes,
three titles highlight new decade

On Monday, February 12, 1900, a new Class B Western League was established at a meeting at the Kirkwood Hotel in Des Moines.[1] Des Moines was among the six franchises to play a 120-game schedule starting May 5 and ending September 4. The other cities with teams were Denver; Omaha; Pueblo, Colorado; St. Joseph, Missouri; and Sioux City. Local sporting goods magnate William Parker Chase represented Des Moines.

Eight other cities had also sought admission to the new league: Cedar Rapids; Colorado Springs, Colorado; Dubuque; Ottumwa; Peoria, Illinois; Rockford, Illinois; Rock Island, Illinois; and Topeka, Kansas. However, the *Des Moines Leader* reported the next day that "experience had proven that baseball in the [eight other] cities applying had not been profitable."[2] At the same time, league officials left open the possibility that the league could expand to eight teams at some point down the road.

In March, construction started on a new ball field on land between Fourth, Sixth, Grand, and Chestnut (now Locust) Streets. The tract was two-and-a-half blocks north of the corner of Fifth and Walnut streets, the city's commercial center and within a block of every street car line in the city. An old house on the south side of the property and several sheds were moved to provide room for the new ballpark.[3]

Improvements to the property, including fencing, grandstand, bleachers, and clubhouse, were expected to cost approximately $3,500. A bicycle track was installed later in the season. The ball field could also be used for football games and other types of athletic entertainment.

"It is claimed for this site that it will be the closest to the business center, the best equipped and the most convenient in every respect of any ballpark in the circuit," the *Register* observed.[4]

Chase cited a letter from a Des Moines board member that said the latter had already "reserved several first class players for the Des Moines team" and had "applications from enough more to assure him of a first class aggregation."[5]

Manager Jay Andrews' initial roster for the Hawkeyes included catchers Fred Holmes and Dave Seisler; first baseman Jay Parker; second baseman Frank Quigley and Bobbie Warner; third baseman Dave Brain; shortstop Art Ball; left fielder Kid Fear; center fielder Jimmie Burke; and pitchers William Harkey, Jack Callahan, Jake Weimer, Jack Roach, Warren Beckwith, Bug Lally, and Jack Brennan. Looking forward to the season opener on May 5, Andrews expressed confidence that he had "secured a good team, and that credible ball will be played."[6]

Catcher Holmes was described as "a big man, a good hitter, fast on his feet" and "an exceptionally good thrower."[7] Seisler, a .300-plus hitter, was known as "Iron Man" for his endurance.[8] First baseman Parker was "large, fast on his feet, and a good hitter."[9] The left-handed-hitting Quigley was "a good infielder."[10] Second baseman Warner was "steady and reliable."[11] Third baseman Brain was "one of the best amateur ballplayers in Chicago."[12] Ball was rated a "star shortstop."[13] All the outfielders will hit over .300, the *Register* predicted.

Callahan had pitched for Rock Island's pennant-winning team in the Western Association. The *Register* predicted Weimer would be the best left-hander in the league. The 225-pound hurler Roach had played several seasons in the Eastern League before signing with Des Moines. Beckwith, too, had considerable minor league experience.

Andrews was supposed to play for Boston in 1900, "but he preferred coming to Des Moines to manage the team to playing ball in the big league," the *Register* noted.[14]

The new version of the Hawkeyes was scheduled to report to Des Moines on Thursday, April 5, and work out for a month, with exhibition games mainly in Des Moines. The team used the Highland Park College ball grounds because the grounds behind the Des Moines auditorium were not ready.[15]

The dedication for the new auditorium on Monday, August 28, 1899, drew approximately 1,500 people. Built primarily for lectures, musical programs, and theatrical performances, it had hosted the Republican and Democratic state conventions before the formal dedication.

Mayor John MacVicar attributed the project's success to the small subscribers, such as "the Italian apple woman who operates a little stand on Locust Street when she subscribed $2 was what encouraged canvassers in their work."[16] In a letter read at the dedication, *Register* editor R.P. Clarkson said the new auditorium had been talked about during the past twelve months more than any other building in the state's history.

"The Auditorium speaks for itself, and it tells the story of the best and most helpful enterprise engaged in by the citizens of Des Moines," Clarkson added. "It tells the story of a divided people ceasing from divisive strife and uniting in an enterprise which is certain to be of more value to the people of the city than any other movement they have ever engaged in."[17]

Governor Leslie Shaw of Denison called Des Moines "an ideal residence city." "Her people are intelligent, refined, and many of them cultured; her men are energetic, honorable and brave; her women are kind, sociable and handsome; her children are well bred, studious and bright; her homes are spacious and well kept, and the doors thereof swing readily to the touch of friendship and hospitality to the stranger within her gates."[18]

Although the National League had cut 140 player positions, it did not mean the lower levels of the minor leagues such as the Western League would benefit due to salary disparities. As Chase pointed out, Baltimore's Steve Brodie had a $2,000 contract, yet his only choice was to return to the minors and receive $900 for four and a half months of baseball.

Nevertheless, the *Register* opined, "Minor league magnates . . . are congratulating themselves to some extent over the change, because it will give them a chance to secure good material for their teams. Minor league ball this season promises to be about as fast as that of the big league."[19]

By mid-March of that year, construction started on a new multi-purpose ballpark between West Fourth and Sixth streets north of Grand Avenue in Des Moines. The Hawkeyes beat the Sioux City Indians, 3-2, in the first game at the new facility on May 5, 1900. The Hawkeyes finished second in the Western League that year with a 59-45 record under three managers: Belden Hill, Jay Parker, and Hunkey Hines.

Called the Undertakers in 1903, manager Joe Quinn's club finished in seventh place in the Western League with a 55-76 record, thirty-and-a-half games in back of the first place Milwaukee Creams. Pitcher Harvey Cushman led the circuit in strikeouts with 195. After the season, a correspondent for *The Sporting News* said, "The local managers have determined that Des Moines shall not have another poor team. The public is as equally certain that if such a thing happens, there will be no base ball [sic] in Des Moines for some time thereafter."[20] The St. Louis-based publication added that putting together a good club was "almost impossible" due to the personal feelings among the franchise's officers and directors.[21] While Quinn wanted his pay to remain the same for 1904, "this the management will not do for another season," *The Sporting News* wrote.[22]

The ballclub was renamed the Politicians as the result of a three-day contest held by the *Des Moines Register and Leader* Thursday, April 7, to Saturday, April 9, 1904. Rock Island Railroad clerk Roy Brown of Des Moines was the first person to submit the name and received a $5 gold piece and free admission to the fifteen remaining practice games before the season opener on April 24 in Denver. "In view of the fact that Iowa stands to the front politically, having a splendid representation, commanding press notices and recognition," Brown explained, "and Des Moines is its capital city and home of our ball team, and also during the last campaign it figured so largely as a political center, being quoted by nearly every press in the state, is suggestive to the name 'Politicians' for our ball team."[23]

More than 250 names were suggested, including "Stand-Patters," "Iowa Ideals," "Iowa Ideas," "Grafters," "Hard Boiled Eggs," "detectives," "Aristocrats," "Resurrectionists," and "Live Wires." Others such as "Harvesters" and "Plowboys" paid tribute to the state's agricultural heritage. A committee comprised of club president W.G. Harrison, secretary C.D. Rawson, and manager Bill Hoffer was responsible for picking the new name. "It is certainly a good name, and one that will stick to the team through thick and thin," Rawson said. "There were many other good ones and the selection was exceedingly hard to make. I had no idea that so many answers could be brought out by so little booming as the scheme has had in the last two or three days."[24] Hoffer liked the new name, too. "If the boys will work like some of these politicians do we ought to see some great ball playing this year," he predicted.[25]

In announcing the contest, the *Des Moines Register and Leader* said a "short, bright and self explanatory [sic]" name was needed to replace the old name, Undertakers, which was "worn out and inadequate."[26] The old moniker matched manager Joe Quinn's offseason occupation. Although some other cities called the team the "Prohibitionists," "that day is past and the name is no longer appropriate," the newspaper argued. "Des Moines must have a new name that will be an honor to the city and it is up to some breezy fan to name the bunch and win the prizes."[27]

Six days after the new name was unveiled, *The Sporting News* predicted the Politicians would be comprised of the men who played in two exhibition games in Des Moines against the Chicago White Sox plus "one or two fast men."[28] Catching appeared to be the ballclub's weakest position. "Four youngsters are in the field and all seem to have the qualifications for the position," *The Sporting News* wrote. "It is possible that three will be released and an experienced man secured."[29]

Des Moines split its two-game series against the White Sox on Sunday, April 10, and Monday, April 11, 1904, winning 7-6 in the first and losing 8-3 in the second. Pitcher Lefty Leifield scattered ten White Sox hits and collected two hits in four at-bats to lead the home team to victory in front of 3,000 fans in the first game. First baseman Babe Towne, who "played in mid-season form," and right fielder Harry McChesney, who had a run-scoring triple in the seventh inning, each had two hits in four at-bats.[30] McChesney also singled to drive in two runs in the third inning. "The Chicagoans showed much better team work and were in better condition as the result of their extensive training trip through the South, but the locals' hitting was more timely," the *Des Moines Register* reported.[31]

Although the Politicians displayed a lack of team work in the field, Leifield, second baseman Frank Shugart, and Towne executed a double play in the seventh that "was the acme of smoothness and perfection."[32] "The Politicians played a loose fielding game, but their work at critical times more than made up for their deficiencies in the other departments," the *Register* concluded.[33] Ironically, Shugart could scarcely move one arm without pain, and had practiced less than any other player on the Des Moines team.

Despite outhitting the visitors, the Politicians could not overcome seven errors in their loss to the White Sox the next day. Chicago's American League representative put the game away early, scoring four runs in the first inning and one in the second. The Pale Hose added one run in the eighth and two in the ninth. Des Moines crossed the plate once in the fifth and twice in the eighth. "Des Moines played loosely, which accounts for the loss of the game, for the Des Moines pitchers, Seymour and [Bill] Hoffer, allowed but nine well scattered hits," the *Chicago Tribune* reported the next day. "The day was cold, with a gale from the west. Occasional showers, not quite heavy enough to stop the game, made it even more uncomfortable for the men."[34]

Three hundred fans attended the game, which took only one hour and thirty-five minutes to complete.

Denver swept the Politicians in the season-opening four-game series in the Mile High city. Des Moines lost the first game on Sunday, April 24, by a score of 4-1. Solly Hofman and Otto Thiel collected the visitors' only base hits. Starter Harvey Cushman surrendered all four Denver runs and gave up seven hits. "The cold and rainy weather played havoc with the crowd, which would have reached great proportions had the weather been good," the *Des Moines Register* noted. "As it was not more than 2,500 people were present. It is figured that the rain kept away thousands."[35]

Denver put the second game away early on Monday, April 25, scoring five times in the second inning and twice more in the third. The Politicians' Harry McChesney went three-for-four at the plate with a home run, triple, and two runs scored in the 9-3 loss. Teammate Lefty Leifield pitched eight innings but was tagged with the loss. Despite jumping out to a 2-0 lead in the first inning, Des Moines lost, 3-2, in the third game of the series on Tuesday, April 26. Denver scored once in the fourth inning and added two runs in the fifth to overcome its Western League rival. Des Moines starter Bill Morrison allowed only six hits, but picked up the loss. Hoffman had two of the Politicians' three hits.

Denver no-hit Des Moines on Wednesday, April 27, as center fielder Fred Ketchum went five-for-five at the plate and scored three runs. Denver wrapped out fifteen hits including eight in the first inning when the team scored eight runs. "The visitors were outclassed and they batted poorly. Their base running too was greatly inferior," the *Des Moines Register* reported in describing the 11-0 blowout.[36]

The Politicians finished fourth in the Western League that season with a 79-69 record, ten games behind the first-place Omaha Rangers. Leifield compiled a 16-17 record in thirty-six games and 313 innings. He allowed 280 hits and walked seventy-six batters. Five Des Moines players saw action in more than one hundred games. Hofman hit .301 in 128 games. Others were McChesney, .289 in 141 games; Josh Clarke, .277 in 143 games; Hans Lobert, .264 in 143 games; and Bob Connery, .219 in 143 games. Del Howard of the Rangers, a key reserve for the Chicago Cubs in the early 1900s, led the circuit in hits with 184 and home runs with nine.

For the first time in franchise history, the Des Moines baseball club had out-of-town ownership in December 1904 when local management sold the team to a group headed by Joe Cantillon of Milwaukee, Wisconsin. During a meeting at the Kirkwood on Saturday, December 10, six officers and directors resigned: W.G.Harvison, president; C.D. Rawson, secretary; George Cooper, treasurer; and fellow directors Frank Flynn, George Van Evera, and Mose Jacobs. The stockholders then elected new directors, including Joe Cantillon and his brother Mike Cantillon, J.E. McDonald, E.B. Bradley, C.H. Myrick, W.W. Sears, John Leahy, John Abbott, and Charles Havenor. The new officers were Joe Cantillon, president, and Mike Cantillon, secretary and treasurer.

"The old directors and stockholders of the club have done well," the *Des Moines Register* observed. "Not only have they been paid all that they originally put into the club, but they now have in the hands of trustees something over $2,000, to be divided among them, and about the same amount will be received in the spring. Besides this, they have enjoyed annual passes to all of the homestands."[37]

Charles Havenor, owner of the Milwaukee franchise in the American Association, provided the financial backing for Joe Cantillon and his group. Mike Cantillon moved to Des Moines to manage the ballclub's affairs for his brother and Havenor. "It is well known that he [Havenor] has great faith in the Cantillons and it is more than probable that it is he who is furnishing the money back of Cantillon in the deal," the *Register and Leader* wrote.[38] Omaha baseball magnate William Rourke spoke highly of the Cantillon brothers when he conferred with Mike Cantillon in Des Moines in December 1904, too. "It's a mighty lucky thing for you people in Des Moines that you have the Cantillons," Rourke said. "I see that they have Herman Long to manage the team and have signed several good men. Des Moines has some good material left over from last year, and with the players that Cantillon can and will bring here I believe that we shall have some very hot games with the Politicians. The Cantillons know baseball players and the baseball players know the Cantillons and will play for them. Yes, Des Moines is very fortunate."[39]

Shortly after taking over the franchise, Joe Cantillon dismissed talk of changing the rules of the game to produce more offense. "Let all the big league teams sell or give away their best pitchers. Fill their places with amateurs," he said tongue-in-cheek. "Do this and there will be more hitting than there are flakes in a good old fashioned snow storm.

"It's not the rules so much as it is the pitchers that hold the hits down and the fans like to see a good pitcher work as well as they like to hear the 'crack of the bat,'" he added. "In fact, the fans don't care much for a hitting game unless there is good pitching as well. Fans like good baseball, and a slugging match is not good baseball. The rules seem to be pretty good as they are."[40]

The team was renamed the Underwriters in 1905 as the result of a contest conducted by the two Des Moines newspapers. The newly-named team won the Western League title that season with a 95-54 record under manager Herman Long. The *Des Moines Register and Leader* fourteen years later said the team "was undoubtedly one of the best minor league teams ever put together."[41]

Claude Rossman had a league-leading .357 batting average and 229 base hits. George Hogreiver scored a league-high 122 runs. Pitcher Lefty Leifield sported a 26-9 record to lead the circuit in wins and winning percentage at .743.

Now known as the Champions, the Des Moines club, along with Milwaukee, came to Des Moines for spring training on Monday, April 1, 1906. The Cantillon brothers accompanied the clubs to assess talent; manager Jack Doyle arrived later. An exhibition schedule was established, starting April 11-13 against Milwaukee and ending April 25-26 versus Duluth, Minnesota, in Des Moines.

The Champions repeated in 1906 under manager Doyle, finishing 97-50, or nineteen games better than the second-place Lincoln Ducklings. George "Red" Andreas led the Western League with eighty-four stolen bases. Pitcher Roscoe Miller recorded a league high twenty-eight wins, and lefthander Lou Manske had the best winning percentage of .697 based on a 23-10 record.

Two years later, the club was sold to Chicago businessman John Higgins and the downtown ballpark on West Fourth Street was demolished due to urban redevelopment. As a result, the team was forced to play at its Sunday ballpark on East Twentieth Street near the State Fairgrounds.

In 1909, Des Moines captured another Western League title by beating Lincoln, 5-3, as Sioux City lost twice to Omaha on the last day of the season. The Boosters' .612 winning percentage (based on a 93-59 record) was slightly better than the Sioux City Soos' .610 winning percentage (based on a 94-60 record). The *Des Moines Evening Tribune* called the pennant race between the two Iowa teams "one of the closest and most exciting finishes in the history of organized baseball."[42] The Boosters entered the decisive game on Tuesday, September 28, with the odds stacked against them. "Two days ago even the most enthusiastic fans would not have taken a ten to one bet that Des Moines would get the flag," the *Evening Tribune* wrote, "for the odds were too great against the home team."[43]

The Boosters snapped a scoreless tie in the fifth inning when player-manager Bill Dwyer scored on "a magnificent slide" at home after reaching base on an error, advancing to second on a sacrifice, and coming home on another fielding miscue by the Soos.[44] Des Moines added four runs in the next inning that started with pitcher Frank Lange's single to left. The next batter, Jack Dalton, walked. Lange was called out when trying to advance to third on Eddie Colligan's bunt. However, the umpire changed his mind when he saw the third baseman's "roughness in touching Lange and his shoving tactics."[45] The next hitter, Wally Mattick, tripled to right center field to clear the bases—his third triple in two days. Mattick scored the fourth run of the inning on Dwyer's sacrifice fly.

The visitors scored three runs in the ninth after Irv Waldron reached base on a bunt single, Boosters' right fielder Dalton lost William Davidson's fly ball in the sun, and Frank Jude lined the ball over Dalton's head for an inside-the-park three-run home run.

The *Evening Tribune* credited Lange with pitching his best game of the year, even though the right hander's statistics may not have reflected it. "He didn't pitch a no-hit game. He didn't have the batters at his mercy. He didn't strike out a dozen of them," the newspaper observed. "He didn't have astounding speed. He was hit hard and often . . . Lange was always there in pinches. He never lost his head."[46] In fact, the Soos outhit the Boosters twelve to five. Left fielder Jude collected three hits alone, while right fielder Waldron, center fielder Davidson, and second baseman George Hogreiver had two hits apiece. Mattick was responsible for two of Des Moines' five hits.

The next day, the Des Moines Baseball Association held a "love feast" for the team and "thirty hoarse, thirty-third degree fans" at the Kirkwood Hotel in Des Moines.[47] Even the team mascot showed up. "Wreathed in smiles and flushed with success, they accepted the congratulations of some of the most prominent men of the city, threw bouquets at the successful young manager, passed off deserved by every man-jack of the bunch in a bashful manner, toasted owner Higgins until the water coolers went dry and feasted to their hearts content," the *Evening Tribune* reported.[48]

The head table included toastmaster and *Daily Capitol* editor Lafe Young Sr., congressman John Hull, the Des Moines mayor and city council members, Greater Des Moines Committee representative Charles Hewitt, postmaster Joseph Myerly, and assistant postmaster John Ryan as well as Boosters fans Herman Huttenlocher, Len Burnett, Harry Frase, and John McDonald. In essence, the mayor and council members said "that Des Moines had the cleanest, ablest, and most deserving bunch of ball players in the league, that their success was well-deserved, and that every man and woman in Des Moines should be proud of the team."[49]

Hewitt promised better support for the team from the business community in the future. "The people at large scarcely realize what a great thing has been accomplished by Mr. Higgins, Manager Dwyer and their lieutenants. There are few things that can do more towards advertising a city than a winning ball team. We have a winning team this year, and as a result Des Moines will be talked of in the headlines of at least fifty newspapers in the next two weeks.

"If the merchants knew just what this meant to Des Moines in future growth, they would take more pains toward seeing that Des Moines had better support in the grand stand. This is realized now to some extent since the pennant is won, and I am confident that the Greater Des Moines committee [sic], for one civic organization, will give Mr. Higgins the support that is rightfully coming to him."[50]

Young predicted the street car company would provide better service for fans next season. He suggested a certain number of street cars should leave the street car waiting room at a certain time each day and arrive at the ballpark before the first batter came up.

Meanwhile, Sioux City's reaction to Des Moines's Western League championship was much less effusive and questioned the capital city's support of the Boosters. "The team is to be congratulated, although most people in the circuit would rather have a town which supports a team well, win the pennant," the *Sioux City Tribune* wrote.[51] The *Sioux City Journal* was even more direct. "Although the Boosters get the pennant the league records fail to show they are the best team. In every department except in the box [pitching] the Packers [Soos] show their superiority," the *Journal* maintained. "Manager [Ducky] Holmes' men are far and away the better batters, the better fielders, the better base runners, and exceed in sacrifice hits. [Frank] Miller and [Frank] Lange have been the big factors in their winning and the two twirlers deserve all the credit that can be heaped on them."[52] Pitching was the Sioux City club's only weakness, the *Journal* added.

The five-foot-eleven, 180-pound Lange had a 29-12 record and appeared in fifty-two of the team's 152 games in 1909. He led Western League hurlers in wins and strikeouts (328). He compiled a 28-25 record with the Chicago White Sox from 1910 to 1913. The six-foot, 188-pound Miller finished 24-16 and pitched in forty-seven games. He had a 52-66 mark with the White Sox, Pittsburgh Pirates, and Boston Braves in 1913 and 1916-1923. "Working in and out of turn, performing tasks that would have put ordinary men in the hospital with dislocated arms, these men [Lange and Miller] have pitched Des Moines within striking distance of the flag, when the team seemed to be down and out," the *Des Moines Evening Tribune* wrote a day after the Boosters won the title.[53] A third pitcher, Clarence Biersdofer, appeared in thirty-five games, won sixteen, and lost eleven.

In general, the 1909 Boosters reflected the Deadball Era of the times, which lasted from the founding of the American League in 1901 to the elimination of the spitball in 1920. The era was distinguished by low scoring and an emphasis on pitching and defense. The Boosters hit only twenty-three home runs—Bert Niehoff had a team-leading seven. On the other hand, the Boosters collected 176 doubles and sixty-eight triples. Bill Dwyer had a team-leading thirty doubles; Wally Mattick struck a team-leading thirteen triples. Jack Dalton was credited with 179 of the Boosters' 1,288 hits. The team batted .260 as a whole, led by Dalton's .308 average. Mattick hit .227 in three seasons with the White Sox and St. Louis Cardinals. However, he batted .273 in eighteen minor league seasons and accumulated 2,254 hits, including 338 doubles, seventy-nine triples, sixteen home runs, and 2,441 total bases. The five-foot-ten, 180-pound St. Louis native struck out only sixty-nine times in 8,262 at-bats.

Chapter 3

Tom Fairweather takes over;
blue law muddles Boosters' future

Charles Sherman, who helped establish Des Moines' first professional baseball team, died suddenly at his home in New York City on Friday, September 1, 1911, at age fifty. After suffering paralysis, he died a few minutes later.[1] After Sherman was admitted to the bar, he began his professional career in Chicago in 1888. He left Chicago in 1904 and moved to Boston where he lived until 1910.

He was a trustee of the Sherman estate but resigned and was replaced by William Griffith of Philadelphia, the husband of his youngest sister. He was survived by his wife, three children, one brother, and two sisters. His body was brought back to Des Moines for burial.

On Tuesday, January 16, 1912, Tom Fairweather and Frank "Bald Eagle" Isbell bought the franchise from Charles Comiskey, a Chicago native who established the Chicago White Sox. The new owners bought a site at Sixth and Holcomb Avenues on the north side of Des Moines for a new ballpark called Western League Park. Now known as the Boosters, the team won the 1915 and 1917 Western League titles.

Called "the patriarch of Iowa baseball," Fairweather started in professional baseball as secretary of the Sioux City Soos in 1907.[2] He was co-owner of the Sioux City franchise in 1910 and 1911. For years, he operated as many as two minor leagues out of his office in the Highland Park area of Des Moines: the Class C Western Association from 1934 to 1942 and from 1946 to 1949, and the Class B Three-I League from 1937 to 1942 and from 1946 to 1950. "Yes, baseball's a great game," Fairweather said in 1949. "It has been kept clean, and that's one of the game's greatest appeals, because the fans know they can always see the better team win."[3]

Fairweather came from Illinois to a Cherokee County farm with his family at age five. After one year of high school, he served in the Spanish American war. Later, he completed high school and graduated from the Drake University Law School in Des Moines as class president. He was elected to the Des Moines City Council in 1916 and 1917, and served as that city's mayor in 1918 and 1919.

During World War I, he organized a Highland Park drill company, a group of boys who marched up and down the streets in that area. "He was more proud of this aggregation than any political office he ever held," a Des Moines publication said.[4] After practicing law in 1921 and 1922, he quit to devote more time and money to his farms northwest of Des Moines. "A blue ribbon to pin on his sleek dairy cattle means more to Tom now than votes," the *Des Moines Register* said.[5] He was a member of the draft and ration boards in Highland Park during World War II. He also served as instructor and president at Highland Park College at Second and Euclid in Des Moines, now the site of the Park Fair Shopping Mall.

Frank Isbell had ten years of experience with Chicago's two major-league teams before taking over the reigns as the Boosters' manager. He played in forty-five games for the Orphans (predecessors of the Cubs) in 1898 and hit .233 with four doubles, eight runs-batted-in, and three stolen bases. The New York native also pitched in thirteen games including nine starts. He compiled a 4-7 record with a 3.56 earned run average, forty-two walks, and sixteen strikeouts in eighty-one innings. He also played every other position on the field.

Isbell played 1,074 games with the White Sox from 1901 to 1909 and hit .308 in the 1906 World Series, in which the White Sox defeated their crosstown rivals, the Chicago Cubs. During his time on the south side of Chicago, Isbell batted .251 and collected 154 doubles, sixty-two triples, thirteen home runs, 447 runs-batted-in, and 250 stolen bases. He retired after the 1910 season and became manager of the Wichita, Kansas, club in the Western League.

In early February 1912, the Boosters traded ex-manager Bill Dwyer and pitcher Andy Owens to Lincoln for pitcher Knapp (sic) and first baseman (Jack) Thomas. *The Sporting News* described

Dwyer as "undoubtedly one of the most popular managers in the circuit." "He is known as 'Smiling Bill' to the 'loop' fans and never fails to get a hand in the other cities."[6] While Owens played well in 1910, "last year, he was dissatisfied with the conditions here [in Des Moines] and refused to get into condition," *The Sporting News* wrote.[7] A ten-year veteran in the Western League, Thomas's "long suit is clouting out three-baggers and home runs with the bases choked," the St. Louis publication added.[8]

With the season scheduled to open April 12 and close September 22, teams were expected to make three trips around the league and play four-game series, rather than four trips around the circuit and three-game series as in the past. The league also capped player salaries at $2,000 starting in 1913. "The new Des Moines owners are starting out in an economical manner and several other clubs in the league are making wholesale cuts," *The Sporting News* noted.[9]

Nearly one hundred fans attended a boosters' meeting at the Press Club in Des Moines on Monday, April 15. The first sixty tickets were auctioned off for $10 apiece; the rest were sold for the regular price. The executive committee used the proceeds totaling more than $600 to offset opening day expenses and other activities. Earlier in the day, Des Moines mayor James Hanna was elected president of the Booster Club. Gilger MacKinnon, president of Mechanics Savings Bank, was selected secretary-treasurer. The rest of the executive board included John Chase; Robert Barrowman; John Ryan; John Sullivan; John Hogan; Leo Stevens; Fred Van Liew, attorney and Department of Public Safety superintendent; Wendell Churchill; Park Bowers; Rube Place, sports editor of the *Des Moines Daily Capital*; Howard Dorward, a cashier with the *Daily Capital*; and Rollie Bales, sports editor of *the Des Moines Register and Leader*.

The Boosters finished in a fourth-place tie with an 82-80 record in their first year of new ownership. The first-place Denver Grizzlies ended up seventeen games ahead of the Boosters and the Lincoln Railsplitters.

Cascade native Red Faber anchored the pitching staff, compiling a 21-14 record and a 3.11 earned run average. The twenty-three-year-old Faber appeared in forty-three games, including thirty-eight starts. He walked only sixty-nine batters in 304 innings. At the plate, he hit .221 with three home runs. He is the only Iowa-born Hall of Famer to play with a Des Moines professional team. He finished his twenty-year career in the major leagues with 254 wins, 213 losses, and a 3.15 earned run average for the Chicago White Sox. He won twenty-one or more games four times, including twenty-five in 1921. He also led the American League in earned run average at 2.48 and the major leagues in complete games with thirty-two in 1921.

Red Faber (Courtesy: John Liepa)

On Saturday, April 15, 1915, Isbell announced he had replaced former captain Red Andreas with third baseman Lee Tannehill, a member of the world champion Chicago White Sox in 1906. In August, the *Des Moines Tribune* editorialized about the city's opportunity for growth in general and the ball club in particular. "The Des Moines ball park [sic] is more conveniently located, and more satisfactory in every way than any in the Western circuit, and Des Moines has a baseball management second to none, not even second to the management of the big league nines," the *Tribune* boasted.[10] The city's growth was linked directly to its ability to promote itself, the newspaper added. "The future of Des Moines is bound up in the things that will attract the great crowds of the middle west in the coming twenty-five years," the *Tribune* wrote, "and the more Des Moines does to popularize its own advantages as a meeting place the better and bigger city it is going to grow to be."[11]

Isbell led the Boosters to a Western League crown with an 87-53 record in 1915. Tex Jones scored 103 runs to lead the circuit. Des Moines hurler George Mogridge tied for the lead league in wins with twenty-four. His 1.93 earned run average was lowest in the league, too. Orient native Dazzy Vance of the St. Joseph Drummers struck out a league-best 199 batters.

J.L. Wilkinson of Algona unveiled his Des Moines-based All Nations Baseball Team at Western League Park on Sunday, May 5, 1912, against a local Moose Lodge squad. Wilkinson's team included Blacks, Native Americans, and Mexicans among several nationalities. The All Nations won, 3-0, in seven innings behind pitcher John Donaldson.

"The lanky colored twirler of the All Nations team was the sensation of the day in his way of pitching," the *Des Moines Capital* reported. "He had a variety of curves that fairly dazzled the Moose team and but one man reached first."[12] The next day, Wilkinson and the team headed west before coming back through the Dakotas and Minnesota into Iowa.

After training in Des Moines in the spring 1913, the All Nations finished with a 119-17 record that season, not counting two ties.[13] While they apparently didn't play in Des Moines, the state of Iowa, or neighboring states, that changed in 1914. That year, many of their games were played in conjunction with fairs and festivals. Primarily a barnstorming team, the group's last game at Western League Park as a Des Moines-based team occurred on Sunday, September 19, 1915. The Chicago Union Giants won, 6-1, for their third victory in five games against Wilkinson's club that season. "Rasmussen was on the mound for the All-Nations and pitched great ball, an error being largely responsible for three of the Giants' runs," the *Des Moines Register and Leader* reported the next day. "Simpson hurled the first five innings for the colored boys and then was succeeded by Rice who finished in good style."[14] The All-Nations club scored its only run in the fourth, which started with a triple to left center by Durham. After a walk, John Donaldson grounded out. Durham crossed the plate when Dunbar bounced a single off Simpson's glove. The Union Giants' pitcher then struck out the next two batters to avoid further damage.

Wilkinson moved his ballclub to Kansas City after the 1915 season and became the only white owner in the Negro National League. The renamed Monarchs ruled the Negro National League for much of its existence and produced such future major league players as Jackie Robinson, Ernie Banks, Elston Howard, and Gene Baker of Davenport. The Monarchs' manager, Buck O'Neil, later scouted and coached for the Chicago Cubs and was inducted into the Hall of Fame in 2022.

After winning the Western League title in 1915, the Boosters finished in fifth place with a 75-75 record the next season. Pitcher Paul Musser led the league's hurlers with 249 strikeouts.

Even with a world war raging in Europe, Des Moines baseball fans were eager for the season to begin in 1917. "Despite the war situation interest in baseball in this city seems to be greater this spring than in recent years," *Des Moines Register* sports editor Sec Taylor observed, "judging by the preseason talk wherever fans congregate and by the increased number of telephone calls at the newspaper offices for scores."[15]

Taylor gave four reasons for the increased interest in baseball. First, co-owner Tom Fairweather bought out Frank Isbell's interest in the club and replaced Isbell as manager with Jack Coffey. Second, the "decadence" of college athletics after many track and field athletes entered military service.[16] Third, Fairweather and Coffey had obtained several new players to replace some veterans. Fourth, the team had just returned from a road trip in which it had won five of nine games and had never lost by more than two runs.

Taylor added that Fairweather and Coffey had assembled "a team of young, peppery ball players" [sic] with nine veterans and six rookies.[17] The more experienced players included second baseman and manager Coffey, third baseman Art Ewoldt, right fielder Bill Hunter, catchers Larry Spahr and Dick Breen, and pitchers Musser and spit-baller Joel Berger. A new hurler, Rudy Kallio, led his league in strikeouts in 1916, the *Register* reported. Kallio pitched 306 innings and posted a 25-9 record and a 1.76 earned run average for Des Moines in 1917. Kallio had a twenty-one-year minor league record of 246-211 and played until he was forty-seven years old.

Opening Day festivities started at noon on Tuesday, May 1, with a public luncheon sponsored by the Chamber of Commerce for the Des Moines and Wichita players. A parade to the ballpark started at Seventh and Park Streets at 1:30 p.m. with a machine gun platoon on motorcycles, three bands, an infantry company, city officials in cars, baseball officials, baseball players, and fans. Once inside the ballpark, soldiers drilled and fired a salute to the American flag. Adjutant general Guy Logan threw out the ceremonial first pitch to mayor John MacVicar.

The Boosters did not disappoint their fans, posting a 2-1 victory in thirteen innings over the Wichita Witches and manager Frank Isbell. In the thirteenth, D.J. Cass scored the winning run when Bill Hunter singled over the head of first baseman Tex Jones. Cass walked to lead off the bottom of the decisive inning. The next batter, Art Ewoldt, bunted, and third baseman Ike Davis' throw bounced over Jones' head. Second baseman Pep Goodwin backed up Jones, however, and held the runners to one base. Then Goodwin mishandled a grounder by Spencer, which loaded the bases with one out. Moments later, Hunter drove in the winning run. "The battle was punctuated with five cute double plays, some startling catches, amazing pitching by [Paul] Musser and [Elmer]

Koestner, and many of the tensest situations imaginable," *Des Moines Register* sports editor Sec Taylor wrote.[18]

Wichita starter Koestner allowed only two hits until Spencer singled to start the bottom of the seventh. Two batters later, Spencer crossed the plate on a single to left by Coffey, which gave the Boosters a short-lived 1-0 lead. With two outs in the ninth, Bert Coy of Wichita homered over the right-field fence after a questionable call. The next day, Taylor said home plate umpire Mike Jacobs "undoubtedly missed a third strike on the Wichita slugger, for the ball was squarely down the groove and almost hip high."[19]

Boosters hurler Paul Musser escaped jams in the eleventh and twelfth innings and gave up eight hits including two by Coy and two by Koestner. In the eleventh, Koestner doubled and reached third with one out, but Kidder White struck out and Jones grounded out. In the next inning, the Witches had a scoring opportunity after a walk, an error, and an infield out. Musser escaped further danger when he knocked down a line drive, and shortstop Bruce Hartford threw the runner out at first.

The Boosters collected seven hits including two by Coffey and a triple by first baseman Sweeney. The Witches turned in three double plays, including an unassisted twin killing by Jones. The Boosters executed two double plays.

While the Boosters and their fans prepared for their second Western League championship in three years, the Iowa legislature, attorney general, and judicial system failed to agree on whether the state's blue law prohibited baseball on Sundays. On April 2, the Iowa Senate voted twenty-seven to eighteen to permit municipalities of 500 or more people to vote on legalizing the operation of baseball, theaters, moving picture houses, and amusement parks on Sundays. The original bill provided for referendums in cities of at least 5,000 people on whether baseball and theaters could operate on Sundays. An amendment to allow cities with populations of 3,000 to 5,000 to do the same lost. Finally, state senator Grant Caswell's amendment to allow all municipalities of 500 or more people to vote on the issue cleared the upper chamber. A publication clause was added so the measure would take effect after it was signed by the governor and published. That way, the Western League, Central Association, and Three-I League could continue to operate in Iowa.

After the Senate acted, the Des Moines Ministerial Association approved a resolution that opposed some of the provisions in the local option legislation concerning the operation of baseball and theaters on Sunday. In particular, the ministerial alliance opposed legalizing certain amusements after 1 p.m. on Sundays and conducting referendums on various Sunday sports. Nine days later, the local trades and labor assembly adopted a resolution supporting the passage of the Senate bill modifying the Iowa blue law. The trades and labor representatives "expressed that the modifications were just and fair to everyone and could not see how any fair minded person could do otherwise than favor its passage."[20]

On Friday, April 13, however, the Iowa House defeated the Senate version that included the referendum option for cities with at least 500 people. Forty-seven of the representatives present voted in favor of the bill, but fifty-seven voted against it after various amendments were rejected. State representative Fred Turner of North English offered an unsuccessful amendment that would have allowed the use of an injunction to enforce the blue laws. Turner's amendment would also have permitted legalization of baseball and theaters by city ordinance. In response to the House's action, the *Des Moines Register* wrote, "It is doubtful . . . whether the laws can be enforced with any degree of success."[21]

In its upcoming season preview, the *Des Moines Register* maintained the biggest problem faced by the Boosters in 1917 was the state's blue law that prohibited baseball on Sundays. "If it is enforced as the state officials say it will be, baseball should suffer here as well as Sioux City, the other Iowa club in the Western League."[22] Noting that the Boosters did not have a profitable season in 1916, the *Tribune* added, "It is doubtful if either of the two cities [Des Moines and Sioux City] can retain a baseball team without Sunday games. If Des Moines and Sioux City are taken out of the league, the Western circuit should be a flivver."[23]

In an editorial on Thursday, April 26, the *Tribune* pointed out that juries had to enforce the blue law, which carried a maximum fine of only $5 per infraction. "That is the most foolish part of the Sunday law," the newspaper argued. "For it makes it practically unenforceable unless the community is dead set on having it enforced."[24] In fact, not one conviction was obtained in seventy blue law cases in one summer resort county in Iowa. "To start on a Sunday enforcing crusade that is not sustained by an overwhelming public opinion will be merely to harass the community and get nowhere under the present law, for juries will not convict frequently enough to make a $5 fine amount to be a deterrent."[25]

If the law was strictly interpreted, any activity on Sunday could be stopped, including street cars, the *Tribune* opined. Calling the old law "outdated and unenforceable," the newspaper said the legislature should have enacted a new Sunday law. "It never has been enforced and not even attorney general [Horace] Havner can enforce it now," the *Tribune* wrote. "It would be a hardship to have it enforced as it reads . . . an attempt to literally enforce the present law will lead to nothing but turmoil, will disgust good people with other and more practical reforms, will end in humiliation, and will do no good."[26]

On Sunday, May 13, Fairweather announced the Boosters would play that day as usual. In response, the authorities said if the team did play, he would be arrested, along with any other participants. "As in the other cases, the arrests were to be purely formal," the *Register* noted, meaning the arrests would not occur during the game.[27] The paper added that "commercial activity throughout the city would be nearer to a standstill than at any former time since the city was incorporated."[28]

Des Moines police chief Charles Jackson planned to arrest all violators of the blue law after being told to do so by county attorney Ward Henry. That gave business owners impacted by the law three options: remain closed all day, stay open a short time to test the law, or stay open as usual, putting the burden on law enforcement. Some businesses agreed to stay closed all day—drug stores, cigar stores, hotel cigar counters, shoe shine parlors, candy stores, soda fountains, gas service stations, and gas and auto repair stations.

Under the direction of former attorney general George Cosson, however, five motion picture theaters agreed to stay open to test the law.

A record crowd was on hand that day to see the Boosters shut out the St. Joseph Drummers, 8-0, behind the four-hit pitching of Rudy Kallio. Just as the authorities promised, two representatives of the attorney general took the names of the players and ballpark employees to file information against them. Des Moines got the only run it needed in the second inning when Jack Coffey doubled to center and Sweeney singled to drive in Coffey. The Boosters added six runs in the seventh on four hits, two walks, and two St. Joseph errors. A single, infield out, sacrifice, and wild pitch produced the final run in the eighth.

One hundred people were arrested for violating the Sunday closing law on May 13. Three paid $1 fines plus court costs. Four days later, Fairweather appeared in court for the first time in his life along with Cosson and attorneys for the five moving picture theaters that stayed open. The defendants and the prosecution stipulated that Fairweather was arrested the previous Sunday by police; a scheduled baseball game was played and the players received their regular salaries; the ballpark's employees were not paid; tickets were not sold that day; baseball is a business for pecuniary profit, but it is not primarily a commercial enterprise; and the Boosters had not earned a dividend since 1909.

Representing the state, attorney W.R. Kendrick said baseball should be called a commercial enterprise. Cosson argued that baseball is a sport, only slightly commercial. Fairweather testified that although he had invested $40,000 in the ballclub, the franchise had not earned a dividend in five years and its existence depended on public donations. Further, Cosson said, the fight for baseball was not in the interest of commercialism, but only in the desire to keep sports alive in Des Moines.

On Friday, May 18, a letter from Havner was mailed to county attorneys throughout the state. The *Des Moines Register* said the letter would be "quite lengthy" and would present "quite an extended argument" to support strict enforcement of the blue law.[29]

Havner did not plan to take sole responsibility for enforcing the law. In fact, the *Register* wrote, governor William Harding was responsible "for at least a portion of the crusade," based on an agreement with Havner that the executive branch would fully cooperate with the attorney general on the enforcement of laws.[30] "The legislature refused to repeal the law, public sentiment did not manifest itself in favor of repeal to any great extent, and Mr. Havner now believes that the only thing to be done is to enforce the law," the *Register* reasoned.[31]

After meeting with the state's Supreme Court justices, Havner issued a list of what was and was not allowed on Sunday. His list banned commercialized baseball or other sports, but not amateur sports such as baseball, golf, and tennis. The list of barred activities also included movies, theaters, farm labor (except when necessary to save crops), drug stores, cigar stores, confectionary stores, and all labor not absolutely necessary. The longer list of acceptable activities also included trains, street cars, interurbans, auto service stations, garages, hotels, livery stables, vessels, telegraph, telephone, electric light plants, gas plants, newspapers, fishing, milk deliveries, and work necessary to preserve life, health, or property.[32]

Havner also advised the Polk County attorney that a concerted effort by any group of businessmen to stay open the next day, Sunday, would be considered "conspiracy to violate the law," punishable by a three-year prison sentence upon conviction. His phone call from Corydon came after being told some druggists and most cigar dealers had decided to remain open on the Sabbath. A spokesman for the cigar dealers, however, denied Havner's claim about that group of businesses. The county attorney also told the police chief that no effort would be made the next day to interfere with Sunday baseball, theaters, motion picture shows, and Jewish merchants because their cases testing the blue law were pending. Other violators should be arrested, county attorney Henry said. "It was pointed out that as soon as information is filed against any violator his status would become virtually the same as that of the various activities exempted and he would be allowed to operate until the courts have handed down their rulings," the *Register* observed.[33]

Given one-day immunity, the Boosters clipped the St. Joseph Drummers 10-8 for their tenth straight victory on Sunday, May 20. "The game was an old fashioned slugging match, punctured by good, bad and indifferent fielding, much wrangling, two or three questionable decisions and many long bingles," sports editor Sec Taylor wrote.[34]

The issue came to a head on Wednesday, May 23, 1917, when Municipal Court judge Joseph Meyer ruled that baseball and movies on Sundays did not violate the state's blue law. Meyer described baseball and movies as "clean, wholesome amusements" and said that any labor associated with them would be categorized as a "necessity," which was exempt under the law. Meanwhile, the Iowa attorney general refused to be interviewed after the judge's ruling. When Havner was finally contacted, he told a reporter, "I have nothing to say to the press. I do not want to be annoyed."[35] His secretary explained that her boss had to write some commencement addresses and a Memorial Day speech and did not want to be disturbed.

Coffey guided the Boosters to another Western League title in 1917. Des Moines finished 84-62; the Lincoln Ducklings were 83-64 during the regular season. Coffey's club beat Hutchinson four games to two in the finals. Musser fanned 337 hitters to lead the league.

Despite the unsuccessful effort by the righteous to protect the sanctity of Sundays, baseball continued. In fact, baseball stars such as pitcher Grover Cleveland Alexander suffered the rest of their lives from the effects of serving in the military during World War I. Alexander's epilepsy was blamed on the shelling he was exposed to in World War I.

Chapter 4

Demons win two titles; Ruth,
Gehrig entertain fans twice

In their first year as the Des Moines Demons in 1925, the Demons rolled to a Western League pennant with a 98-70 record, one game ahead of the second-place Denver Bears. Des Moines placed six players on the all-star team: first baseman Charles Stuvengen, who hit .349 with 229 hits and eighteen triples; outfielder Elton "Sam" Langford, who batted .339 and scored a league-leading 160 runs; outfielder Francis "Pug" Griffin, who hit .320 with twenty-three home runs; catcher Homer Haworth, who batted .295; pitcher Herm Holzhouser, who sported a 19-8 won-loss record; and pitcher Claude Thomas, 19-6. There were two notable all-star omissions: Dutch Wetzel, who collected thirty-two home runs and batted .353, and hurler Leo Moon, who compiled a 22-13 record and 127 strikeouts.

Babe Ruth did more than belt three balls over the outfield fence at Western League Park on Wednesday, October 27, 1926. After arriving by train in Des Moines at 8 a.m., he ate breakfast with Demons' president Lee Keyser among others, and visited disabled soldiers in a Knoxville hospital before suiting up for the exhibition game at 2:30 p.m. that day. When he arrived at the hospital by car, he made a short speech to the residents who were able to leave their rooms. "Afterwards Ruth visited some of the patients who were bedfast or could not leave their wards," *Des Moines Register* sports editor Sec Taylor wrote the next day. "Unfortunately some of them were unable to recognize him but many did, and apparently enjoyed and appreciated the opportunity to shake the hand and hear the voice of the great baseball player."[1]

After skipping lunch, Ruth put on a football uniform and had his picture taken at the ballpark with captain Gail Fry, Chuck Everett, and Clarence Simpson of the Drake University football team. After changing into a baseball uniform, Ruth hit three balls over the outfield fence in batting practice, and played all nine innings of the exhibition matchup against Dutch Wetzel's all-stars. The "Sultan of Swat's" three home runs in the main affair propelled his all-star team to a 14-9 victory with approximately 2,500 spectators on hand. "It didn't take Ruth long to get the range of the farthest corner of the park as he drove six balls out of the lot in less than ten minutes and all of the clouts were terrific liners," the *Des Moines Tribune* reported.[2]

In the first inning, Ruth was retired after his slow roller died in front of home plate. Two innings later, he homered on a three-ball, no-strike count with a runner on first. He flied out to shortstop Chalmer Cissell in the fourth and struck out swinging in the sixth. Two innings later, he drove in Al Van Camp from second with a tape-measure clout that cleared the right-field fence near the foul line. With runners on second and third in the ninth, Ruth hit "the longest home run ever seen at the Sixth Avenue park."[3] In the field, the New York Yankee star played first base for seven innings and pitched the final two innings for his all-star team.[4] "Ruth took things easy while on the mound, allowing one run and three hits," the *Tribune* recounted. "He fanned two batters in the eighth and one in the ninth."[5]

Second baseman John Hart aided Ruth's all-stars with a single, double, and triple. Despite playing on the losing team, Cissell collected five hits and Art Ewoldt had four. Wetzel had three singles. Mike Schreck, a former Western League umpire, and John McMahon, an ex-Des Moines City League arbiter, covered home plate and the bases, respectively. After the exhibition, Ruth participated in a Drake University football team practice at Drake Stadium. After playing left tackle on offense, he shifted to fullback and scored on a twenty-yard run for a touchdown. Later, he played defense. "In addition to this, the Bambino was forced to pay the usual price of popularity by shaking hands with hundreds, autographing dozens of balls, pictures and sometimes mere scraps of paper, answering hundreds of foolish questions and posing for pictures many, many times," the *Register's* Sec Taylor observed. "But he did it all graciously and without the slightest sign of impatience."[6]

The Yankee slugger led the American League in eight offensive categories that season with forty-seven home runs, 153 runs-batted-in, 139 runs scored, 144 walks, a .516 on-base percentage, .737 slugging average, 1.253 on-base-plus-slugging average, and 365 total bases. He hit .372.

The Demons repeated as Western League pennant winners in 1926, but fell to Three-I League pennant winner Springfield (Illinois) Senators in the Mid-Western Championship three games to one. Player-manager Shano Collins' club finished 99-64 in the regular season, a half-game ahead of the 100-66 Oklahoma City Indians. Oklahoma City claimed that the Wichita Izzies, Lincoln (Nebraska) Links, and Tulsa (Oklahoma) Oilers threw games to the Demons, but league president Mike Sexton cleared them all.[7]

Moon had a Western League-best .750 winning percentage based on a 24-8 pitching record and was named to the all-star team. Griffin also was an all-star thanks to his .345 batting average and eighteen home runs. Wetzel contributed to the Demons' offense with a .352 batting average, eighteen home runs, and 394 total bases.

The Demons slipped to third place in the Western League a year later with an 82-72 record, nineteen games behind first-place Tulsa. However, all-star Sam Langford led the circuit with a .409 batting average and collected 250 hits, including forty-seven doubles and 377 total bases. All-star catcher Joe Sprinz hit .314, and all-star utility player Al Van Camp batted .309. All-star pitcher Fred Ortman posted a 21-11 record, good for the second most wins in the circuit. Teammate Claude Davenport finished 21-10 and pitched the second most innings in the league, 289.

Coming off a record-breaking season, New York Yankees slugger Babe Ruth and teammate Lou Gehrig came to Des Moines on Sunday, October 16, 1927, to play in an exhibition game at Western League Park the following afternoon. Ruth's sixty home runs that season exceeded the totals of twelve major-league teams, including seven in the American League and five in the National League.

Ruth, Gehrig, and Des Moines Baseball Association president Lee Keyser were among ten persons in a box at the Berchel Theater in Des Moines that night who watched "Merry Minstrel Maids," a fundraiser for the Des Moines Federation of Women's Clubs. The show had a baseball skit and "A Bit of Nonsense" by "Two Komical Koons." A parade with blackface minstrels standing on the cars' running boards illustrating the show's features was held in the afternoon preceding the performance.

More than one hundred letters from Des Moines area orphans awaited the two stars upon arrival in the capital. Children at the Des Moines Home for Friendless Children at 21st and High Streets and the Iowa Children's Home, who were old enough to attend the game, had been invited.

Ruth's "Bustin' Babes" and Gehrig's "Larrupin Lous" were comprised of professional and semipro players, including Elton "Sam" Langfold, who played twenty games with the Cleveland Indians at the end of the 1927 season; popular semipros Al Van Camp and Johnny Powers of Davenport; Ed Wetzel, who was slated to have a tryout in the spring with the Philadelphia Athletics; and three players who were on the Des Moines Demons' roster at the end of the 1927 season (pitcher Sam Dailey, catcher Ralph Brandon, and infielder O.H. Peterson).

Despite hitting the ball over the fence in batting practice, neither Yankee star duplicated the feat during the game, which ended 15-7 in Ruth's team's favor. In four at-bats, Ruth hit into a double play, doubled off the left-field fence near the foul line, beat out a roller down the third base line, and singled in right field.

"I shouldn't have swung at it," Ruth said later about hitting into the double play. "It was a bad one. But that pitcher looked so solemn and ambitious he had me hypnotized.

"Ordinarily, I just stand up there naturally and step into it [the ball] when it gets to me," he added. "But when I have only ten or fifteen balls pitched to me in an afternoon, and want to make a homer out of one of them, why, it's up to me to take a step or two or three if the ball isn't coming to my liking."[8]

Gehrig went four-for-five, doubling to center; singling in the third, fifth and sixth innings; and popping out with Ruth pitching.

Both Yankee stars started the game at first base and fielded their position without making an error. Ruth pitched two perfect innings at the end of the game. Gehrig was less effective, allowing five runs in two-thirds of an inning.

Third baseman Van Camp of Ruth's team hit the only home run in the game, a second-inning blast off Dailey that cleared the left-center-field fence. Former Demon Walter Genin almost hit an inside-the-park home run for Gehrig's team.

Afterwards, *Des Moines Register* sports editor Sec Taylor called the game "a baseball atrocity." "Most of the players were not in good condition, errors were frequent and the affair quickly resolved itself into a long wait for the two visitors from New York to take their turn at trying to conjure home runs out of bush league pitching."[9]

The *Tribune*'s Miller had a slightly kinder view of the game and Ruth in particular. "At close range, Mr. Ruth appeared to take the exhibition game, with nondescript lineups, as seriously as most players take a regular major league game. Not for one moment did baseball seem a laughing matter."[10]

Approximately 3,000 fans including 400 youngsters attended the game featuring the "Sultan of Swat" and his teammate.

In 1928, the Demons ended up in last place in the Western League at 63-98 despite Al Van Camp's .351 batting average, league-leading nineteen triples, and fifteen home runs. Lute Boone, Archie Yelle, and Lee Fohl managed the team at one time or another that season. The Demons finished the decade in seventh place with a slightly improved 72-86 record in 1929.

Chapter 5

Night baseball arrives; Feller, Paige square off;
Black Barons, Tigers play first MLB game

The Des Moines Demons and Independence (Kansas) Producers both claim the honor of hosting the first professional baseball game played under permanent lights in Organized Ball. On Friday, May 2, 1930, the Demons beat the Wichita Aviators, 13-6, under permanent lights at Western League Park (also known as Holcomb Park and League Park) at the corner of Sixth and Holcomb Avenues. The audience included Branch Rickey and Cincinnati Reds president Sidney Weil.

Two days earlier, the visiting Muskogee (Oklahoma) Chiefs defeated Independence, 13-3, under permanent lighting. The latter game in Kansas did not receive as much publicity as the game in Des Moines. Nevertheless, the Demons did have the first nationwide radio broadcast of a minor-league night baseball game.[1] The NBC Radio network carried the last half of the contest, which did not end until after midnight due to the 8:30 p.m. starting time. "Unlike the game in Independence, the game in Des Moines was partially broadcast live on NBC radio," author Mark Metcalf noted in the *Fall 2016 Baseball Research Journal*. "That broadcast put Des Moines in the national spotlight, while the achievement in Independence went mostly unnoticed by the mainstream media."[2] The game was also broadcast by shortwave radio overseas to Europe, South America, South Africa, Australia, and the Orient. "The Independence lights were adequate for professional baseball, but the system Keyser used in Des Moines was superior," Kraft said in his 2016 comparison of the two ballparks' permanent lighting systems.[3]

Coming off a five win-six loss road trip to start the season, the Demons and their management expected the new lights to attract a record crowd for the home opener. "Tests have indicated that the playing conditions will be as suitable as the customary daylight," the *Des Moines Tribune* reported.[4]

A lot was at stake. "Many [of the minor league presidents] have looked upon the innovation as the salvation of minor league baseball whose attendance has been shrinking in the last few years," the *Tribune* said. "The magnates are hoping night baseball will become a fixture, allowing more persons to attend the games. This is especially true in the smaller circuits."[5]

At the time, twenty-four baseball leagues with 176 teams were recognized by Organized Baseball. "Not one of the 176 club owners in Organized Baseball saw the possibility of night baseball in the same light as [Demons' president] Lee Keyser and not one of them are [sic] willing to risk his finances in promoting the new venture until Keyser plunged into the project," the *Des Moines Register's* Bert McGrane opined. "Now that he has taken the venturesome step, baseball authorities from far and wide have interested themselves in the project. They are coming here Friday to sit in and witness the result of engineering ingenuity and Lee Keyser's courage."[6]

The *Register's* McGrane clearly credited the Demons' president with bringing night baseball to Des Moines, calling Keyser "the pioneer of night baseball."[7]

"He did not conceive night baseball, nor did he have much of a part in the development of the project," McGrane said. "yet, had it not been for Lee Keyser, night baseball might never have passed the novelty stage and the dream of the engineers who saw the possibilities of baseball under artificial lights might never have been realized."[8]

Engineers adjusted the new lighting system on the preceding Monday, Tuesday, and Wednesday under the direction of F.D. Crowther from Schenectady, New York, and F.W. Ralston of Lynn, Massachusetts. Two light towers were located behind the grandstand. Each tower had fourteen 1,000-watt bulbs in horizontal rows. Towers with thirty-six bulbs each were erected behind first and third base. Two more towers, each with twenty-four bulbs, were located behind the left- and right-field fences, 350 and 400 feet from home plate, respectively.[9]

"Each of the 146 projectors must be focused and the visor adjusted, one at a time," *Register* sports editor Sec Taylor explained. "Then each battery of projectors on the six towers is tested and lastly all of the lights are turned on, candle-foot tests [are] made and further adjustments to equalize and regulate the light are made."[10]

On Thursday, May 1, 1930, Taylor reported that police turned away hundreds of cars of curious fans at the corner of Holcomb and Sixth Avenues the previous night "when all of the lights were throwing their 53,000,000 candle-power of illumination on the ballpark and into the air above it."[11]

When all the lights were first turned on the previous Tuesday night, thousands of birds starting flying around the ballpark and made the sky dark, apparently believing it was sunup, Taylor added.

Two days before the game, Keyser announced that all of the box and reserved seats at Western League Park had been sold, leaving about 5,000 unreserved seats in the 7,000-seat stadium. On the morning of the historic game, the *Des Moines Register* said 11,000 "whooping, howling men and women" were expected to attend the contest.[12]

Depending on the source, the highly anticipated game on May 2 attracted 10,000 to 12,000 spectators, or twice the normal number for a typical home opener. "In lieu of skybox suites, men in suits and fedoras sat on the ground along the foul lines and formed a human warning track in front of the outfield walls, partially obscuring advertisements that decorated them," Mike Wellman wrote in the *Des Moines Register* in 2015.[13]

The Demons put the game away early, scoring eleven runs with seven hits and five walks in the first inning off three Aviator pitchers. In fact, Wichita hurler Rufus Meadows was removed before he could retire a batter. His successor, John Cano, walked the only two batters he faced after reaching three-and-two counts. Former Demon Charles Newbill walked Des Moines starter Bud Tinning to force in a run.

The Demons' Leo Norris, Jim Oglesby, and Stan Keyes each had two hits in the inning, but Tom Hughes was retired on a force out for the second out. Hill Windham then flied out for the third out. "The hitting of the entire team in that inning was of the same variety of hitting that comes on a midsummer day," the *Des Moines Tribune's* Gayle Hayes reported the next day.[14] Wichita scored four of its six runs in the seventh; otherwise, Tinning displayed a "fine assortment of stuff," Hayes added.[15]

Tinning, the winning pitcher that night, sported a 24-2 won-loss record in 1931 and eventually reached the big leagues with the Chicago Cubs. "There doesn't seem to be any difference to me [between day and night baseball]," Tinning told the *Des Moines Register* after the game. "When I dived after that one drive which knocked me over, I located the ball instantly when I searched for it. Even though the bingle came like a rifle shot, it was clearly outlined."[16]

Keyes, who got four hits that night, won the Western League Triple Crown in 1931 with a .369 batting average, thirty-eight home runs, and 160 runs-batted-in.[17] Neither Keyes nor outfielder Tom Hughes had difficulty judging the "soaring fly balls" or the "bullet-like smacks," the *Register* reported.[18]

Demons manager Dave Davenport pointed out that night baseball would give thousands of fans who worked during the day the opportunity to see baseball games. "Many of the summer days are scorching hot and not many people like to sit through the blistering heat," Davenport added. "The cool of the evening affords a much better condition for the thousands who work all day long."[19]

Speaking from the batter's viewpoint, Demon shortstop Hughie Nielsen said, "To me, it seemed easier to hit curves. I don't mean that the curve balls were easier to swing on exactly, but it seemed easier to follow the ball as it broke."[20] Home plate umpire Swazina saw no difference between night and day baseball games either. "I experienced no difficulty in seeing the plays," he observed.[21]

Although the Demons committed four errors that day, they "were errors that happen at any time and in no way could be attributed to the lighting of the park," the *Des Moines Tribune's* Hayes reported.[22]

Even the scribes in Wichita were impressed that night. "The six electrical beacons surrounding the playing field pale a bright summer moon into insignificance without dazzling the players," the *Wichita Beacon* said the next day. "Even when the batters lifted the ball high in the air, the light cast by the beacons enabled the fans to watch the path of the horsehide."[23] *Beacon* columnist Roy Sourbeer waxed "the setting of approximately 12,000 fans afforded a great spectacle."[24]

Two other sports editors were not so sure night baseball under permanent lights would endure. Calling night baseball "a novelty," *St. Paul (Minnesota) Pioneer Press* sports editor Lou McKenna wrote, "The question in my mind is whether it will stand up. I am well pleased with this test, however, and can see the day when night baseball may be generally adopted if the fans accept it as the club owners hope they will."[25] Ralph Wagner, sports editor of the *Omaha Bee*, believed night baseball was a big improvement compared to night football. "It [night baseball] needs more of a tryout, however," Wagner said. "Players can follow the ball and can hit just as well as in the daytime, it is true, but will the fans take to night baseball enough to justify club owners in making the great expenditure necessary to equip their fields?"[26]

Cleveland scout Cy Slapnicka, who signed Van Meter native Bob Feller five years later, predicted, "Within a year, every Class A and Class B ballpark in the country will be equipped with lights."[27] Slapnicka pitched for Cedar Rapids Washington High School from 1902 to 1905 and scouted for the Cleveland Indians from 1921 to 1941 and from 1947 to 1960. In addition to Feller, he signed other Iowans, such as Bill Zuber, 218-game winner Earl Whitehill, and Hal Trosky.[28]

St. Louis Browns business manager Bill Friel was also impressed with the Demons' first attempt at night baseball under permanent lights. "I look for it [night baseball] to spread all over the country in the very near future," Friel said.[29]

"There is no doubt that the game can be played satisfactorily at night," said Mike Sexton, president of the Professional Baseball Association. "This game here may be the first step in vastly changing playing conditions in the minors."[30]

Western League president Dale Gear was pleased, too. "The demonstration tonight was very practical," Gear said. "I am confident that night baseball will succeed."[31]

Club and city officials also expressed optimism. "I am very confident that the lovers of outdoor sports have a tremendous treat in store for them in these lighting installations," said Demon president Joe Christy.[32] Admitting that he had not seen a baseball game in several years until the Demons-Aviators game, Des Moines mayor Parker Crouch commented, "Now that they will play at night, I expect to see many more [games]."[33] Des Moines police chief Henry Alber said, "It's o.k. I have been looking forward to this game and I was not in the least disappointed."[34]

Even representatives of other sports were impressed. "This is going to be a great thing for the baseball fans of Des Moines, and there are many who cannot attend afternoon games during the week," Des Moines Boxing Commission member Harry Searle said.[35] Referring to the Des Moines Demons' owner Lee Keyser, Chamberlain Hotel manager Chester Hartnagel added, "I think Lee Keyser has started something that will spread far and wide. I was well satisfied with the playing of the game and believe it to be practical in every way."[36]

A survey conducted by four men from Drake University from 7:30 p.m. to 12:30 a.m. on Saturday, May 3, showed that 3,311 cars were parked by people who saw the game that night. Cars from Polk County numbered 2,635; Story County, fifty-nine; Dallas County, forty-two; and Warren County, twenty. A total of 676 autos came from outside Polk County, while forty-six were from outside Iowa's borders.[37] The next night, 1,200 fans turned out to see the Demons beat the Aviators, 6-5, under the lights, and the "players again had no difficulty in seeing the ball."[38]

Tornadoes that ripped across Iowa, Nebraska, Kansas, Missouri, Illinois, Wisconsin, and Minnesota killed sixteen people the previous day. Three separate twisters struck northeast Kansas and northwest Missouri alone. Although Des Moines received a "violent downpour of rain and hail," meteorologist Charles Reed said on Thursday, May 1, that the deadly storms in the Midwest and Plains would not impact the next night's home opener under lights.[39]

Des Moines' experiment with night baseball was so successful that several other minor league clubs including Bloomington, Illinois; Decatur, Illinois; Houston; Omaha; and Wichita started planning for their own permanent lighting systems. The Class D Mississippi Valley League's attendance increase of 52,470 that season was attributed to night games played under artificial lights.[40] At least thirty-eight teams in fourteen minor leagues had introduced night baseball that summer.[41]

In 1930, the Demons finished in the Western League's first division for the first time since 1927. Managers Claude Davenport and Shano Collins guided the club to a 77-71 record. All-star outfielder Stan Keyes led the league with thirty-five home runs, 140 runs-batted-in, and 358 total bases. He also hit .340, clubbed eighteen triples, and scored 123 runs. Al Van Camp had a solid season with a .344 batting average and eighteen home runs. Bud Tinning posted a 16-11 record from the mound.

On Monday, June 18, 1934, William Parker Chase, who headed Des Moines' franchise in the new Western League, died in New York City at age 64. The cause of death was listed as pneumonia.[42]

Chase left Des Moines in approximately 1904 and had lived in New York City about twenty years. He worked in the mail order business. "He is remembered in Des Moines as the organizer of an early baseball club, proprietor of a sporting goods store and as manager of a theater in the building, now demolished, which housed the old city auditorium," his obituary in the *Des Moines Register* stated shortly after his death. Besides his business ventures, Chase wrote music, including several musical comedies.

He and his brother were the only survivors of a family with ten children. He was also survived by his wife, the former Nellie Rawson.

On Wednesday night, October 7, 1936, Bob Feller and Negro Leagues pitching star Satchel Paige squared off in an exhibition game at Western League Park. "The colored team is of major league caliber and Wednesday night's contest will afford fans of this vicinity their first opportunity to see the Van Meter star pitch against the heavy hitters," the *Register's* Sec Taylor wrote before the game featuring Negro National League and major league all-stars.[43] The Negro N.L. all-stars had previously played three games in Des Moines in 1936.

The Negro N.L. all-stars topped the (white) major league all-stars, 4-2, although the seventeen-year-old Feller outpitched Paige. "What really matters is that 5,000 Iowans got to see just how great a pitcher 17-year-old Bob Feller of Van Meter, Iowa, really is," the *Register's* Leighton Housh wrote the next day.[44]

Facing some of the best Black hitters in Negro Leagues baseball, Feller struck out eight batters in three innings of work. He gave up a scratch hit when he failed to cover first base after a pop up fell between him and first baseman Johnny Mize, who got to the ball in time to make the play. Paige fanned seven of the eleven batters he faced and allowed one hit, a single by former St. Louis Browns third baseman Heinie Mueller.

The Negro NL all-stars jumped out to a 2-0 lead when Earl Caldwell replaced Feller on the mound. After doubles by Sammy Hughes and Jim West, West was trapped between second and third as Bill Perkins reached first on a fielder's choice. Perkins then advanced to second as West was being retired in the rundown. After

Perkins moved to third on a grounder, he scored on Chester Williams' smash to right-center field.

The major league all-stars tied the game in the fifth after Andy Porter had replaced Paige on the mound. The Cardinals' Mike Ryba singled to left center and scored when the Pirates' Al Todd doubled to left. Todd scored the tying run when the left fielder's throw home eluded the catcher. The major league all-stars eventually loaded the bases, but skipper Rogers Hornsby and the Cardinals' Mize failed to drive them in.

The Negro NL all-stars regained the lead in the sixth with one run off Ryba, who played left field the first four innings and then pitched the final five frames for Hornsby's crew. Hughes singled and scored on Perkins' triple to the left-center-field fence.

The major league all-stars missed a scoring opportunity in the seventh when Drake University alumnus Lynn King beat out a slow roller toward third and moved to second on the third baseman's errant throw to first. King was picked off second, however, with one out and Hornsby at the plate. Hornsby then singled to center, which would have scored King.

The major league all-stars missed another chance in the eighth when Goodman walked, but was thrown out at the plate after Ryba's double. The Negro NL all-stars padded their lead in the ninth when Felton Snow singled and crossed the plate on Cool Papa Bell's two-base hit.

Ryba had two of his team's six hits off three Negro NL all-star pitchers. Although Mize and Gus Suhr hit .328 and .312 during the regular season, neither got a hit off Paige and his two successors. The Negro NL all-stars collected twelve hits off Feller, Caldwell, and Ryba. Bell and Hughes each had three hits to lead the Negro NL all-stars' attack. The game took only two hours and five minutes.

The Negro NL all-stars defeated a group of major league all-stars, 5-2, on Friday, October 2, 1936. Leroy Matlock went the distance and struck out nine major leaguers, so Paige was not called upon to pitch. Major league all-star Jim Weaver fanned eleven in a losing effort.

Feller was supposed to pitch for Prager Beer, the state semipro champions, against the Page Fence Giants the following Sunday. The Prager Beer team was supposed to use the same lineup that won the state title. However, the game was cancelled due to inclement weather.

Feller was coming off a brilliant rookie season at age seventeen. He nearly tied Rube Waddell's American League record for most strikeouts in a game by a pitcher with fifteen against the St. Louis Browns on August 23. Three weeks later, he struck out seventeen Philadelphia Athletics to break the AL record and tie the major league mark set by the Cardinals' Dizzy Dean. Overall, Feller finished 5-3 with a 3.34 earned run average, appeared in fourteen games including eight starts, completed five, earned a save, and fanned seventy-six batters in sixty-two innings.

Feller's status became unclear when the Des Moines club protested that its efforts to sign the teenage sensation had been frustrated by Cleveland's signing of Feller in violation of major-minor league rules. However, Cleveland argued that Fargo, North Dakota, of the Northern League had actually signed Feller so the rules had not been broken. Feller's contract was shifted to New Orleans in the Southern League. However, he did not report to either minor league club. Instead, he spent the summer of 1935 playing with a Cleveland semiprofessional team and working out with the Cleveland Indians[45].

In December 1936, though, commissioner Kennesaw Mountain Landis ruled that Feller was Cleveland Indians' property and Cleveland must pay the Des Moines club $7,500.

Landis explained "that from the beginning of this inquiry the player and his father [who also signed the contract because Feller was a minor] have exclusively sought and supported validation of the Cleveland contract."[46] The $7,500 awarded to the Des Moines club was based on the amount offered for Feller's contract as a free agent, Landis said.

The Associated Press said Landis's decision "was regarded as a great triumph for the major leaguers who are in the midst of a campaign to open the baseball market even down to the sandlots for major league scouts."[47]

Calling the ruling "wise" and "just," Des Moines Demons president Lee Keyser said, "I was fighting for a principle that was right and am well pleased with the verdict of the judge."[48] (Landis served as a U.S. federal judge from 1905 to 1922.)

Landis's decision, however, didn't please Feller or his father. "The Des Moines club had no more claim on me than some club out on the Pacific Coast," the young protégé told the *Des Moines Tribune*. "I suppose if I had been born near St. Louis, they'd have awarded it to that club.

"I never signed a contract with Des Moines, never played with Des Moines, and never would sign a contract with Des Moines," he added.[49]

The elder Feller agreed. "I don't believe $7,500 should have been paid to Des Moines, for Bob never had a contract with Keyser and never worked out with the team. Des Moines had no more right to Bob's contract than any other minor league club."[50]

Sportswriter Paul Mickelson of the *Des Moines Register* indicated after the October 7 exhibition game that some major league clubs were willing to offer as much as $100,000 for Feller.[51] The Associated Press also claimed that Keyser tried to sign Feller and even had the lad work out at League Park in 1935.[52]

In his book sixty-five years later, Feller said he received a check for $1 to make the contract legal. He was also given a baseball signed by all of the Cleveland Indians. "I didn't care about how much money I was getting or the amount of the signing bonus," Feller wrote. "I just wanted the opportunity to play, even at the lowest level in Class D in Fargo, North Dakota, the Indians' farm club."[53]

Feller also praised Slapnicka, the scout who signed him to his first contract, and Paige, his mound opponent in the October 1936 exhibition game. "He [Slapnicka] was one of the best scouts of all time," Feller said. "He signed some of the best players: Herb Score, Lou Boudreau, Mel Harder, and Hal Trosky."[54] Feller rated Paige one of the top five or ten pitchers of all time. "There was nobody better than Satchel when it came to the art of pitching, or preparation for that matter. Nobody did their homework so well," Feller recalled. "He knew the scouting report on everybody. He knew the hitters and their tendencies, and he could spot a hitter's weaknesses very quickly, quicker than anyone I ever knew. He was respected by everyone all over the baseball world as one of the game's greatest pitchers."[55]

In 1937, the Demons were affiliated with the major-league St. Louis Browns, the first time a Des Moines ballclub had been connected to a major-league team. The Browns had thirteen other farm teams that year, while their in-state rival, the St. Louis Cardinals of the National League, had a major-league high thirty-three.[56]

On May 16, 1937, the *Des Moines Register* announced that the Chicago American Giants and Cincinnati Tigers from the Negro Leagues would play that Wednesday and Thursday night at Western League Park. Two days later, *Register* sports editor Sec Taylor described the contests as "major league games" in his column, "Sittin' In With the Athletes."[57] "It was claimed before the [Chicago American] Giants appeared here a year ago that at least six or seven of their players would be in the National or American leagues if they were white," Taylor observed, "and after the Negroes defeated the Des Moines Western leaguers and the House of David, there were few who would dispute those claims."[58] Lee Keyser, president of the Des Moines Demons, arranged for teams from the Negro Leagues to play in Des Moines and elsewhere after the Chicago club's exhibition games in the Iowa capital in 1936.

However, both games were rained out. A week later, the *Register* disclosed that two new games featuring the Tigers and the Birmingham Black Barons would be played on the following Wednesday and Thursday nights. The Black Barons were champions of the Negro Southern League in 1936. Once again, the games were regularly-scheduled games in the Negro American League and would count in the standings, but the first game of the two-game series was rained out.

Hence, the first game in Iowa between major league teams was not the Field of Dreams game pitting the New York Yankees against the Chicago White Sox on August 12, 2021, outside of Dyersville. The game actually occurred eighty-four years earlier in Des Moines after three postponements. The Black Barons, a recent addition to the Negro American League, came from behind to defeat the Negro League's Tigers, 8-4, on Thursday, May 27, 1937, at Western League Park. Major League Baseball finally recognized the Negro Leagues as a "major" league in December 2020 when commissioner Rob Manfred Jr. announced that Major League Baseball was correcting "a longtime oversight" in the game's history.[59] Approximately 3,400 players competed in the Negro Leagues from 1920 through 1948—the time span officially recognized by Major League Baseball.

Trailing 2-1, the Black Barons responded with five runs in the fifth inning. "The Barons jumped on [Cincinnati pitcher] Gene Bremmer in the fifth, after he had hurled brilliant ball, and shelled him from the mound," the *Des Moines Register* recounted the next day. "Birmingham bunched five hits and took advantage of a pair of Tiger errors to push across their five tallies."[60]

Cincinnati scored twice in the eighth to narrow the gap to 6-4, but Birmingham added two runs in the top of the ninth and held the Tigers scoreless in the bottom of the ninth. "Herman [Red] Howard, husky Baron hurler, stopped the Cincinnati batters with his southpaw slants and scattered nine hits," the *Register* wrote.[61] In recording the win, Howard struck out seven, walked four, and uncorked two wild pitches. The five-foot-ten, 198-pound native of Birmingham, Alabama, had a 3-2 record and a 7.65 earned average that season, his first in the Negro Leagues. In five games and thirty-seven and two-thirds innings, Howard allowed forty-four hits, walked fourteen, and struck out twenty-five.

The Des Moines newspaper described the game as "a colorful exhibition" and noted that "Ted Radcliff [sic] [the Tigers' catcher] showed why he is ranked as one of the finest catchers in the game with his sparkling work."[62]

Third baseman Parnell Woods and first baseman Jim Canada collected three hits each to pace Birmingham's ten-hit attack. The Black Barons rapped out six doubles, including two by Canada and one each by Woods, catcher Harry Barnes, right fielder David Whatley, and left fielder Sylvester Owens.

Right fielder Lloyd Davenport, a .342 hitter in 1937, had four of Cincinnati's nine hits. Shortstop Sonny Harris and his replacement, Howard Easterling, a .351 hitter that season, had two-base knocks for the Tigers. The teams committed nine errors; Tiger second baseman Cowan Hyde had four alone. The Tigers played home games at Crosley Field, the home ballpark of the Cincinnati Reds, and used second-hand Reds uniforms. The team from the Queen City was founded by DeHart Hubbard, the first Black to win an individual Olympic gold medal. The Tigers disbanded after just one season in the Negro Leagues.[63]

One year later, the Western League folded, marking the first time since 1900 that Des Moines did not have a professional baseball team.

On the morning of Thursday, July 28, 1938, the *Des Moines Register* previewed that night's game between the Kansas City Monarchs and the Chicago American Giants. The newspaper said "several members of the two clubs are of major league ability, but because of their color they are not in the top circuits."[64] The Monarchs were described as "a well balanced club, sprinkled with veteran stars with one of the greatest Negro pitchers of many years [Hilton Smith]." Although the Chicago American Giants had won seventeen world Black championships, the club was coming off two substandard seasons. When the first half of the Negro American

League season ended on the Fourth of July, the Memphis Red Sox led the Monarchs by a half-game. Meanwhile, Chicago completed the first half with a .500 record.

Chicago had lost three straight to Kansas City coming into the game that night at Western League Park. The American Giants' fourteen-hit offense was too much for the Monarchs, though, and Chicago won, 11-4. The victors had two home runs, two triples, and four doubles off three Kansas City hurlers. The Monarchs were not at full strength; right fielder Ed Mayweather and second baseman Newt Allen were out with injuries.

Chicago scored three times in the first on a walk, hit batsman, an error, and three singles. Kansas City responded with four runs in the second and knocked out starter Jesse Houston. His successor, Tommy Johnson, retired the side, gave up only four hits in seven innings of relief, and earned the win. The American Giants added two runs in the third with the help of the first of two triples by Alex Radcliff. Chicago scored four more runs in the fifth, one run in the seventh, and one run in the eighth. Radcliff, Ed Young, and Sparks each had three hits for Chicago. The losing pitcher Vet Barnes was charged with eight hits and eight runs in four and two-thirds innings.

In 1939, the Kansas City Monarchs' roster included five future Baseball Hall of Famers: player-manager Andy Cooper, pitcher Hilton Smith, left fielder Willard Brown, center fielder Norman "Turkey" Stearns, and first baseman John "Buck" O'Neil. On Thursday, May 26, Brown, Stearns, and O'Neil helped that season's Negro American League pennant winner beat the Indianapolis A.B.C.'s, 11-2, at Western League Park. Brown alone slugged two triples and two doubles in five plate appearances. "All of the blows, which brought in three runs, rattled off the center-field fence," the *Des Moines Register* reported the next day. [65]

Kansas City scored in every inning except the fourth. In the second inning, catcher Jesse Green homered over the left-field fence. Indianapolis pitcher Tee Mitchell "managed to whiff five rivals with his 'nothing' ball but walked four, three of which were eventual runs."[66] On the other hand, Monarchs starter George

Walker, "a sidearm specialist with a sizzling curve," had only one bad inning.[67] In the fifth, Indianapolis loaded the bases on a walk, double, and poorly-fielded bunt. "Walker, puzzled, couldn't decide where to throw with the result that all hands were safe," the *Register* wrote.[68] The next batter, Red Moore, sacrificed Tommy Butts home for the team's first run. After Gabby Kemp struck out, Monarch catcher Green three out Spencer Davis at third to end the threat. The A.B.C.'s scored again in the sixth on a double and sacrifice fly by Oscar Boone.

The best fielding play came in the first inning when Kansas City's first baseman caught a sharply-hit drive by Monk Davis and stepped on first for an unassisted double play. Six hundred spectators turned out to see the Negro American League contest that was played under threatening skies.

On Thursday, July 6, the *Register* previewed the next night's game between the St. Louis Stars, a "high class defensive team," and the Kansas City Monarchs, a "hard hitting ... team."[69] The article noted that the Stars had defeated the Monarchs, 6-0, on the previous Sunday in Cleveland, Ohio.

St. Louis' fielding prowess was displayed when it beat Kansas City, 9-5, at Western League Park. In the fifth inning, shortstop Buddy Armour made a one-handed grab of Rainey Bibbs' smash with a runner in scoring position. In the same inning, right fielder Bill Bradford ran back into the right-field corner to haul down Turkey Stearns' drive. In the ninth, left fielder Dan Wilson made a shoestring catch of a drive off the bat of Henry Milton.

Right-hander Robert Dean scattered seven Monarchs hits, allowed three earned runs, struck out seven, and walked five to pick up the win for the Stars. "Dean's mates snuffed several Monarch uprisings, most notable of which came in the fourth and seventh frames," the *Register* wrote the next day. In the fourth, the Monarchs tied the game, 4-4, after scoring a pair of unearned runs. In the seventh, Armour stopped an apparent hit through the mound and cut down the advancing base runners.

Armour also starred at the plate, collecting three hits, including a double, and driving in five runs. Wilson also had three of the Stars' twelve hits. Milton and Willard Brown had two hits each for the Monarchs. Lefty Moses was tagged with the loss. Kansas City's hurler gave up seven hits and seven runs (four earned), struck out six, and walked four in four-and-third innings.

Spurred by their owner, J.L. Wilkinson, the Kansas City Monarchs thrashed the Chicago American Giants, 20-7, in a battle of Negro American League titans on Friday, July 28, 1939, at Western League Park. Before the game, Wilkinson, the only white owner in the circuit, pointed out his club had not won a game in the Iowa capital in two years.

The Monarchs jumped out to an early lead, scoring five runs in the first inning on four hits including a home run by Turkey Stearns . Kansas City wrapped out nine more hits in an eleven-run sixth inning to lead, 19-4. After Kansas City knocked out Chicago starter Jesse Houston in the big inning, right fielder Henry Milton homered off the new pitcher, Lemuel Williams. Before the inning ended, Lefty Bowe replaced Williams and eleven runs crossed the plate.

In all, the Monarchs pounded three American Giant pitchers for twenty hits and twenty-nine total bases. Chicago had seventeen hits good for twenty-three total bases. "But the latter played poorly in the field, committing eight chargeable errors against one for the Kansas City aggregation," the *Des Moines Register* reported the next day.[70]

Milton had a double and two singles as well as the home run for the victors. Stearns had two singles in addition to a home run. Teammate Ted Strong chipped in with four singles. Two other Monarchs, third baseman Rainey Bibbs and catcher Paul Hardy, each had two hits. For Chicago, shortstop Joe Sparks had a triple and two singles. Third baseman Alex Radcliff collected a double and two singles, and left fielder Brown was credited with three hits. Three other American Giants had two hits each: left fielder Wilson Redus, first baseman Stubby Byes, and catcher Pepper Bassett. On the morning of the game, the *Register* wrote that Bassett would work behind the plate while seated in a rocking chair, which he had done several times. However, the story the next day did not mention anything about Bassett's catching during the game.

Kansas City starter Big Train Jackson allowed three runs and five hits in one-and-two-thirds innings. Frank Bradley, the winning pitcher, gave up one run and six hits in four-and-a-third innings. The Monarchs' third pitcher, Willie Hutchinson, surrendered three runs and six hits in three innings of work. American Giants starter Tommy Johnson was tagged with eight runs and ten hits in four innings and got the loss. Houston gave up seven runs and six hits in one-and-two-thirds innings. Lemuel Williams faced only five batters but was nicked for four runs and three hits. Chicago's last hurler, Lefty Bowe, allowed one run and one hit in three-and-a-third innings. Neither of the expected starters, Hilton Smith for the Monarchs nor Ted Trent for the American Giants, saw action. Smith won twenty-seven games in 1938, and Trent averaged thirty wins a season for several years.

In 1939, the Monarchs won the Negro American League title with a 42-25 record and beat the St. Louis Stars four games to one to win the Negro Leagues championship.

Chapter 6

*Monarchs, Western League
return; Stabelfeld tosses no-hitter*

Frank "Fireball" Bradley's arm and bat were too much for the Chicago American Giants on Monday, June 10, 1940, at Western League Park. As a result, the Kansas City Monarchs defeated the Chicago club, 7-3, in a Negro American League game. Bradley scattered five hits, struck out ten, and hit a home run in the fourth inning off American Giants starter Wadel Miller.

The Monarchs got a dozen hits off losing pitcher Miller, including another four-bagger by first baseman Buck O'Neil and two doubles. Jojo Green, who was being compared to Rogers Hornsby, led the way with three hits including a double and two singles. Bradley and left fielder Fred McDaniel each had two hits.

The Monarchs led 1-0 after the first inning and added two runs in the second on three hits including Jesse Williams' double. A double by Green and a single by Newt Allen accounted for another run in the third. In the seventh, Green singled and scored on O'Neil's home run over the right-field fence. Chicago scored twice in the fourth on two hits. In the eighth, Willie Sims singled and scored on a triple into center field by Ted Bond. "Sparkling fielding plays kept the 700 shivering spectators in the stands until the final out," the *Des Moines Register* wrote the next day. "Leroy Morney, former Pittsburgh Crawford star now shortstopping with the Chicago crew," handled nine chances, two of them jewel stops, without an error."[1]

In addition to striking out ten Chicago batters, Bradley walked one, and unleashed two wild pitches. Miller struck out four, walked two, and hit one batter.

In June 1940, *Register* sports editor Sec Taylor predicted professional baseball would not return to the capital until the masses felt they needed a Class A or another Class B league. He also speculated that the major-league clubs would own and operate most of new minor league clubs outright.

"I would oppose baseball here if it were necessary to beg the finances from business men to keep the team going," Taylor wrote in his popular column, "Sittin' In With the Athletes."[2]

If a big league club wanted to run a team in Des Moines, he made this proposal: "The franchise is yours, the team is yours. Des Moines will see that you get a ballpark at reasonable rental and we might try to sell some tickets for the opening game or a special day. But you'll be on your own. If you give us a good team, you won't lose money; you'll probably make some. But if you give us a lousy club, you'll lose money. And it will be you, not us, who loses it."[3]

On a perfect day for a baseball game, the thirty-three-year-old grandstand at the old Western League ballpark at Sixth and Holcomb Avenues was sold at auction for $2,200 on Thursday, April 26, 1945. "I never thought I'd own a grandstand, but I do now," said W.F. Kucharo, president of Kucharo Construction Co. of Des Moines.[4] The auction was conducted by George Garton, secretary of the Des Moines Independent School Board, the owner of the property.

"Going once, going twice, going three times and gone for $2,200 to the gentleman [Kucharo] in the tan coat," Garton exclaimed.[5] After bidding $2,100, Kucharo started to leave the ballpark, telling Garton, "Let us know if we get it, George."[6] However, someone in the crowd of approximately fifty men raised the bid by $50. Kucharo stayed and increased his bid to $2,200. Afterwards, he said he would probably dispose of the old lumber and light structural steel in a piecemeal manner. Under the school board's stipulations, the grandstand had to be torn down and removed within sixty days. That included the dilapidated wood and iron benches, legless wooden chairs that had served as reserved seats, and the press box on top of the grandstand, except for the fence around the ballpark and a few small outbuildings.

The grandstand was built by Tom Fairweather and Frank Isbell in 1912, when the two men took over the franchise. They sold the ballpark and grandstand to the Des Moines Independent School District in 1920 for about $8,000 and other real estate owned by the school district. They were also given the right to keep using the site as a ballpark for ten years. For several years until the auction, the vacant ballpark had been used by North High School for an athletic field and for softball and twilight league ball. The light towers were moved earlier to a World War II ordnance plant in Ankeny.

The Western League came back to life in 1947 and Des Moines' franchise was named Bruins, reflecting the Chicago Cubs' ownership.

The Bruins shut out Lincoln, Nebraska, 9-0, in their first Western League game at Pioneer Memorial Stadium, the site of today's Principal Park, on Friday, June 20, 1947. A crowd of 4,262 turned out for the first night game in Des Moines in ten years. Bruins shortstop Roy Smalley smacked a home run and double to lead the home team's offense. Des Moines starting pitcher Bill Bonness gave up three hits, walked five, and struck out six Athletics. Smalley went on to play in the majors with the Chicago Cubs among other teams.

In his account of the historic game the next day, *Des Moines Register* sports editor Sec Taylor noted that the four ticket-sellers could not handle all of the late-arriving crowd fast enough to get all of them into the stadium before the first pitch.[7] All of the ballpark's box seats were sold by that afternoon.

Pioneer Memorial Stadium had a seating capacity of about 5,000 on opening night, including 2,184 in the bleachers, 2,000 in the grandstand, and 356 in chairs in the box seat area. The field was about 330 feet from home plate down the foul lines to the left- and right-field corners and 380 feet to center field. In addition to a substantial, well-built grandstand, Pioneer Memorial Stadium featured a concession stand, restrooms, clubhouses for both home and visiting teams, and an umpires' room.

The neighborhood around Pioneer Memorial Stadium was much different than it is today around Principal Park. "In those days, the area around the park was full of factories and lumberyards and warehouses," former majority owner Michael Gartner said in 2014. "The roads were dirt, and there were train tracks everywhere. There were neighborhoods across the Raccoon River and the Des Moines River, but no one lived on the ballpark side of the rivers."[8]

In the summer of 1954, the 15-year-old Gartner started working in the sports department at the *Des Moines Register*. Besides answering the telephone and taking dictation, he would occasionally cover high school sports from "the tiny and rickety press box plopped down atop the metal roof at the ballpark."[9] "It was still a grimy part of town dominated by factories and warehouses."[10]

Bruins 1948 (Courtesy: Scott Sailor/Iowa Cubs)

The Bruins actually played their first home game that season at Birdland Park on the north side of Des Moines on Saturday, May 10, 1947. A crowd of 2,200 saw the home team beat the Denver Grizzlies, 13-10, in ten innings. After hitting a game-tying homer in the ninth, Bruin Clifford Aberson's 400-foot blast with two on in the tenth inning provided the margin of victory. Additional bleachers were installed at Birdland Park for the opening game. There were no box or reserved seats.

The Bruins finished second in the Western League in 1947, four-and-half games behind the first-place Sioux City Soos. They lost to Pueblo three games to one in the first round of the playoffs. The Western League all-star team included four Bruins: third baseman Les Peden, outfielder Carmen Mauro, utility man Russ Burns, and pitcher Herb Chmiel, who had a league leading 2.23 earned run average and .778 winning percentage, thanks to a 14-4 record.

Negro League teams made their last appearance in Des Moines on Thursday, June 24, 1948, at Pioneer Memorial Stadium. Down 4-1, the Kansas City Monarchs scored six runs on one hit in the bottom of the eighth inning to beat the Memphis Red Sox, 7-4. Tabbed a day before as "two of the fastest teams in the Negro baseball leagues," the Monarchs featured player-manager Buck O'Neil, Hank Thompson, and Willard Brown.[11]

In the bottom of the eighth inning, Red Sox starter Buddy Woods walked the first three batters he faced and was taken out of the game. Reliever Ray Sharp then picked Brown off first base. The Monarchs cut the score to 4-3 on a Memphis error, two walks, and a fielder's choice, which loaded the bases with two outs. Pinch-hitting, O'Neil ran the count to three balls and two strikes before hitting a single that drove in three runs. Moments later, the thirty-six-year-old Negro Leagues veteran stole third and scored when the catcher's throw to third went into left field.

Kansas City recorded six hits including doubles by Thompson and catcher Mickey Taborn. Memphis tallied seven hits including a triple and double by Colas and a double by first baseman Bob Boyd. Willie Wells Sr. had two hits for the Red Sox.

The winning pitcher, twenty-year-old Gene Richardson, allowed four runs and seven hits. He struck out six and walked one. Sharp was tagged with the loss despite facing only two batters.

The Monarchs repeated as Negro American League title holders in 1948 with a 67-34-3 record. However, the Birmingham Black Barons beat them in the championship series four games to three with one tie. The Red Sox finished last in the league with a 43-65-4 record.

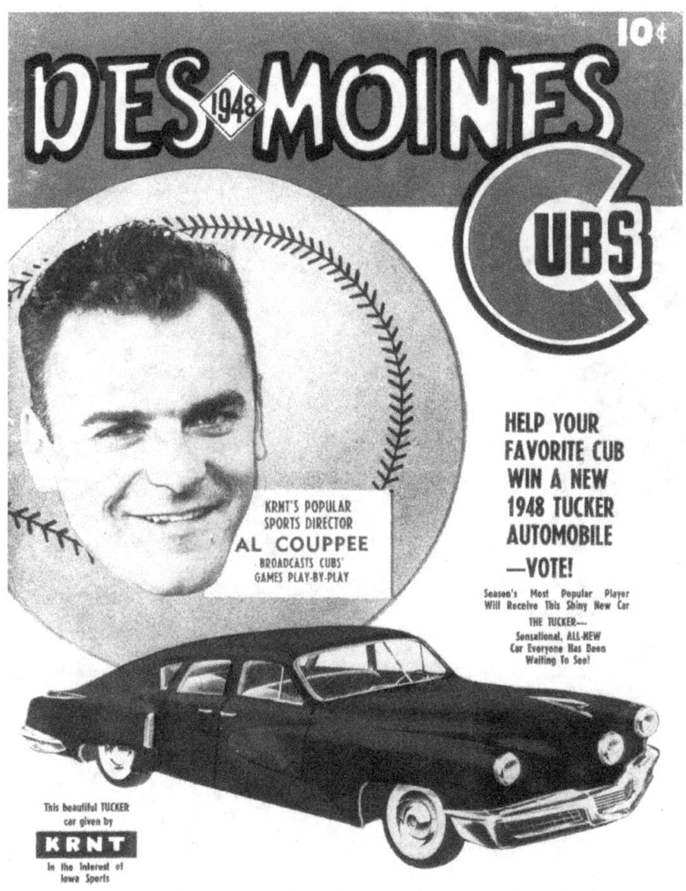

1948 Bruins program (Courtesy: Scott Sailor/Iowa Cubs)

With the help of six former minor leaguers, the House of David baseball team from Benton Harbor, Michigan, defeated the Harlem Globetrotters nine on Friday, June 17, 1949, at Pioneer Memorial Stadium. Dick Mullins had pitched for San Diego in the Pacific Coast League, and Jim Hayes and Zank Glossenger had played in the Pittsburgh Pirates and Chicago Cubs organizations, respectively. Jerry Sebring, Stretch Jansen, and Hugh Cook had played at the Class D level at one time or another. The House of David team came into the game with a .738 winning percentage over thirty years.

Carl Sawatski April 1948 (Courtesy: Scott Sailor/Iowa Cubs)

Brushing off a leadoff walk on a three-ball, two-strike count, northwest Iowa native Elvin "Stubby" Stabelfeld retired the next twenty-seven batters in a row in route to a no-hitter at Pioneer Memorial Stadium Tuesday, August 17, 1949. The Bruins won, 7-0, cutting the Pueblo Dodgers' second-place lead to two-and-a-half games. "Stubby, as placid all the way as one of the cows on his dad's farm up near Aurelia, mixed his crackling curve with a down-swerving fast ball and a pitch that is known in the trade as a 'slider.' This is a junior-size curve, which darts just far enough to keep the hitters off balance," the *Register's* Bill Bryson wrote afterward.[12]

Throwing his fourth shutout of the season, Stabelfeld only had two close calls when Pueblo was at bat. "The fans had a scare when [Dick] Teed lashed a hard shot to the left of shortstop Frank Whitman who was playing despite a painfully swollen left forearm," Bryson wrote. "An inch or so farther and it would have been a hit. But Whitman snagged it on the first vicious bounce, snagged it in the webbing of his glove, and threw Teed out."[13] In the first inning, Bruin second baseman Danny Lynch speared a sharp grounder between first and second base and threw the runner out at first. A crowd of 3,272 fans was on hand for Stabelfeld's brush with perfection.

Despite adverse playing conditions, the Des Moines Bruins beat their major-league brethren from Chicago, 7-4, on Tuesday, September 6, 1949, at Pioneer Memorial Stadium. The record 7,915 spectators could not fit into the grandstands and bleachers, so many fans had to stand or sit eight to ten deep on damp grass around the outfield fence.[14] "The infield was so sticky and slippery that the players could scarcely move out of their tracks," *Des Moines Register* sports editor Sec Taylor said.[15] Although gasoline was burned on the wet playing field before the game, "the going was treacherous and players were skidding around like kittens on a waxed floor," the *Register's* Bill Bryson wrote in his post-game summary.[16]

Bruins pitcher Paul Schneiders allowed nine hits and walked seven batters but was saved by four double plays and catcher Les Peden's work behind the plate. (Peden threw out four Cubs who tried to steal a base.) The Bruins scored once in the fifth inning to take the lead for good at 2-1. They added three runs in the seventh and two tallies in the eighth that featured doubles by Peden and Bob Talbot. Talbot went five-for-five at the plate off Cub rookie hurler Ed Kowalski, who had played in the Pacific Coast League in 1948. Former Des Moines infielders Roy Smalley and Wayne Terwilliger went a combined zero-for-three with one walk for the Cubs. Smalley, who was named to the major-league all-star rookie team in 1948, grounded out and drew a walk; Terwilliger struck out and grounded out to short.

Bruins shortstop Clayton Johnson also made a "sensational, twisting backhand catch of a fly" that brought the crowd to its feet.[17] The *Register's* Bryson said the five-foot-six infielder "was running, twisting, turning all at once when, in some incredible manner, he grabbed Hank Sauer's Texas leaguer near the left-field foul line— ending up in a fancy somersault that failed to dislodge the ball."[18]

49 Bruins Tony Jacobs and Rigelsby (Courtesy: Scott Sailor/Iowa Cubs)

Bryson described the Bruins' victory over their big league cousins as "merely pleasant and artistic."[19] "Eliminate the big difference in the throwing of the two teams and one would not have known which was the major league club," Taylor opined. "Even though the Chicago club is a tail-end outfit, there is a distinct difference between a minor league club and a major league club, though on occasions the minor leaguers will defeat their big brothers."[20] Although the Bruins' win pleased him, it meant nothing to him, Taylor added. While the Bruins were battling for a Western League playoff position, the Cubs were mired in last place in the National League with a 52-82 record, thirty-one-and-a-half games behind first-place St. Louis.

In the nightcap, Des Moines edged Sioux City, 4-1, to lock up a spot in the playoffs. Fewer than 2,000 spectators were on hand for the game that did not end until 11:44 p.m. Talbot was hitless in the second game, but Peden's double down the left-field line brought in two Bruins in the fifth. Des Moines moved into a third-place tie with Denver, three-and-a-half games in back of league-leading Lincoln.

The next day, last place Sioux City beat the Bruins twice, 6-4 and 7-4. But Des Moines still had a shot at second place thanks to Denver's win over the Pueblo Dodgers. However, the Bruins finished in fourth place, five games behind Lincoln, the regular season champion. The club had revenge on its mind when the Governor's Cup playoffs started two nights later in Lincoln; Des Moines manager Stan Hack's crew won the regular season pennant in 1948, but lost in the first round of the playoffs to Lincoln that year.

In 1949, though, the Bruins reached the finals, but lost to Pueblo four games to three. The Western League's all-star team did not include any Bruins, but first baseman Fred Richards had a circuit-leading 178 hits and pitcher "Stubby" Stabelfeld tied two other hurlers for most wins with seventeen. The club drew 210,204 fans, the third highest total in the league.

Chapter 7

*Baker debuts; Fear throws
gem; Bruins repeat as champs;
stadium named after Taylor*

In 1950, infielder Gene Baker became the first Black to play for Des Moines. The twenty-five-year-old Baker hit .321 in forty-nine games for the Bruins, who lost in the first round of the Western League playoffs, after finishing 84-70 under manager Charlie Root during the regular season.[1]

Baker had a bunt single and a double in his Bruins debut at Sioux City on Tuesday, May 16, 1950, although the Bruins lost, 5-4. The Davenport native had played sparingly for former Bruin manager Stan Hack at triple-A

Gene Baker (Courtesy: John Liepa)

Springfield (Massachusetts) in the International League.

"He's just the type of player we've needed all season," said Root, referring to Baker's scoring from first base after two errant throws by the Soos' pitcher and first baseman in the second inning. "Did you see how he ran those bases? And did you see him slide into third? [It was the] most beautiful slide I ever saw in my life."[2]

Baker's "sizzling" single ignited the Bruins' three-run fourth inning.[3] Immediately after reaching base, Baker recorded the club's first intentional stolen base in twenty-five games. Later in the game,

Baker collected a double, which "was never more than four feet above the ground, yet it carried to deep left-center."[4]

The *Des Moines Tribune's* Bill Bryson said the former Davenport High School track star's "sloping shoulders and long arms have unexpected power."[5] Despite making four errors in six games, Baker "can glide faster and farther back or to his left better than any other shortstop in the league," Bryson wrote six days later. [6]

The Bruin shortstop drove in four runs in the second game of a doubleheader loss at Denver on May 29, 1950. He cleared the bases with a triple in the sixth inning and doubled to knock in Des Moines' fourth run. During his time in Des Moines, he collected seventeen doubles and six triples, drove in twenty-four runs, and reached base more than 40 percent of the time. He drew thirty-seven walks and struck out only nineteen times. He made twenty-two errors in the field, but his teammate Johnson made even more—thirty-two to be exact—in the same number of games. Although the inclusion of Black players in major-league baseball was a touchy subject in some quarters, Wichita had the only hotel on the road that refused to accept Baker.[7]

Baker played three years of basketball at Davenport High School and was named an all-state guard in 1943. He was on the 1942 Davenport High team that lost to Ottumwa, 37-30, in the championship of the state basketball tournament.

The parent Chicago Cubs used three unearned runs to defeat the Bruins, 4-1, at Pioneer Memorial Stadium on Tuesday, July 11, 1950. Former Des Moines player Bob Borkowski had three of the major league team's eight hits, including a double off fifty-one-year-old starter Charlie Root. "Charlie, still a reasonable facsimile of the Root who pitched for the Cubs from 1927 through '42, escaped handily from that one-out situation," the *Register's* Bill Bryson reported. Gordon Van Dyke, Ray Bauer, Leon Foulk, Tom Kerr, Vern Fear, Paul Schneiders, and Fred Baczewski followed Root to the mound for the Bruins.

Chicago broke a scoreless tie with two runs in the sixth. The Bruins' lone run came in the eighth. The Cubs added a two-run ninth highlighted by a single up the middle by Borkowski. Clayton Johnson had two of Des Moines' four hits; Vern Morgan and Dwight Maxhimer collected the others. A total of 5,903 fans turned out for the exhibition contest.

The twenty-four-year-old Fear survived two errors and three walks to record a seven-inning no-hitter in the first game of a doubleheader on Friday, July 21, 1950. Although five Denver Grizzlies reached base, none got past first base. One runner was erased on a double play and Bruin catcher Bob Zuber threw out another on an attempted steal. Fear contributed at the plate, too. His single was part of a three-run sixth inning that made the final score, 5-0.

Fear faced a formidable task in the seventh and final inning when three Denver hitters with .300-plus batting averages came to the plate. After running the count to three balls, two strikes, Denver's Danny Holden flied out to right field. The next hitter, Pete Whisenant, was retired on a ground ball to short. The last batter, Moose Womack, who came into the game hitting .330, took three balls at first. However, Fear recovered and threw three straight strikes, with Womack swinging futilely at the last offering.

Fear was making his first athletic appearance in Des Moines since he was a member of the Everly High School basketball team that reached the state tournament. The Bruins won the nightcap, 6-5, in ten innings. Fear led Western League pitchers with a 2.83 earned run average and a .750 winning percentage that season.

Former Prohibitionists owner Tom Fairweather died on Thursday morning, January 24, 1951, at his farm home approximately two miles north of Des Moines after suffering a heart attack. "The death of Fairweather removes from the midwestern scene a colorful and popular personality and ends a long and varied career," the *Des Moines Tribune* wrote.[8] In an editorial the following day, the *Tribune* said, "Tom Fairweather took a whack at a lot of things, and did them rather well. He made a business of enjoying life, and of doing worthwhile things. And thousands of the rest of us learned to enjoy life more, and to do things better, for having known him."[9] Services for Fairweather were held on Saturday afternoon, January 27, at the Highland Park Presbyterian Church. Burial and additional services were held in Cherokee two days later.

A day after Fairweather's death, five minor leagues met at the Savery Hotel in Des Moines and proposed holding national bat boy and beauty contests as well as a Lou Gehrig Day in 1951. The afternoon session on Saturday was canceled so the representatives could attend Fairweather's funeral. "His loss to baseball was a great blow," said Bob Finch, promotional director of the National Association of Professional Baseball Leagues. "He was a man of wisdom and his experience in baseball legislative manners was invaluable to baseball."[10]

The slogan, "The American way—baseball today," was adopted to recognize the golden anniversary of minor-league baseball. The baseball officials proposed that the winner of the national batboy contest would get a trip to the Baseball Hall of Fame in Cooperstown, New York. The golden girl beauty contest would last approximately two-thirds of the season and conclude with an event resembling the Miss America Contest in Atlantic City, New Jersey. Coincidentally, Finch was behind the first Drake Relays beauty contest in 1926 when he was a member of the Drake University staff.

Two weeks after the minor league meeting, *Des Moines Register* sports editor Sec Taylor reminisced about Fairweather. The two met first in 1909 when Taylor was secretary of the ballclub in Wichita, Kansas, and Fairweather had a similar position with the ball team in Sioux City. "Even at that time," Taylor wrote, "Tom was a large, jovial man who could get a good laugh out of a jest or prank although he was not a prankster."[11] The longtime journalist described the former owner of the Des Moines franchise as "conscientious" and "sensitive."[12] "If he had a fault, it was that he did not like to make enemies," said Taylor. "It hurt him to make decisions that hurt others."[13]

Initially, Fairweather opposed the farm system set up used by major-league teams. "Like Jack Holland, Frank Isbell, [Lee] Keyser and others in the Western League, he realized that local ownership was the only sound foundation on which a minor league club could be built and that the chain [farm] system, wherein a major league club owns and runs several teams, would eat at the vitals of the smaller leagues and would eventually force the individual club owner out of business," Taylor recalled.[14] In 1951 alone, the sixteen major league teams in the National and American leagues had a total of 182 farm clubs.[15] Today, the thirty major league teams have a total of 120 full-season affiliates. Later, as president of the Western Association and Three-I League, Fairweather changed his position, "but [he] would frequently express a longing for the old days in baseball, with local owners, street parades, band contests and the like, making a gala event of coming days and flag-raising days."[16]

Aided by six Des Moines errors, the Chicago Cubs shut out their single-A affiliate, 9-0, on Monday, June 25, 1951, at Pioneer Memorial Stadium. Former Bruin hurler Bob Kelly gave up doubles to Bob Lee and Harry Chiti and walked one batter in his complete-game performance for the Cubs. Still, Kelly was not completely satisfied. "My curve ball was breaking too much," he said afterwards.[17] Despite a sore shoulder, Wes Carr started for the Bruins and was tagged with two home runs by Hank Sauer and another by Eddie Miksis, before leaving after the fourth inning with the Bruins trailing, 6-0.

Sauer's two round-trippers came on "seemingly nonchalant swings."[18] "The first, not fair by much, was one of the longest ever knocked over the northern obstacle in Pioneer Memorial Stadium," *Des Moines Register* sportswriter Bill Bryson said.[19] Former Bruins Bob Borkowski and Ransom Jackson played the entire game for the Cubs. Borkowski struck out twice and drew a walk in the second inning. Jackson singled twice and drove in the Cubs' first run with a grounder past second in the first.

Chiti, the eighteen-year-old Bruin catcher, cut down two of the four Cubs' base stealers. Two of his throws, however, went into center field when Chicago's Gene Hermanski stole second. On the other side, the Cubs' fielding was "workmanlike rather than brilliant."[20]

A season-high 5,398 spectators had to sit through rain during the first two innings. Nevertheless, the moisture did not spoil the Cubs' jocular mood, with the Bruins serving as "embarrassed guinea pigs."[21] For instance, after Kelly pitched to Des Moines' five-foot-six shortstop Clayton Johnson, Kelly said, "Gosh, Clayt is getting smaller every time I see him. I've got to aim the ball at ground level to get a strike over when he's at bat."[22]

The entire Cubs team with the exception of pitcher Dutch Leonard arrived in Des Moines at 7:45 that morning. Bruin business manager John Holland treated the forty-person contingent and Des Moines sportswriters and sportscasters to breakfast at Hotel Savery. The game that night started at 7 p.m. so the Cubs could catch a night train to St. Louis after the exhibition in Des Moines.

Bob Feller entertained 1,640 fans at Pioneer Memorial Stadium on Sunday, October 14, 1951, in an exhibition in conjunction with his hometown's annual homecoming. Pitching for the semi-pro Linden Merchants, Feller gave up eleven hits in seven innings in an 8-5 loss to a group of all-stars including Jack Dittmer of Elkader, a former All-Big 10 end at the University of Iowa.

Sportswriter Bill Bryson said the thirty-two-year-old Feller "displayed little of the strikeout skill which earned him a flock of major league records in his earlier years."[23] Feller came into the game as a twenty-two-game winner for the Cleveland Indians, who finished second in the American League with a 93-61-1 record in 1951.

The all-stars coached by Drake University baseball coach Shan Deniston pounded out thirteen hits, including three by Herb Adams and two each by Dittmer, Marty Carlson, and Bob Anderlik. Anderlik led the Bruin regulars with a .317 batting average in 1951. Feller's Linden team collected eight hits. The Merchants' record fell to twenty-eight wins, and twelve losses with the defeat. They had an eighty-eight win, thirty-six loss three-year record coming into the game.

Carlson, a former East High School and Drake athlete, stole home in the three-run sixth inning that led to a 5-5 tie. Dittmer scored the tie-breaking run on a single to right by former Bruin Roman Bartkowski. Feller's former Cleveland teammate Jack Weik and Vern Fear, a Bruin in 1948 and 1949, struck out seventeen Linden batters. Weik fanned twelve in five innings, and Fear added five strikeouts in four innings. Weik, up from Fort Leonard Wood, reached a three ball, two-strike count on five of the first six Linden hitters. He walked three of them and struck out the other three. After fanning three more Linden batters, Weik gave up five runs and five hits in Linden's third inning. Other all-stars from Fort Leonard Wood included catcher Vern Rapp and center fielder Herb Adams.

Don Neumann pitched two innings of relief after Feller, struck out two, walked one, and allowed one run and two hits. He also collected one hit in his only at-bat. Joe Fisher and Franz Linden umpired the game, which lasted two hours and twenty-three minutes.

Feller flew his own plane from Cleveland and stopped in Iowa City first to refuel. Before the game, the Van Meter native received a golden replica of an ear of corn with the inscription "To Iowa's Favorite Athlete, Bob Feller. From his friends in Des Moines."[24] His mother, Lena Feller of Van Meter, got a bouquet of roses during the pre-game ceremony, which included a concert by the Van Meter band. Proceeds from the game went toward a new community center in Van Meter named after the major-league pitching star.

On July 8, 1952, the Bruins avenged their defeat in the previous year's exhibition against the Chicago Cubs at the hands of pitcher Bob Kelly. This time, the Des Moines squad managed by Harry Strohm shut out the visitors, 2-0, on the same day the National League all-stars beat the American League all-stars in Philadelphia.

Semi-regular pitcher John Kuncl held the Cubs to two singles and did not allow a runner past first base. "A grounder to right field by Bill Serena in the fourth inning and a delicate fly to short left by Gene Hermanski represented all the effective bat-swinging by the Cubs," Bill Bryson of the *Des Moines Register* reported.[25] Serena was thrown out trying to steal as Roy Smalley struck out. Hermanski started the seventh with a bloop single, but John Pramesa and Bruce Edwards struck out. Then Kuncl fanned Serena on three straight pitches. Kuncl, who struck out seven, had not started since June 21 when he beat the Pueblo Dodgers, 4-3. Bruin pitchers had shut out only one Western League opponent coming into the exhibition seen by 4,801 fans.

Kelly, who shut out Des Moines in 1951, lasted only three innings and gave up six hits and the Bruins' two runs. In the second, Hank Nasternak of Des Moines singled to left center and moved to second on Dick Johnson's groundout. The following hitter, Bob Dant, hit a line drive over Kelly's head and Nasternak beat outfielder Hall Jeffcoat's throw home for the first run. In the third, John Magliolo reached first on a drag bunt between Kelly and Cubs first baseman Phil Cavarretta. Magliolo advanced to third on Red Lavigne's single and scored the Bruins' second run when Fred Richards singled to center. The inning ended when Lavigne was picked off second and Charlie Teague hit into a double play. The Bruins threatened again in the eighth when Cubs hurler Bob Schultz issued three walks with one out. But Nasternak grounded into an inning-ending double play.

In Philadelphia, meanwhile, Hank Sauer of the Cubs hit a two-run, 430-foot home run that gave the National League its third straight All-Star Game victory. Sauer came into the game leading the National League in home runs with twenty-three and runs-batted-in with sixty-nine. He ended the season as the NL's Most Valuable Player with a league-leading thirty-seven home runs and 121 runs-batted-in. Another Cub, pitcher Bob Rush, was credited with the win. The All-Star Game that year was stopped due to rain after five innings.

Catcher-turned-outfielder Joe Garagiola homered in the six-run sixth inning as the Chicago Cubs blasted the Des Moines Bruins, 12-

4, Monday, August 17, 1953, at Pioneer Memorial Stadium. A few minutes before Garagiola's clout, catcher Clyde McCullough, who played the outfield that night, sent a ball over the outfield fence with two on base and Hal Jeffcoat, an outfielder by trade, tripled. Afterwards, Garagiola boasted that the trio of Jeffcoat, McCullough, and himself was "the greatest assemblage of power in the outfield since the '34 All-Star game."[26]

Des Moines scored twice in the fourth inning to take a 2-1 lead when John Magliolo scored on a double by Paul Schramka and Schramka crossed the plate on a wild pitch. But Bruin pitchers Ed Funal and Dick Verbic were unable to stop the major leaguers from the Windy City. Two ex-Bruins, shortstop Roy Smalley and catcher Carl Sawatski, played for the Cubs. Smalley executed the defensive play of the game when he leaped to his right and made a backhand stab of a liner by the Bruins' player-manager, Bruce Edwards. "The was one of the finest plays I've ever seen a shortstop make . . . and I've seen quite a few," said Cubs manager Phil Cavarretta.[27]

The next day, *Des Moines Register* sports editor Sec Taylor estimated the Bruins would lose between $25,000 and $40,000 in 1953 for their owner, the Chicago Cubs. "Will they [Cubs] withdraw as owners of the Des Moines club or will they exercise their option in their contract with Des Moines Enterprises, Inc., to continue in the Iowa capital?" Taylor asked in his column.[28] When he presented the same query to Wid Matthews, the Cubs' director of player personnel, Matthews responded, "As far as I'm concerned, we'll be back in Des Moines in 1954. I see no reason why we shouldn't return here."

The Bruins under managers Kemp Wick and Edwards captured the Western League title in 1953. After finishing fourth during the regular season, the Bruins defeated the Denver Bears three games to one in the playoff championship. Bob Zick made the all-star team as a utility player. At the time, the parent Chicago Cubs had ten farm teams compared to four today.

First baseman Steve Bilko, playing for the injured Dee Fondy, knocked in three runs with two home runs and a double to lead the Chicago Cubs to a 9-3 victory over the Bruins on Monday, July 12,

1954. Solo homers by Bob Speake, Ed Winceniak, and Solly Drake accounted for Des Moines' only runs in the nearly 100F heat. Dave Cole singled in the tie-breaking run in the fifth and pitched seven innings to earn the win.

The Bruins' starter, Don Elston, struck out the first four batters he faced and tossed three scoreless innings. Outfielder Hank Sauer of the Cubs was not surprised that the right-hander set five batters down on strikes and allowed only one hit, a single by shortstop Ernie Banks. "We've faced Elston before at spring training," Sauer said. "He's got a dandy sinker and he keeps it low. That's a good pitch."[29]

The Cubs also got a run-scoring double from Frankie Baumholtz and two unearned runs on a passed ball and an error by Bruin second baseman Casey Wise. The Chicago lineup featured several former Des Moines players. Center fielder Bob Talbot went two-for-four, shortstop Gene Baker was hitless, catcher El Tappe went one-for-three, and Jim Brosnan pitched. Manager Stan Hack guided the Bruins in 1948 and 1949. The exhibition drew 5,256 to Pioneer Memorial Stadium.

The 897 fans who watched the Indianapolis Clowns and Kansas City Monarchs play at Pioneer Memorial Stadium on Wednesday, August 11, 1954, got more than a baseball game between two Negro American League rivals. Ed Hamman, playing King Tut, his sidekick, Spec Bebop, and the Flying Nesbit, an acrobatic troupe, entertained the fans before the game and between innings.

On the field itself, the Clowns overcame an early 3-0 deficit and won, 6-3, with three runs in the tenth inning after tying the score in the eighth inning. The Clowns' George Wanamake, who had three hits in four at-bats, drove in Verdes Drake and Ray Neil with a two-out double in the decisive tenth inning. Erwin Ford singled moments later to score Wanamake. "The sideliner was King Tut, whose exhibition of a praying mantis, seeking help for his teammates, directly behind the umpire failed to even bother the plate official," the *Des Moines Register* reported the next day.[30]

The Flying Nesbit thrilled the crowd midway in the seventh inning. Spec Bebop, described as a "midget," was chased twice by a "policeman" for stealing chickens.[31] However, he did not get caught, the *Register* reported.

Bill Bell, who attended East High School in Des Moines, started for the Monarchs. He struck out eight Clown batters, issued twelve walks, and allowed six runs including four earned runs. Indianapolis left fifteen runners on base; Kansas City, thirteen. The Clowns committed five errors; the Monarchs, two. The game took two hours and fifteen minutes.

Hy Cohen June 1954 (Courtesy: Scott Sailor/Iowa Cubs)

Each team featured a female at second base: Connie Morgan for the Clowns and Toni Stone for the Monarchs. Founded in 1919, Kansas City was managed by Buck O'Neil, who later coached for the Chicago Cubs. The Clowns, established in 1929, were piloted by Oscar Charleston. Both O'Neil and Charleston were eventually inducted into the Baseball Hall of Fame—Charleston in 1976 and O'Neil in 2022.

The Bruins under manager Les Peden repeated their Western League title in 1954 by beating Denver three games to one in the championship. Des Moines finished second during the regular season at 88-66, eight games behind first-place Denver. Hy Cohen led the league's hurlers with a 1.88 earned run average. The team drew 113,691 compared to 98,972 the previous season. "I want to thank the Des Moines fans for supporting the club," said Bruin president John Holland at the end of the season. "My bosses [the Chicago Cubs] are pleased with the support we received here this year."[32]

In 1955, the Bruins under managers Peden and Pepper Martin were swept by Wichita in the Western League playoff finals. They had finished in fourth place during the regular season with a 77-74 record. Joe Stanka led the circuit's pitchers with seventeen victories. Second baseman Bob McKee made the Western League all-star team.

The hiring of Martin in mid-July spurred attendance as well as the Bruins' performance on the field. The Wild Horse of the Osage was well remembered as a member of the St. Louis Cardinals and their "Gas House Gang" during the 1930s. "The advance [ticket] sale is one of the best we've had all year," said president and general manager Salty Saltwell, as the club prepared to play Lincoln in a doubleheader at Pioneer Memorial Stadium. "For one thing, I think the Bruins, under Pepper, will give the fans a livelier type of performance. He'll take advantage of the potential speed on our club, I believe, and play a more daring brand of ball."[33]

Les Peden 1955 (Courtesy; Scott Sailor/Iowa Cubs)

In fact, the Bruins' attendance more than doubled over the last thirty-five games. Des Moines drew 25,510 fewer fans overall than the year before, but it finished third in the Western League in attendance at 88,181. "I'll bet our entire loss came in the first half of the season," Saltwell said. "If we'd been drawing in May and June the way we did the last two months, we'd have finished ahead of '54."[34]

Pepper Martin July 1955
(Courtesy: Scott Sailor/Iowa Cubs)

Des Moines Register executive sports editor Leighton Housh started his coverage of an exhibition game on Saturday, August 12, 1956, featuring the Bruins against their wives and significant others this way: "Never underestimate the power of a woman."[35] Described as a "burlesqued game," the wives and children of the players shut out their husbands and fathers.[36] "The male team had no chance to score, batting wrong-sided, one-handed with a shovel, with a feminine ump behind the plate," Housh wrote. "On defense, the Bruins had one hand tied behind their backs and a boxing glove on the other hand. Female outfielders used fish nets."[37]

Five days before the game, Estelle Klein, wife of the Bruins' Lou Klein, expressed concern that her team would not have enough players, forcing a cancellation. "I've only got seven able-bodied players among the wives," she said, "and two of them absolutely refuse to play."[38] As a result, Estelle Klein had to recruit her fourteen-year-old daughter, Nerlyn, and Betty Saltwell, the wife of the Bruins' general manager, Salty Saltwell.

The Bruins had their last winning season as an affiliate of the Chicago Cubs in 1956. They finished in third place with a 72-67 record under Lou Klein. Klein later become one of the coaches in the Chicago Cubs' "College of Coaches," which replaced the customary managerial position until the Cubs hired Leo Durocher in late 1965. Outfielder Eddie Haas represented Des Moines on the Western League all-star team that season.[39]

The Bruins' last two seasons in the Western League did not end well; the ballclub finished in the cellar and last in attendance. Although pitcher Dave Stenhouse led the circuit with 184 strikeouts in 1957, the Bruins were 60-92 under managers Lou Stringer and Hershel Martin. They ended up thirty-seven games behind first-place Lincoln and drew 79,965 to Pioneer Memorial Stadium.

On Saturday, April 12, 1958, the San Francisco Giants outlasted the Cleveland Indians in ten innings at Pioneer Memorial Stadium. A crowd of 7,165 watched the Giants score the winning run in the tenth inning when a double by Andre Rogers scored Willie Kirkland, who had walked. For most of the game, five or six spectators-deep stood in the back of the outfield. The spectators had been removed, however, by the time the Giants came up to bat in the tenth.

Only a half dozen fans were standing in center field when Chico Carrasquel of the Indians doubled with the bases loaded and two outs in the ninth. The hit appeared to have driven in the tying and game-winning runs, but the runner who scored the last run was put back on third base. Twelve Indians batted in the six-run inning. Four walked, one was hit by a pitch, and two left-handed pinch-hitters singled off lefty Mike McCormick.

The unusual ending overshadowed twenty-year-old Orlando Cepeda's big day at the plate. Cepeda went four-for-four, was hit by a pitch in his last at-bat, and drove in three runs. His two-run, 365-feet blow keyed San Francisco's five-run fifth inning. Willie Mays smacked a two-run home run earlier in the inning. Starting pitcher Johnny Antonelli's perfect squeeze bunt accounted for the fifth run in the inning.

The Giants collected sixteen hits; the Indians, thirteen. In addition to Cepeda's four hits, the Giants got two hits each from Mays, Rogers, Daryl Spencer, and Bob Schmidt. Former Des Moines player Bob Speake added a two-run homer for the Giants "that made the natives happy," Walter Judge of the *San Francisco Examiner* reported. Bobby Avila had two of Cleveland's hits. The Indians' lineup also included Minnie Minoso, Rocky Colavito, Roger Maris, and Hoyt Wilhelm.

Des Moines became an affiliate of the Los Angeles Dodgers in 1958, but the Western League disbanded after the season. Once again, Des Moines, then known as the Dodgers, came in last, this time with a 61-83 record under skipper Roy Hartsfield. Only 35,039 spectators saw the Dodgers finish twenty-four-and-a-half games behind first-place Colorado Springs in 1958.

A year later, the Des Moines Demons joined the Class B Three-I League as a Philadelphia Phillies affiliate, only to see the league go out of existence in 1961. However, the Demons captured first place during the regular season and had the Three-I League's Most

Valuable Player in first baseman Cal Emery in 1959. Des Moines had a 78-48 mark under Manager of the Year Charlie Kress, but lost to Green Bay in the playoff three games to one. Emery turned in a league-leading twenty-seven home runs and 129 runs-batted-in. He also tied for the league lead in runs scored with 107. Outfielder Bill McGuckin, twenty-six, and catcher Al Kenders, twenty-two, joined the twenty-two-year-old Emery on the Three-I League all-star team.

On Tuesday, September 1, 1959, Pioneer Memorial Stadium was renamed Sec Taylor Stadium after the popular *Register* sports editor. Des Moines mayor Charles Iles made it official by presenting a proclamation to Taylor in ceremonies that evening at Hotel Fort Des Moines. The festivities had to be moved from the ballpark to the hotel due to rain. Only 698 fans showed up to see the abbreviated game's twelve pitches.

After starting his career as a general assignment reporter for the *Wichita (Kansas) Beacon* in 1904, Taylor took over the baseball beat of the *Wichita Eagle* in 1909. One year later, he quit and became the baseball club's secretary. The next year, he became the secretary of the St. Joseph's, Missouri, baseball team and wrote for the *St. Joseph Gazette* in the offseason. Taylor started with the *Register* in 1914, earning $22 a week.[40]

He started writing his "Sittin' In With the Athletes" column in the early 1920s and soon became known nationally, especially for his knowledge of baseball. Under his leadership, the *Register* sports section was considered one of the best in the country.[41] He also helped bring pro baseball back to Des Moines after World War II. In 1957 he received the Grantland Rice Memorial Award for excellence in sports writing. "I'm extremely proud to have my name linked with that of Grantland Rice in any way," he said on the night he accepted the award, "but I'm unworthy of this honor—the greatest I've ever received in my long career."[42]

Chapter 8

Kerrigan hurls no-hitter; Texan
buys franchise; Oaks introduced

The Demons tied for last place in the Three-I League in 1960 with a 64-74 mark under skipper Andy Seminick. They drew 53,828 to the newly-named Sec Taylor Stadium and placed first baseman Jerry Reimer and second baseman George Williams on the all-star team.

Twenty-year-old Jack Kerrigan survived three Demon errors in one inning and pitched the first no-hitter at home in ten years on Sunday, July 10, 1960. A crowd of 1,784 at Sec Taylor Stadium witnessed the masterpiece against the Cedar Rapids Braves. In improving his record to 8-2, Kerrigan walked only one batter, leadoff man Hub Hubbard in the eighth inning. He struck out eight Braves to raise his season strikeout total to 101 in eighty-eight innings.

Cal Emery 1959
(Courtesy: Scott
Sailor/Iowa Cubs)

Errors by Demon first baseman Reimer, catcher Bob Lipski, and shortstop Nolan Campbell gave the visitors a short-lived, 1-0 lead in the fourth inning. The Demons scored all they needed in their half of the inning on third baseman Fred Walters' two-run smash over the right-field fence. Second baseman Williams' triple highlighted Des Moines' three-run sixth inning. Williams added a two-run double in the seventh. Center fielder Don Lightner snared Brave pitcher Hank Fischer's drive in the sixth inning to keep the no-hitter intact.

The Demons won the first game, 4-0, on a five-hit shutout by eighteen-year-old Ray Culp. Between games, Demon general manager Clay Dennis received an award as executive of the year in the lower minor leagues for 1959. Vern Hoscheit, the new Three-I League president, presented the honor on behalf of *The Sporting News*.

Des Moines finished its short-lived Three-I League experience with a last-place finish in 1961, going 37-93 under Kress. The team ended forty-two-and-a-half games behind first-place Topeka and attracted only 33,337 fans to the ballpark. Nevertheless, twenty-one-year-old outfielder Dick Haines led the league with a .355 batting average, and catcher Pat Corrales was named to the all-star team after hitting .305.

On Friday, February 26, 1965, *Des Moines Register* sports editor Sec Taylor died at a Miami, Florida, hospital after apparently suffering a heart attack. Taylor and his wife, Hazel, had flown to Florida the previous Thursday afternoon to cover spring training. He became ill at approximately 3 a.m. Friday and was taken by ambulance to Mercy Hospital in Miami. Hospital officials said Taylor passed away in the emergency room shortly after arriving at the hospital.[1] He was seventy-eight-years-old.

"He was an institution in the field of sports, and he was an institution in The Register and Tribune," the *Register* said in an editorial two days later. "His death leaves a place which never can be filled in these newspapers and world of sports and sports writing."[2] In an age when sports writers were often mouthpieces for the teams they covered, Taylor provided "accurate, impartial reporting of news instead of puffery."[3] He also insisted that sportswriters refuse favors and expense accounts from promoters. The *Register* described the late sports editor as "a force for clean sports" and "a vigorous enemy of the fixers, the gamblers and the crooks who tend to cluster around many branches of professional athletes."[4]

Funeral services were held at 11 a.m. Monday, March 1, at Dunn's Funeral Home in Des Moines. Twenty men served as honorary pallbearers, including Bert McGrane, Jack North, Brad Wilson, Maurice White, Bill Bryson, Robert Price, Leighton Housh, George Yates, Paul George, Parker Crouch, M.B. Cornelison, Vic Talerico, Dr. M.B. Cramer, Herman Wallace, Werner Woods, Joseph Rosenfield, Sam McGinn, Harold Neu, Phineas Henry, and Hal Chase. Gardner Cowles, president of the Des Moines Register and Tribune Company, sent a cablegram from Singapore that said, "Spec's death makes me very sad. He was a wonderful, wonderful man."5

Sec Taylor "office" (Courtesy: Steve Dunn)

Four years later, Des Moines had another pro baseball team called the Iowa Oaks in the modern-day triple-A American Association thanks to Texan Ray Johnston. The association also included the Denver Bears, Indianapolis Indians, Omaha Royals, Oklahoma City 89ers, and Tulsa Oilers, who were managed by Warren Spahn.

In November 1968, the *Des Moines Tribune's* Bill Bryson described Johnston as "a smallish man, mild but quietly dynamic."6 Clearly, looks could be deceiving. "He doesn't smoke. His strongest drink is a tame sherry. His strongest epithet is in the gee-golly-goodness sakes range," Bryson said. "Yes this man from Dallas is a gambler willing to risk a good-sized chunk of his capital that triple-A baseball will succeed in Des Moines."7 Des Moines had rejected an invitation sixty-six years earlier to join the original American Association.

Iowa Oaks (Courtesy: Scott Sailor/Iowa Cubs)

Despite not having official approval, Johnston was willing to start a franchise in Des Moines as long as civic groups were willing to sell $100,000 of tickets before the season started in 1969. The sale of approximately 70,000 tickets would provide less than half of the anticipated budget for the first year of operation.[8]

The fifty-three-year-old Johnston was no stranger to professional baseball. After graduating from high school in his native Detroit, Michigan, Johnston worked in the concessions department of the Detroit Tigers. After working at higher levels for the Tigers and Boston Red Sox, he became general manager of triple-A clubs in Toledo, Ohio; Charleston, West Virginia; Louisville, Kentucky; Indianapolis, Indiana; and Dallas, Texas.

He owned the Dallas-Fort Worth franchise in the Class A Texas League in the early 1960s. After he sold the club, he was involved with his travel agency and real estate interests in Dallas. He brought professional baseball back to Toledo in 1964 after a nine-year absence and stayed on as general manager for one year.

In announcing that Johnston had obtained a working agreement with the Oakland Athletics to provide players, the *Des Moines Tribune* said in an editorial in late November, "The city's good fortune is the result of expansion of the major leagues to 12 teams apiece next year, and the need for each to have a top-level minor league player training ground. By the time Des Moines got into the act, only Oakland and the Chicago White Sox were looking for affiliates. An agreement with the White Sox would have been better from the standpoint of sustaining local interest, but the Sox didn't like the looks of the somewhat rundown Sec Taylor Stadium and went to Tucson [Arizona] instead."[9]

Under a proposed lease, the City of Des Moines would spend $25,000 to repair the ballpark and would maintain the facility and grounds. Johnston would handle concessions and pay for utilities, parking, and policing as well as $10,000 in rent.

In its November editorial, the *Tribune* expressed optimism that the franchise would succeed. "With good promotion, a competent team, and the stimulus of being so close to the major leagues, 175,000 customers are not too many to expect," the *Tribune opined*, referring to the number of paid admissions a triple-A ballclub needed to break even. "If this kind of baseball can survive anywhere in the era of televised big league games and growing interest in professional football, it should be able to make a go in Des Moines."[10]

Johnston spent three days in Des Moines in early December 1968 laying the groundwork for a franchise that, technically, was "still floating in air."[11] Although neither the league nor the Des Moines franchise technically existed, player rosters were available, a constitution was adopted, and a schedule was set. An agreement had to be reached on compensation to the Pacific Coast League for giving up the Seattle, Washington, and San Diego, California, territories to Major League Baseball for expansion.[12] In turn, the PCL would not release the Denver, Indianapolis, Oklahoma City, and Tulsa franchises until there was an agreement on payment.[13]

Season box seat ticket orders started coming in mid-December. Prices were set at $120 for a full-season box seat, or $1.71 per game, and $60 for a half-season box seat. Under the latter plan, the buyer could have the seat on even or odd days. Season ticket holders could also access a reserved parking area. The price of admission for children was set at $.50, $1 less than the standard triple-A price.

By mid-December 1968, the Des Moines franchise had a general manager: Bob Morris, a former pitcher at the pro level. In 1968, Morris served as general manager of the Atlanta Braves' farm team in Shreveport, Louisiana. The affiliate of the Oakland Athletics finished fourth in the AA under manager Jimmy Williams at 62-78 and drew 129,432 to Sec Taylor Stadium in 1969.

Chapter 9

*Blue sets strikeout marks; Oaks
host exhibitions; Kucek makes history*

The Oaks remained affiliated with Oakland under Williams and former major league catcher Sherm Lollar through 1972. They finished second in the Eastern Division in 1970 and 1971 and third in 1972. They drew only 89,477 in Oakland's last year in Des Moines.

Nevertheless, the Oaks produced such noted players as pitcher Vida Blue, first baseman Joe Rudi, catcher Gene Tenace, second baseman Manny Trillo, and outfielder George Hendrick. Another player and manager, Tony LaRussa, eventually compiled a Hall of Fame managerial career with Oakland, the Chicago White Sox, and St. Louis Cardinals.

Blue still holds the Des Moines franchise records for strikeouts in a single game (sixteen) and season (165), which he accomplished in 1970. His 2.17 earned run average that year still ranks second in franchise history. He is also among the top five all-time single-season club leaders in shutouts (four) and winning percentages (.800).

The twenty-year-old left-hander from Mansfield, Louisiana, struck out fourteen Oklahoma City batters in his triple-A debut on Wednesday, April 29, at Sec Taylor Stadium. In the process, Blue broke the old franchise record of twelve strikeouts in a game set by George Lauzerique in 1969. It was Blue's first appearance since April 11, when he pitched four innings in an exhibition game. "Because of [six months of] military duty, he didn't get to spring training till March 18," Oaks manager Sherman Lollar noted. "And he'd only pitched eleven innings in three exhibitions."[1]

Blue missed a chance for a fifteenth strikeout in the fifth inning when the Oaks lost an appeal with nineteen-year-old Oklahoma City outfielder Cesar Cedeno at the plate. "Cedeno went clear around on that first pitch to him in the fifth," Oaks catcher Gene Tenace said. "We wanted the plate umpire [Buster Sanchez] to get the opinion of Mike Shirmer [the first base umpire], but he wouldn't do it. He said he'd seen it."[2]

Given new life, Cedeno homered after the count reached three balls and two strikes. Blue's fourteen strikeouts were six short of the American Association record of twenty set by Maury McDermott for Louisville against St. Paul in 1949.[3]

The *Des Moines Register's* Bill Bryson said afterwards that Blue's command of the curve ball surprised the Oaks and the Oakland A's minor-league pitching coach Warren Hacker, a former major league hurler. "Vida had a tremendous deuce (curve ball)," Tenace concurred. "It's the best I've ever seen him throw."[4]

Glancing at Blue, Tenace asked, "We got at least half the third strikes with the curve, didn't we, Vida?" Blue nodded. "Yes, that's probably the best my curve has ever worked for me," the Oaks' young pitching ace responded.[5]

Joe Rudi (Courtesy: Steve Dunn)

Blue put Oklahoma City runners on second and third in the second inning, but he fanned three 89ers to end the threat. He averted more trouble in the fifth when he struck out Jack Lind on three pitches and Rich Chiles on five with the bases loaded. Blue was replaced by reliever Mike Olivo with one out in the seventh inning. "We had decided that Vida should throw in the range of 116 to 130 [pitches] in his first outing," manager Lollar explained. "He had just about reached 130 when Torres got that single in the seventh and we didn't want to risk having Vida hurt a great arm because of fatigue."[6]

Tenace led the Oaks' thirteen-hit attack with a run-scoring single in the fourth and a two-run home run in the eighth. A double by Jim Driscoll and singles by Dwain Anderson and Gonzalo Marquez produced two runs in the fifth. Tommy Reynolds' single brought in two more runs in the eighth.

Vida Blue (Courtesy: Steve Dunn)

On Wednesday, May 6, 1970, Blue tossed a three-hitter and struck out ten batters in the Oaks' 4-0 win over visiting Tulsa. He had to get up at 6:30 that morning to catch a flight to Des Moines after four days of military reserve duty in Oakland, California. "He was more consistent tonight than he was in his first game," Oaks skipper Lollar said. "Vida threw 127 pitches—about the same total he had in six and two-thirds innings last week."[7]

Tulsa loaded the bases in the second, but John Olerud hit into an inning-ending double play, one of three by the Oaks that night. Blue struck out at least one hitter in every inning except the fifth, as the Oaks improved their record to 13-2. Iowa's Tommy Reynolds extended his hitting streak to fourteen games with two singles. Teammate Bill McNulty delivered a run-scoring single in the third and a two-run home run in the fifth.

Blue captured his fifth straight win by striking out eleven and allowing only four hits in Iowa's 2-1 decision at Omaha on Thursday, May 21. He also scored the winning run on a force out in the fifth inning.

Omaha managed only one hit in the first five innings, and four Royals struck out in the first two innings. After Steve McMillan reached base on a single in the seventh, Blue retired the last nine Royals. Oaks infielder Tony LaRussa was called up to Oakland after the game.

On June 25, another pitching gem by Blue ended Iowa's five-game losing streak. The southpaw struck out twelve and allowed only four singles as the Oaks beat Oklahoma City, 2-0, at Sec Taylor Stadium. "He has a chance to become one of the great left-hand pitchers of all time," Iowa owner Ray Johnston exclaimed.[8] At that point, Blue sported a 9-1 record while striking out 116 and giving up only fifty-eight hits in ninety-two innings.

His manager called the performance Blue's best game so far. "He walked four, but he was keeping ahead of the hitters better than he has before," Lollar said. "Two of the hits off him were infield choppers.

"He also threw fewer pitches than in any other game. Yep, he threw 120 pitches," Lollar added. "That's his lowest. And he looked stronger at the finish than he did at the start."[9]

Blue agreed after thinking to himself for a few seconds. "Yes, I believe it was [his best game of the season]. I think I had my best stuff and I had to bear down to keep a shutout going so long till 'The Hammer' [Bobby Brooks] saved me again."[10]

The game was scoreless until the eighth when Gonzalo Marquez singled and Brooks homered off Oklahoma City hurler Scipio Spinks.

Blue helped the Oaks get back in the American Association Eastern Division's pennant race by shutting out the Evansville

Triplets in the second game of a doubleheader on Thursday, August 28. The Oaks moved within two games of division-leading Omaha by winning, 9-2, in the opener and 5-0 in the nightcap.

Blue struck out eleven Evansville hitters and permitted only a second-inning double by Cotton Nash and a seventh-inning single by Hoss Bowlin. "It was kind of a test," Oaks manager Lollar said, "and I think he passed, don't you?

"He hadn't pitched in over a month. He had a little arm trouble, spent a couple of weeks in the military and was up with the big club [Oakland] for a while, before we got him back a few days ago," Lollar added. "He didn't pitch any with the A's and we've had him pitch batting practice a couple of times, so we didn't know how he'd go. But he looks all right to me."[11]

Evansville's Hoss Bowlin agreed. "That's the best stuff we've seen all season. How can that guy not be pitching in the major leagues? He was firing faster at the finish than he was at the start," Bowlin said. "He was really burning them at the end."[12]

The Triplets got two runners on base for the first time in the seventh on Bowlin's single and an Oaks' error. Blue came back and fanned the next three hitters. "I was just out there fooling around," Blue said later. "If I'm back here next year, I'll show you some real pitching."[13]

Blue fanned the franchise-record sixteen Omaha Royals and pitched a shutout in his last appearance of the season in 1970. The 3-0 win upped his record to 12-3. Beating Omaha for the fifth time that season, he allowed four hits and walked four Royals. He had a no-hitter until Charlie Day tripled with two outs in the sixth.

Blue walked two batters with one out in the second. However, Bill Harris struck out and Pat Skrable was caught stealing to end the Omaha threat. Blue escaped another jam in the seventh when the leadoff hitter walked and Harris singled with two outs.

The Oaks scored twice in the fourth, when Bill McNulty tripled to left-center and scored on Jim Driscoll's double to the right-field corner. Driscoll scored when Don Young singled to center. The Oaks added an insurance run in the seventh on Gonzalo Marquez's infield single, Bobby Brooks' force out, and McNulty's single.

Although he received "about forty" scholarship offers to play football in college, Blue passed up the sport after throwing thirty-five touchdown passes in his senior year at De Soto High School.[14] He was drafted by the Kansas City Athletics in the second round of the major-league amateur draft in June 1967.

He had already played two full seasons of professional baseball by the time he reached Triple A with the Oaks. In 1968, he struck out a league-leading 231 batters in 152 innings for Class A Burlington in the Midwest League, but had a modest 8-11 record. A year later, he compiled a 10-3 mark with Birmingham in the double-A Southern League.

Despite their 13-2 start, the Oaks finished in second place in the American Association Eastern Division with a 70-68 record, three games behind first-place Omaha. Blue, Marquez, McNulty, and Tenace represented Iowa on the American Association all-star team.

Judy Borwick of Des Moines still has fond memories of those early years in the 1970s. The daughter of a former semi-pro baseball player, Borwick worked in the ticket office rather than serve as an usherette at Sec Taylor Stadium while she was attending Iowa State University in Ames.

"They started the usherettes in the spring of 1972, which would have been at the end of my freshman year in college. I was driving back and forth [to work] to Des Moines in my Volkswagen before school got out," she recalled. "They had an audition for the usherettes, which was an interview process.

"My dad saw it in the paper and thought it would be a good summer job for me. The interviews were held in February or March at [Hotel] Fort Des Moines in one of the big ballrooms. We went around from table to table and they asked us questions about our work experience, baseball, and things like that," she added. "Then they selected about twenty girls before baseball started in April, followed by a group meeting. We had to wear white shorts, which they furnished, and a Navy blue, short-sleeve shirt.

"They needed two people to work in the ticket office; the rest would be usherettes. The ticket office staff got paid $6 a game, and the usherettes got paid $4 a game. I needed the money, so I asked to be in the ticket office. We were only employed during home games. It was a great summer job because I was off when the team was out of town."[15]

She worked the same job the following summer between her sophomore and junior year of college.

"If it was a night game, we had to be there at 4 o'clock. There were no computers so it was all paper tickets. We usually had three [ticket] windows open. We were done at the end of the sixth inning when the ticket windows were closed and you could go to the game for free," she recalled. "There was a machine that counted the tickets, and it always counted the tickets wrong. We basically had to hand count the tickets, and the money in our drawers [from ticket sales] had to match the number of tickets we sold. A lot of times on a slow night we would do a tally mark on the number of tickets we sold. If we were really busy, we couldn't do that.

"All the money was put into a bag, and I was in charge of depositing the money. The security guard who was there drove his motorcycle or moped, and I had to hop on the back of that," she added. "He would take me to a bank in uptown Des Moines with this bag of money, and I would put it in the night deposit. The guy driving the motorcycle probably couldn't have outrun a child. He was not a lot of protection, but we didn't get into any trouble. Once he brought me back [to the ballpark], I could leave."[16]

Later, she did clerical work part-time in the Oaks' office when she changed career paths and attended AIB (American Institute of Business) in Des Moines the next two years.

"I worked for Bob Martin, the [office] manager, and his full-time secretary, and I ran errands all over town because I had a car," she said. "Tony LaRussa was the manager, and his kids were really little at the time. He was a super neat guy. I babysat his and his wife's kids a couple of times. A lot of the players were great; some, not so great.

"It was a real fun place to work. They were caring. Bob Martin was one of the neatest guys I was able to work with. I think he continued on [with the Oaks] after I left. Then [owner] Ray [Johnston] sold the team, and they changed affiliations."[17]

Crediting her father with her love of baseball, a lack of opportunities for females to work in the game prevented her from pursuing the sport as a vocation. Softball wasn't available either for girls when she moved to Des Moines in junior high.

"I don't think my dad ever missed a game when I worked there," she recalled. "There just weren't any women in that field then. I would have loved it [working full-time in professional baseball] because I loved baseball."[18]

Her father even had reserved seat season tickets. The programs for the games had numbers in them, and prizes were awarded to the winners of drawings. The winners received envelopes with coupons.

"A lot of times the coupons weren't claimed, so the Oaks would let us take the coupons. At least every other night I'd take the coupons home to my dad, and he just thought the craziest thing in the world was to get the lucky number. He'd come into a good restaurant [with coupons] around Second and Euclid and they'd wonder."[19]

Tony LaRussa
(Courtesy: Steve Dunn)

The Oaks were affiliated with the Chicago White Sox in 1973, 1974, 1976, 1977, 1978, 1979, and 1980 under managers LaRussa, Joe Sparks, Loren Babe, Pete Ward, and Sam Ewing. The team was a Houston Astros' affiliate in 1975. The Chicago Cubs' affiliation started in 1981 with managers Randy Hundley and Roy Hartsfield.

The first exhibition game with a major-league team in thirteen years was a homecoming of sorts for seven Oakland A's, when they played their triple-A affiliate in Des Moines on Thursday night, August 3, 1972.[20] In the end, the A's scored twice in the tenth inning to beat the Iowa Oaks, 5-3, with 7,277 fans on hand. "It was a good show, so good, in fact, the kids got carried away and streamed onto the field every time the A's took it and besieged them for autographs," said Howard Kluender of the *Des Moines Register*. "One even approached pitcher Gary Waslewski as he made his warmup pitches in the tenth."[21]

Waslewski, a former Oak, was credited with the win despite giving up three runs in the eighth. The inning started with a walk and singles by Gaylen Pitts and Manny Trillo. The Oaks' second run scored on an error by first baseman Mike Hegan. Rene Lachemann then tied the score with a single to left. A double by Pitts in the first inning was the only extra-base hit of the game, which lasted two hours and thirty-five minutes. Mudcat Grant was charged with the loss after giving up the decisive two runs in the tenth.

In that inning, second baseman Trillo went deep into the hole and threw out Hegan, but Bill Voss scored on the play to break the 3-3 tie. Angel Mangual then singled to drive in Oakland's fifth run. The rally began with a walk and a single by Don Mincher, who had replaced third baseman Sal Bando in the fourth. The A's scored two runs in the first, which was highlighted by Joe Rudi's single. The world champions added a run in the fourth on a run-scoring single by former Oak Tim Cullen.

Ex-Oak Mangual collected two hits, drove in two runs, and stole a base. On the other hand, former Iowa player George Hendrick went hitless in five at-bats. Two other Oakland players, injured outfielder Reggie Jackson and catcher Dave Duncan, who missed the plane to Des Moines, were not available. Before the game, Blue—the 1971 American League Cy Young Award winner and Most Valuable Player—answered questions from the media and signed autographs after asking the autograph-seekers to form "one big line."[22]

Iowa native and Oakland relief pitcher Bob Locker also was a center of attention before the game. (Locker's parents, Mr. and Mrs. H.W. Locker, and wife Judy's parents, Mr. and Mrs. Rich Swaive, had homes in George in northwest Iowa.) At that point, Locker had appeared in 389 major league games, all in relief.

The Oaks won the AA's Eastern Division in 1973 with an 83-53 record. The team, which included Bucky Dent, Rich Gossage, Jerry Hairston, and Denny McLain, was beaten by the Tulsa Oilers in the AA championship series four games to three. Iowa lost two one-run decisions to open the seven-game series in Oklahoma. The Oaks rebounded by beating the Oilers, 4-3, behind the pitching of Joe Henderson. Iowa moved ahead three games to two by winning 7-3 and 5-0 at home. However, Tulsa pitcher Bob Forsch shut out the Oaks, 16-0, to even the series. The Oilers locked up the American Association championship with a 4-1 victory before 3,125 fans at Sec Taylor Stadium.

Twenty-eight members of that Oaks team eventually played in the major leagues. Hugh Yancy and Ewing hit a team-leading .292; Ewing topped the club with seventy-five runs-batted-in. Pitcher Stan Perzanowski led the Oaks with fourteen wins; Ken Frailing had a team best 2.86 earned run average.

Fans at the exhibition game between the Houston Astros and Iowa Oaks on Thursday, August 21, 1975, had to wait until the eighth inning to see the offenses come to life. Houston starter Doug Konieczny scattered three hits and lasted seven innings. Iowa starter Larry Elenes, a half-Cherokee Native American, gave up a home run by Cliff Johnson in the fourth. Two of the four runs allowed by Elenes were unearned, due to second baseman Larry Milbourne's wild throw to third after Johnson was apparently picked off second. Elenes's successors gave up six runs in the final two innings as the Astros won, 10-2.

Houston manager Bill Virdon, who had replaced the fired Preston Gomez two days earlier, said his starter's performance "was encouraging."[23] However, Virdon was reluctant to talk about the future. "I'm just glad that I got the job with about six weeks of the season left so I can become familiar with the personnel and see what we need for next year," he said.[24] Virdon himself had been fired a few weeks earlier as manager of the New York Yankees.

Ken Boswell of Houston clouted a three-run home run off Oaks reliever Carlos Alfonso with two outs in the ninth. The Oaks did not score until the bottom of the ninth when Art Gardner and Bob Gallagher hit pitches by Houston reliever Jose Sosa over the fence. Bob Watson of Houston tested his badly bruised wrist as a designated hitter and struck out twice and singled twice. Among the National League leaders in batting average and runs-batted-in, Watson was injured when he was hit on the wrist by pitcher Bruce Kison of Pittsburgh a few weeks earlier.

Goose Gossage
(Courtesy: Steve Dunn)

The Oaks under manager Joe Sparks were last in the East Division of the American Association with a 56-79 mark in 1975, twenty-and-a-half games in back of first-place Evansville.

Approximately 3,000 fans went home early when rain stopped the Chicago White Sox and Iowa Oaks exhibition after four innings on Wednesday, May 12, 1976. The teams were tied at 3-3 when wet field conditions made the game unplayable. "Roland Hemond [White Sox general manager] and I agreed that the field conditions were becoming poor, and there was no reason to risk injury," Oaks owner Ray Johnston said.[25] Rain in the afternoon pushed the game's start back an hour, and rain started falling again in the third inning.

The White Sox scored twice in the first when Pat Kelly and Jim Spencer singled and scored on singles by Carlos May and former Oak Pete Varney. The Oaks got a run back in their half of the first when Alan Bannister tripled and scored on an infield grounder by Nyls Nymans. Iowa jumped ahead, 3-2, in the second when starting pitcher Paul Patterson singled in two runs. With one out, Morris Nettles walked and Kevin Bell singled. After a passed ball moved the runners to second and third, George Enright struck out. But Patterson knocked the first pitch into left-center field to drive in Nettles and Bell. Jim Spencer's home run in the third for the White Sox tied the score at 3-3.

Three days earlier, Chicago's number one starter, Wilbur Wood, sustained a broken knee cap; he was put on the injured list on the day of the game. As a result, the White Sox turned to Jesse Jefferson, who had not appeared in a game in weeks. "It was really kind of hard to tell how Jefferson performed," said coach Jim Busby, filling in for manager Paul Richards. "I think he threw well considering the conditions. He didn't exactly look all that good, but he hadn't pitched since spring training, either."[26] Jefferson gave up three runs and three hits in two innings of work. His replacement, Francisco Barrios, allowed two harmless singles in two innings. Patterson surrendered three runs and seven hits in three innings. His successor, Bill Moran, allowed one hit in the final inning. Spencer, May, and Varney each had two hits in two at-bats for the

White Sox. Nettles, Bell, and Patterson went one-for-one for the Oaks.

All ticket holders were offered a raincheck for a future game. "All our idea was to offer the people a chance to see the White Sox. For sure, we're not out to grab anyone's money," Johnston said. "Unfortunately, the weather was bad, but we think these exhibition games are good. We tried to show our appreciation for the crowd turnout tonight by having the players from both clubs go up into the stands and give autographs."[27]

In 1976, the Oaks came in second in the East Division of the American Association at 68-68, ten games behind first-place Omaha. Iowa had one player on the AA all-star team: outfielder Sam Ewing who hit .351 with twenty-six doubles, fifteen home runs, eighty-one runs-batted-in, and fifty-one runs scored in 101 games. He also had a .958 on-base-plus-slugging average.

A seven-run seventh inning propelled the parent Chicago White Sox to a 12-5 victory over their triple-A affiliate, the Iowa Oaks, on Monday, May 16, 1977. Iowa's third pitcher, Duane Shaffer, gave up seven hits in the inning, including a three-run home run over the left-center-field fence by Oscar Gamble. Tommy Cruz homered on White Sox starter Wilbur Wood's second pitch of the game, but Wood allowed only one more run in his five innings of work. Wood was coming back from a season ending kneecap injury in May 1976, but he showed no ill effects while covering first base for a putout on second baseman Jack Brohamer's throw. Most Chicago regulars played only the first two or three innings.

Jim Spencer led off Chicago's half of the second inning with a shot off Oaks starter Jack Kucek over the right-field fence. A little later in the inning, Brian Downing clubbed a three-run home run over the left-field fence. The Oaks' second hurler, Bob Polinsky, tossed three innings of scoreless, one-hit relief after Kucek. Iowa's fourth pitcher, Greg Terlecky, allowed one run and three hits in two innings. The fifth, Randy Wiles, pitched a scoreless, hitless ninth.

Kevin Bell of the Oaks hit one of White Sox pitching coach Stan Williams' breaking pitches over the center-field wall with two out in the ninth. "I was lucky that was the only run off me in two innings," the forty-year-old Williams said. "[Catcher Wayne] Nordhagen was tipping the batters off on every pitch that was coming. But I will say that Kevin hit the heck out of a good curveball."[28]

The son of a former Des Moines Bruin doubled and scored his team's first run against the Iowa Oaks seven days later, but the Oaks defeated the Minnesota Twins, 6-5, in seven innings at Sec Taylor Stadium. The Twins, who were ahead 9-6 at the start of the eighth inning, left the field to catch a plane and beat a 1 a.m. curfew for a doubleheader in Boston two nights later. Since the Oaks did not get an opportunity to bat in the bottom of the eighth, the game reverted to the end of the seventh when Iowa led, 6-5.

Despite a .195 batting average at the time, Twins' shortstop Roy Smalley III batted in the cleanup spot for Minnesota on Monday, May 23. Twins manager Gene Mauch explained that he put Smalley into the fourth spot in the batting order "because our regulars wouldn't play the whole game and I wanted them to hit as much as they could."[29] The son of former Bruins shortstop Roy Smalley Sr. came to Minnesota in 1976 in a trade with the Texas Rangers. The elder Smalley hit .244 in 114 games for Des Moines in 1947 and played eleven years in the major leagues including six with the Chicago Cubs. "My dad has talked to me about playing in Des Moines," the Twins' shortstop said. "He said he enjoyed this city very much and that the people treated him very well."[30]

The Oaks jumped out to a 2-0 lead in the first inning when Nyls Nyman drove in Mike Wolf with a single and Kevin Bell doubled to bring in Steve Staggs. In the third, Mike Squire's run-scoring single increased Iowa's lead to 3-0. Minnesota trailed by only two runs after scoring a run in the fourth inning. Wolf and Bee Bee Richard hit back-to-back solo homers in the bottom of the fourth to put the Oaks ahead, 5-1. The Twins countered with a run in the fifth and three runs in the sixth to tie the score, 6-6. Glen Adams' solo home run and Bob Gorinski's two-run shot accounted for the Twins' sixth-inning fireworks. Left fielder Jim Fuller of the Oaks provided the game-winning hit with a blast off the flagpole in the seventh inning. "It was a good night for me," Fuller said. "I hit a breaking pitch."[31]

Oaks skipper Joe Sparks called on pitcher Bobby Combs to start the eighth inning. Combs retired two batters and then was replaced by Rick Thoren, who gave up four hits and four runs. When Sparks went to the mound to take out Thoren, the Twins walked off the field so they could get to the airport to catch a plane to Boston.

David Frost pitched the first six innings for Iowa and struck out five-time American League batting champion Rod Carew before giving up a run-scoring single by Carew. "I'm sure Carew would have been more pepped up if he would have been playing in a league game," Frost said. "But you saw what he did with the runner on second. He laid into it good."[32] The thirty-one-year-old Carew just missed winning the AL batting title in 1976, hitting .331 compared to .333 for George Brett and .332 for Hal McRae of Kansas City.

Joe Sparks (Courtesy: Steve Dunn)

Wolf led the Oaks' attack with two hits in three at-bats, two runs scored, and one run-batted-in. Bell went two-for-three with one run scored and one run-batted-in. Squires contributed two hits in four at-bats and drove in a run. The start of the game was moved up to 6 p.m. to accommodate the Twins' travel schedule. The clubs also agreed the game would be called at 8:30 p.m. no matter how many innings had been played for the same reason.

After walking four batters in the first inning, Iowa Oaks pitcher Jack Kucek appeared to be on his way toward an early exit on Friday, May 26, 1978. But after Stan Butkus started warming up in the Oaks' bullpen, Kucek got a force out and retired the next fifteen hitters on his way to a no-hit, 6-1, victory over Oklahoma City at Sec Taylor Stadium. "I hope this breaks us loose," an ecstatic Kucek said afterwards. "The way the guys played behind me tonight, anyone could have gotten a no-hitter."[33]

Not only did Kucek make history, but also the Oaks, then an affiliate of the Chicago White Sox, broke an eight-game losing streak. "When [Manager] Joe [Sparks] came out to talk to me in the first inning, he said I was standing up too straight," Kucek said. "He said I should bend over after I released the ball."[34]

Designated hitter Jim Breazeale provided all the offense the Oaks needed with a mammoth homer to right in the third inning that gave Iowa the lead for good. Breazeale finished with three hits and two runs-batted-in and scored three times. Third baseman Kevin Bell and catcher Mike Colbern added back-to-back homers for the Oaks in the eighth. "I've been coming out early every day for hitting," said Bell, who entered the game batting only .204. "I was wondering when the first one [homer] would come. I hope this gets us turned around."[35]

Two fielding gems secured the no-hitter for Kucek. In the third inning, left fielder Mike Eden made a diving, shoestring catch on Mike Anderson's sinking line drive. As he caught the ball, Eden rolled over and held the ball high in the air as the umpire signaled an out. In the fifth inning, Oaks first baseman Mike Squires stabbed Bobby Brown's line drive toward right field. Other than those two plays, Kucek was in control the rest of the way. He struck out seven of the final fifteen batters he faced. A crowd of 1,172 witnessed Kucek's gem. Kucek has the fourth lowest ERA in club history (3.04), and is tied for the most complete games (sixteen).

Coincidentally, former Oaks pitcher Silvio Martinez of Springfield threw a no-hitter against Omaha at Johnny Rosenblatt Stadium the same night. Martinez retired the first twenty-three

Royals he faced before Darrell Porter reached base on an error in
the eighth

Chapter 10

In 1981, the team signed a working agreement with the Chicago Cubs, and the ballclub was renamed the Iowa Cubs the following year.

Ray Johnston agreed to sell the franchise to a local group of investors headed by Ken Grandquist and Dick Easter on Thursday, December 3, 1981, for $600,000. A signing ceremony was held at the Greater Des Moines Chamber of Commerce to mark the occasion. At that time, the local group had raised about half of the money needed to complete the transaction.

"I guess what it comes down to is that I really didn't want to take the Oaks out of Des Moines," said Johnston, who indicated he was not worried about getting the rest of the money. "I have a lot of confidence that the people here can raise the money."[1]

John Homeier, president of Bi-Petro Inc. in Springfield, Illinois, had also offered $600,000 for the franchise. Johnston received a similar offer from a group in Memphis, Tennessee.

On the day of the signing, Johnston said he was not convinced Des Moines had enough money to buy the franchise until shortly before midnight the previous day. "The key came when I got a chance to meet Dick [Easter]," Johnston told the media. "Until then, I was very doubtful."[2]

Forty-two years later, Grandquist's daughter, Cindy Grandquist, attributed her father's success in landing the franchise to his years-long friendship with Johnston. "A good friend of his was Ray

Johnston," she said. "I don't know how they connected originally, but they got to be pretty good friends."3

Selling the franchise to a local group and keeping it in Des Moines was "very important," she added. "I am sure [Johnston] trusted that dad would do a good job. I doubt that it would have come back to Des Moines [if the franchise had been sold to an out-of-state group]. The fact that he was able to get the triple-A Chicago Cubs here made a huge difference. I think that's one reason it will stay here. Des Moines has always had a big Cubs following."4

The elder Grandquist said at the time he hoped to give a check for $450,000 to $500,000 to Johnston when the deal was closed on January 2, 1982. There was no deadline to pay the rest of the money. Two days earlier, Grandquist hoped Johnston would take $300,000 then and the rest of the money over a three-year period. However, Johnston wanted the remaining $300,000 within one year.5

The fifty-eight-year-old Grandquist headed a twenty-member steering committee formed to keep the franchise in Des Moines. The Roosevelt High School graduate and real estate magnate agreed with other business people that the Oaks' advertising and promotion under Johnston's ownership had been "real bad."6

Earlier, *Des Moines Tribune* columnist Marc Hansen said that Johnston "promoted the Oaks with slightly more zeal than Iowa State promotes Iowa."7 "I'd say there's justification in that," Johnston said. "I've kind of let the community down by not being here. I wanted to move to Des Moines [from Dallas, Texas] six or seven years ago, but my wife's arthritic condition couldn't take the Iowa winters."8 Plus, his travel agency's brisk business in Dallas the past three years had made it more difficult to get away, Johnston added.

"For years, Iowa Oaks baseball has been the best entertainment buy in town," Hansen observed. "But it could have been better, and Ray Johnston knows it."9

"I know I didn't spend as much time here as I should have," Johnston said. "It's time for the ballclub to be owned by someone in Des Moines. I'm an outsider, and I'll always be an outsider."[10]

Johnston called selling the team one of the most difficult decisions he ever made. "I've never offered it to anybody until today," he explained. "I'm going to miss it. That was the hardest part of the decision. I've spent my life in baseball and I've enjoyed it."[11]

In an editorial in the *Des Moines Tribune* on December 4, 1981, the newspaper attributed the previous day's ceremony to the relationship between Grandquist and Johnston. The *Tribune* added that Des Moines had a "gentleman's agreement" between Johnston and Grandquist, "who is confident that an additional $300,000 can be raised to match the money in hand."[12]

Noting that Dick Easter of Easter Foods had pledged $100,000, the *Tribune* added, "The support given to Sec Taylor Stadium by the city of Des Moines and Polk County also bodes well for the future of professional baseball in central Iowa.

"Grandquist, Easter and others who worked to assure that the Oaks would stay in Des Moines played Santa Claus to baseball fans here. The gift came several weeks before Christmas, but that just gives people more time to say thank you."[13]

Cindy Grandquist managed the ushers, program sales by the ushers, and ticket sales shortly after her father assumed ownership of the team. At first, the office staff worked in a trailer outside the entrance to the stadium. Bob Reynolds was her immediate supervisor when the office was outside the ballpark; then current president and general manager Sam Bernabe succeeded Reynolds. "I would show up, go to my office, pick up the money from the front office [when the front office moved inside the stadium]," she recalled. "When the ushers came in, I would give them the number of programs each of them got to sell. The ticket takers also checked in with me. After that was done, I spent most of my time outside walking around and checking to make sure they had what they needed."[14] She described her dad as "kind of a tough guy" when it came to purchasing or selling things. "But I didn't see that side of him," she added.[15]

Cindy Grandquist also taught high school special education at her alma mater, Hoover High School, in Des Moines while the club was owned by her father's group. After the club was sold, she continued to teach at Hoover High School and ended her teaching career at Valley High School in West Des Moines. She was inducted into the Hoover High School Hall of Fame, a list that also includes the late major-league umpire Eric Cooper and former major-league pitcher Jeremy Hellickson.

Officials announced on Monday, January 12, 1981, that an exhibition game between the Chicago Cubs and Oaks would be played in May at Sec Taylor Stadium. Appearing at Hotel Fort Des Moines, Cubs general manager Bob Kennedy said his team would fly from Chicago to Des Moines the afternoon of May 18, play the game starting at approximately 6 p.m., and set a time limit so the team could fly back to Chicago that night. The Cubs came with six players: Bill Buckner, rookie Leon "Bull" Durham, reliever Lee Smith, catcher Tim Blackwell, reserve infielder Steve Dillard, and rookie pitcher Mike King from Sioux City. In addition to Kennedy, the Cubs brought former star player Ernie Banks, manager of group sales and a member of the board of directors. "The bottom line is love," Banks said after thanking the crowd for its warm reception. "Despite the negative things you see and hear about the game and some of the players, it still is the greatest game in the world."[16] Cubs broadcaster Milo Hamilton, a native of Fairfield, introduced Banks.

Fans also got their first look at manager Randy Hundley, a catcher on the Cubs' pennant-contending teams of the late 1960s and early 1970s. "I'm so excited about this job I want to go to spring training tomorrow," Hundley said at a dinner in the evening. "We may not win the pennant but we'll split a gut trying and we'll have some fun."[17] Hundley also promised to move his family, including three children, to Des Moines once school was out in late spring and make public appearances. The former catcher managed the Midland, Texas, club in the Texas League in 1979 and 1980. In

1979, Hundley's team finished 76-59 and captured the division title in the second half of the split season.

"It is no secret that I would like to manage a big league club someday," he said. "I can't play anymore. I would like to manage the Cubs, but I am not trying to get anybody's job."[18] Wichita, Kansas, was Chicago's triple-A farm club in 1980 and finished last in the Western Division of the American Association, thirty-one games out of first place. "My philosophy is to run and steal bases— to put pressure on the other team with speed and defense. Home runs are nice, but we aren't going to sit around and wait for someone to hit one out of the park. I want to create offense by running."[19] In 1979, his Midland team swiped more than 200 bases in 136 games.

Two teams with a combined record of 14-45 squared off at Sec Taylor Stadium on Monday, May 18. In the end, the Oaks came from behind to defeat the parent club, 6-5, before 4,464 fans. "I loved it," said Hundley afterwards. "But we have to play like we did tonight when we get against teams in our own league."[20] The Oaks came into the game at 9-20, having lost ten of their last eleven contests. Meanwhile, the Cubs under manager Joe Amalfitano were 5-25 and fifteen games out of first place in the Eastern Division of the National League.

Carlos Lezcano of Iowa tied the game with a two-out home run over the left-field fence in the bottom of the ninth off Ken Pryce, who had been called up from Class A Quad Cities for the matchup. The next batter, Tye Waller, singled and moved to third when a throw by Cub catcher Jody Davis sailed into the outfield on Waller's stolen base attempt. Waller scored the winning run seconds later on an infield single by Bill Hayes of the Oaks. The victory was only the Oaks' second in the past twelve games.

The Cubs scored single runs in the second and third innings. In the second, Hector Cruz walked, moved to second on Mike Lum's single, and scored on a single by Joe Strain. In the third, Steve Henderson drew a walk, went to second on a single by Jerry Morales, and crossed the plate on a single by Leon "Bull" Durham.

Left-hander Ken Kravec was pitching for Chicago in the third inning when the Oaks scored four runs, of which only two were earned. Waller started the rally with a single and advanced to third on a double by Joe Hicks. The next hitter, Butch Benton, hit a grounder to third that Cubs third baseman Cruz mishandled. At that point, Waller streaked for home and the throw by Cruz hit Waller in the back. Hicks scored when Kravec uncorked a wild pitch, and Benton came home on a single by Scott Fletcher. After Fletcher stole second base, Mike Turgeon singled to drive in Fletcher.

Down 4-2 in the eighth, the Cubs got a run back when Steve Macko hit a grounder to the right side, which scored Mike Tyson. Macko was undergoing cancer treatment at the time, but occasionally went on road trips and worked out with the Cubs whenever possible. Lum put the Cubs ahead momentarily with a two-run home run in the ninth. The Cubs had signed the fourteen-year major-league veteran on the previous Sunday when the team was in Houston. He had been released by the Atlanta Braves three weeks earlier.

Perhaps no one was more excited about the Oaks' win over their big brothers than Lezcano. "We wanted to beat them real bad [sic]," he said, "and they wanted to beat us, too. You bet they did."[21] Amalfitano claimed the loss was no worse than the defeats his club had absorbed in the National League that season. "No, I'm just thinking about who I am going to play tomorrow," he said, referring to the series opener against the Cincinnati Reds in Chicago. "If I felt that way, I would have started Rick Reuschel tonight."[22] Rather than come to Des Moines, Reuschel stayed in Chicago to prepare for his next pitching assignment against the Reds the next day.

Bill Buckner, the National League batting champion in 1980, did not play for the Cubs. Teammate Ken Reitz, who was hitting only .186 at the time, was also held out of the exhibition. The Cubs obtained third baseman Reitz in the deal that sent reliever Bruce Sutter to the St. Louis Cardinals. "Most of the Cubs would rather not have been in Monday night's game, and even some of the Oaks were not all that thrilled about braving the forty-degree temperatures and frigid winds," the *Register's* Mark Hansen concluded the next day.[23]

In 1981, the Oaks came in last in the Eastern Division of the American Association with a 53-82 mark, nineteen-and-a-half games behind first-place Evansville, managed by Jim Leyland. The AA all-star unit included two players who went on to star with Chicago: shortstop Ryne Sandberg and outfielder Bob Dernier of Oklahoma City. Former Oaks skipper Joe Sparks of Omaha was named the manager of the year.

All-star first baseman Bill Buckner doubled and singled twice, but it was not enough to lift the Chicago Cubs to a victory over their triple-A affiliate in Des Moines on Thursday, June 3, 1982. The Iowa Cubs outhit their major-league brethren eleven to six and won, 7-2, with 6,228 on hand at Sec Taylor Stadium. "This game is for the minor league affiliate," said John Cox, assistant to Chicago general manager Dallas Green. "This is our way of thanking and supporting the Des Moines people who operate this team."[24]

Mel Hall of Iowa collected three hits, scored once, and drove in a run. Teammates Scott Fletcher and Randy LaVigne each had two hits. Pat Tabler and Tom Grant were credited with two runs-batted-in apiece. I-Cub starter Craig Lefferts gave up two hits and struck out two in three innings of work. The winning pitcher, Ken Pryce, allowed four hits and two runs in four innings. Larry Jones walked one Chicago player in the eighth inning, but escaped further damage. Jim Gerlach was touched for one hit and struck out one in the ninth. Pryce and Gerlach had been called up from double-A Midland for the exhibition.

The I-Cubs scored the first run of the game on singles by LaVigne, Jack Upton, and Bill Hayes in the second. The home team scored again in the third inning on doubles by Fletcher and Hall. A sacrifice fly by Tabler produced the winning run in the fifth. Meanwhile, Chicago scored twice in the seventh on singles by designated hitter Buckner and Bob Molinaro, walks to Steve Henderson and Scot Thompson, and a run-scoring groundout by Dan Briggs.

Iowa roughed up Cubs pitchers Bill Campbell and Dick Tidrow for six hits. The triple-A Cubs added five hits off two more Chicago hurlers, Scott Johnson and Russ Brahms, who had been summoned from the Quad Cities club in the Midwest League.

Thanks to the biggest crowd of the season, the I-Cubs management realized approximately $25,000 in profits from gate receipts. The next day, *Des Moines Tribune* columnist Marc Hansen described the atmosphere at Sec Taylor Stadium. "The Chi-Cubs left their game faces in Chicago and the I-Cubs were feeling the effects of a three-game winning streak," Hansen wrote. "In other words, it wasn't a pressure-packed event. What it was, was a fun time for all at the old ballyard."[25] And, he said, the I-Cubs were winners in several ways. "Sure, it's only an exhibition," he said, "but the win showed 6,228 eyewitnesses and another goodly sum in television land how well the locals are capable of playing."[26]

Mel Hall (Courtesy: John Liepa)

Six weeks later, president Ken Grandquist expressed satisfaction with his investment in the team. "Heck, yes, I'm happy with my investment," he said. "I think everybody who invested feels we've got the Cubs here and hopefully they'll never leave."[27] The club passed the 100,000 mark in attendance July 14, more than 22,000 ahead of the same period in 1981, and was on pace to break the season record of 136,138 in 1979. "We're expecting 155,000 to 160,000 attendance for the year if we can stay in the [pennant] race," Grandquist said. "One thing about Des Moines is that they like a winner, and they haven't had one for a long time."[28]

Spending more on advertising and promotions than in the past, the new ownership group even used Cadillacs to take the players, wives, and girlfriends from the Des Moines airport to the front gate of Sec Taylor Stadium for a doubleheader against Denver. "We're taking care of our boys," Grandquist said. "We've got to when they're playing like this. They've got the whole town buzzing."[29]

The I-Cubs' management, however, did not expect Braniff Airways to collapse after the club bought approximately $5,000 worth of greatly-reduced price tickets for road trips. One trip through Indianapolis, Evansville, and Denver alone cost $12,000, about $4,000 more than the Braniff rates. To cut costs, manager Jim Napier agreed to travel by bus to Wichita twice rather than by plane. Travel to sixty-eight road games was expected to cost approximately $55,000, at least $10,000 more than estimated originally.[30]

The $50,000 to install plank bleachers along the left-field and right-field foul lines was the biggest unexpected expenditure, not travel expenses. Grandquist said that partner Dick Easter convinced the board of directors to install the additional seating after discovering it would cost $11,000 to erect temporary seating for special promotional events. By mid-July, the club had already had three highly successful promotions: the exhibition game with the Chicago Cubs, San Diego Chicken Night on June 13, and the Fourth of July fireworks night. In line with the new emphasis on promotion, management added a second novelty stand and an expanded line of merchandise for sale.

Iowa finished second in the AA Eastern Division in 1982, finishing 73-62 and one-and-a-half games behind first-place Indianapolis. Pitcher Jay Howell was selected pitcher of the year after compiling a 13-4 record and 2.36 earned run average with five complete games and two shutouts. Outfielder Mel Hall was named rookie of the year based on his thirty-two home runs, thirty-four doubles, six triples, 125 runs-batted-in, .329 batting average, and nineteen stolen bases. The I-Cubs also had five all-star picks:

Howell, Hall, third baseman Pat Tabler, catcher Butch Benton, and manager Jim Napier. Tabler hit .342 with seventeen homers, thirty-two doubles, eleven triples, 105 runs-batted-in, and fifteen stolen bases. Benton hit .330 with eleven home runs and fifty-seven runs-batted-in. As a team, the I-Cubs hit .294 with 749 runs scored, 140 homers, 262 doubles, forty-one triples, 699 runs-batted-in, and 128 stolen bases. The pitchers had a combined 4.90 earned run average and gave up 1,208 hits, 714 runs, and 144 homers. They struck out 754, walked 497, compiled nineteen complete games, and shut out six opponents.

In early September 1982, the Des Moines City Council agreed unanimously to spend $300,000 to renovate Sec Taylor Stadium and to loan $100,000 to the club's owners to help build a new clubhouse. Shortly afterwards, the ballclub's board of directors voted unanimously to accept the deal. City manager Richard Wilkey explained the city would issue $150,000 in general obligation bonds to erect new lights plus $150,000 in bonds for upgrades including new bathrooms, bigger dugouts, new fencing and screening, and better parking and grandstand facilities.

Before the crucial city council vote, it appeared the Chicago Cubs might move their triple-A affiliate to Oklahoma City, forcing Des Moines baseball leaders to come up with another major-league affiliate, such as the Chicago White Sox.[31] In July 1982, the parent club's general manager, Dallas Green, and Gordon Goldsberry made four recommendations concerning Sec Taylor Stadium: improve the lighting, build a new clubhouse, renovate the playing surface, and install a new fence. The latter two were already in the city's capital improvement budget for the year.

Fortunately for central Iowa baseball fans, the upgrades were finished by the start of the 1983 baseball season. In fact, Eliot Nusbaum of the *Des Moines Register* wrote on April 14, 1983, that the new facilities "have elevated the stadium from the bush league to the major league in comfort. The real hit of the season is going to be the new clubhouse out in left field. The teams, both home and visiting, will enjoy twice as much space as in the old facilities."[32]

In addition, a new restaurant, the Cub Club, was built into the left-field wall. The old clubhouses were converted into concession stands and ninety-six new box seats were installed. The "new" Sec Taylor Stadium also featured three times as many restrooms and a regraded, leveled, reseeded, and resodded playing surface. The old eighty-five-foot-high lights were replaced with 110-foot-high lights that produced three times as much light on the infield and twice as much light on the outfield. With the improvements, club officials hoped to increase 1982's attendance from 203,169 to at least 250,000 in 1983.

The Iowa Cubs beat the Chicago Cubs for the third straight time on Monday, May, 1983. This time, Carmelo Martinez and Mike Diaz hit homers to lead the local team to a 7-5 win over the visitors from the Windy City.

The I-Cubs got on the scoreboard in the first when a sacrifice fly by Joe Carter scored Dave Owen, and Martinez singled and scored on Tom Grant's single. The Cubs pulled ahead 5-2 in the top of the second, which included a three-run homer by Jerry Morales. Jay Johnston singled and then scored on a triple by Steve Lake. Moments later, Lake came home on a single by Ryne Sandberg. Iowa regained the lead in the third on a solo homer by Martinez and a two-run blast by Diaz with Grant on base. Iowa's final run came in the sixth on Martinez's single that scored Jay Loviglio.

Iowa hurler Tony Chestnut got the win; Chicago's Dickie Noles was the loser. The game was carried by Iowa Public Television at 6:30 p.m.

The I-Cubs ended the 1983 season by losing to the Denver Bears three games to one in the semifinals of the American Association playoffs. The teams split the first two games in Denver; the I-Cubs manhandled the Bears, 15-2, in the first game and lost, 12-11, in the second contest. Home runs by Henry Cotto and Dave Owen of Iowa were not enough in the third game at Sec Taylor Stadium as the I-Cubs fell, 9-5. Denver moved on to the finals by beating the I-Cubs, 5-3, in the fourth game. Joe Carter homered twice for Iowa.

Third baseman Ron Cey clubbed two home runs and knocked in five runs to spark the Chicago Cubs to an 11-3 drubbing of the I-Cubs on Monday, May 14, 1984, at Sec Taylor Stadium. The win snapped a three-game losing streak to Chicago's triple-A affiliate.

First baseman Bill Buckner provided the "feel good" story with four doubles and a single. Buckner was benched when right fielder Leon "Bull" Durham was moved to first base, and the Cubs obtained outfielder Gary "Sarge" Matthews in a trade with the Philadelphia Phillies. Coming into the exhibition game, Buckner was hitting .220 in only forty-one at-bats.

Known for hitting to all sides of the field, his five hits included two opposite-field doubles. He also scored four runs, and twice he went from second base to third on fly outs. The game ended on his running catch of Trey Brooks' liner. "That's what the fans came to see," said I-Cub manager Jim Napier. "They wanted Ron Cey to hit home runs and Buckner was unbelievable."[33]

Cey lofted a three-run homer to left off Iowa starter Derek Botelho in the first inning and added a two-run shot off Botelho in the second. Botelho, one of six I-Cubs pitchers, gave up nine hits and eight runs in two innings. Richie Hebner replaced Cey at third and contributed a two-run home run and a run-scoring single in Chicago's sixteen-hit attack. The Cubs got eight runs-batted-in from the fifth spot in their batting order that night. Billy Hatcher and Pete Mackanin had two hits apiece for Iowa.

Iowa's Don Werner caught the last four innings for the Cubs. Backup catcher Steve Lake was sent home to Chicago after complaining he did not feel well. Pitcher Scott Sanderson was the only Chicago player who did not make the trip to Des Moines. He was scheduled to start the next night in Cincinnati. The game drew 7,249 and lasted two hours and fifteen minutes.

On Tuesday, August 21, 1984, I-Cub Reggie Patterson threw the first no-hitter in six years by an Iowa pitcher at Sec Taylor Stadium, as Iowa beat Omaha, 2-0. Patterson nearly recorded a perfect game, walking Omaha's Rondin Johnson with two out in the ninth inning after getting head in the count, no balls, two strikes. The only other Omaha runner to get on base was John Morris, who reached first on an error by second baseman Trey Brooks in the second inning. "I'm tired, but excited," Patterson said afterwards. "I had all my pitches working. After six innings, I was thinking no-hitter."[34] "Reggie had command of all his pitches—

Reggie Patterson
(Courtesy: John Liepa)

fastball, slider, screwball, changeup, and knuckle-curve," catcher Bill Hayes said. "Getting ahead of hitters is the key to pitching. We were able to set up pitches. This was a lot of fun."[35]

Patterson threw first strikes to twenty-seven of the twenty-nine Royals he faced. He threw 114 pitches in all. The crowd of 2,413 held its breath in the ninth when Patterson mishandled Jim Scranton's bouncer back to the mound. However, third baseman Pete Mackanin grabbed the ball after it caromed off Patterson's glove and threw out Scranton by a whisker.

The I-Cubs scored their first run in the third on a leadoff double by Shawon Dunston, a bunt single by Billy Hatcher, and a groundout by Ricky Baker. Joe Hicks smashed his thirtieth homer of the season in the fourth inning to pad the lead. The last out came on a fly ball to Hatcher in center field, with Patterson turning and staring in that direction. "I was just thinking, geez, there it is," Patterson said.[36]

Patterson pitched the most shutouts in club history (six). He also ranks third in innings pitched (553 2/3); fourth in hits allowed (612); third in runs allowed (361), earned runs allowed (306), and wild pitches (twenty-six); first in walks (228); and fourth in strikeouts (364).

In 1984, the Denver Bears beat the I-Cubs three out of four games in the American Association semifinals. After losing the first two games at home, 8-3, and 9-0, Iowa came back to clip the Bears, 3-1, at Denver. Iowa hurler Ken Pryce outpitched Guy Hoffman of Denver, and Dave Owen homered for the I-Cubs. Despite home runs by Don Werner and Tom Grant, the I-Cubs lost the decisive fourth game, 5-2, at Denver.

Holding the I-Cubs to only two hits, the Chicago Cubs beat the host team, 5-1, on Thursday, May 30, 1985, in front of a record crowd of 8,639. The previous largest turnout in Des Moines baseball history was 8,424 for Farm Bureau Night on June 4, 1983. "It's about a $50,000 night," said Iowa president Ken Grandquist. "It sure beats the $10,000 the Chicago team pays if it doesn't come here to play."[37]

Two players who had been I-Cubs until recently had big games for Chicago. Left fielder Brian Dayett doubled in the third inning and homered in the sixth. Second baseman Chico Walker went two-for-three and scored two runs. Dayett's two-base hit led off the three-run third inning for Chicago. Larry Bowa grounded out, and then Dayett was out at third on a fielder's choice by Bob Dernier. Walker singled, and Davey Lopes also singled to drive in Dernier.

The next hitter, Leon "Bull" Durham, was hit by a pitch from Greg Maddux, who had been called up from Class A Peoria, Illinois, for the game. With the bases filled, Ron Cey's liner skimmed off the glove of Iowa third baseman Julio Valdez, rolled into the crowd in the left-field corner, and was ruled a ground-rule double that scored Walker and Lopes. The I-Cubs scored their lone run in the third when Marc Gillaspie doubled and came home on a sacrifice fly by Dave Hostetler. Tom Lombardi had Iowa's second hit, a single in the second. In the seventh, Walker drew a walk from Iowa pitcher Joe Hausey, who had been called up from double-A Pittsfield,

Massachusetts, for the exhibition. Walker advanced to third on a single by Durham and scored when Chris Speier hit into a double play.

Chicago starter George Frazier, who allowed two hits and one run in three innings, was the winning pitcher. His successors, Larry Sorensen, Warren Brusstar, and Drew Hall, allowed no runs and no hits the rest of the way. The left-handed Hall, Chicago's first pick in the previous year's summer draft, was brought up from Class A Winston-Salem, North Carolina, for the special game. Maddux, Chicago's second pick in the 1984 summer draft, was charged with the loss. The nineteen-year-old future Hall of Famer allowed six hits and three runs in three innings of work. I-Cub reliever Dave Gumpert struck out the side in the eighth.

I-Cub shortstop Shawon Dunston went hitless in two at-bats and saw no significance in the game even though he had started the season with the Cubs in Chicago. "This game means nothing to me," he said beforehand. "It's just another game. Even if I hit two home runs."[38] Dunston was sent down to Des Moines two weeks earlier after hitting .194 and committing nine errors in twenty-three games at the major-league level. For the I-Cubs, he was hitting .271 with six stolen bases and four errors.

In 1985, the I-Cubs under skipper Larry Cox finished last in the Western Division of the American Association at 66-75. Despite having all-star designated hitter Dave Hostetler, Iowa ended twelve-and-a-half games behind first-place Oklahoma City.

The Iowa Cubs turned the tables on their big league brethren on Thursday, May 15, 1986, winning 5-1 at Sec Taylor Stadium. The Chicago Cubs did not get a hit until former Iowa Cub and Iowa Oak Thad Bosley tripled with two outs in the sixth inning. The three-base hit came off pitcher Jeff Hirsch, who had been called up from Class A Peoria of the Midwest League for the game.

Iowa scored all of its runs in the sixth. First, Chico Walker doubled to left; then Dave Martinez drove in Walker with a single to center. Steve Hammond doubled to left, and Martinez stopped at third. A single by Joe Hicks brought in Martinez and Hammond. Then Tom Lombarski homered off six-foot-seven Chicago pitcher Dave Pavlas, who had been brought in from Class A Winston-Salem for the game. Chicago scored its only run of the game in the seventh when Chris Speier doubled, Steve Lake singled, and Manny Trillo hit a sacrifice fly. Lake, an I-Cub, wore a Chicago uniform and played for the major-league team that night.

The I-Cubs collected doubles from second baseman Walker, right fielder Martinez, designated hitter Hicks, catcher Hammond, and outfielder Pookie Bernstine; a triple from Walker; and the home run by first baseman Lombarski. "This might get us going," said Iowa manager Larry Cox. "This might do something for Hicks. Our guys do get pumped up for this game. They want to show the people of Des Moines they play decent baseball."[39] Hicks was mired in a three-for-thirty-six slump going into the game. Hammond had collected hits in twenty of his twenty-four games with Iowa. "Sure, we get pumped up for this game," he said. "These are guys you've watched on TV. It's better than playing Buffalo."[40]

Only catcher Jody Davis had the night off among Chicago's regular players. Still, it appeared the major-league version of the Cubs was playing at half-speed at times. "As usual, the farm club was the more spirited of the two teams on the field," the *Register's* Hansen observed. "To illustrate how serious the Chi-Cubs took the game, Keith Moreland, pinch-hitting for designated hitter Ryne Sandberg, batted left-handed. For the record, he swings from the right side."[41]

Chicago did not arrive in Des Moines until 5 p.m. due to a thunderstorm in the Windy City that delayed the flight. At the time, Chicago was in last place in the Eastern Division of the National League, ten games behind the first-place New York Mets. The I-Cubs were sixth in the eight-team American Association with a record of 64-74, fourteen games behind first place Denver.

Coming back from a sore right arm, Chicago Cubs starter Scott Sanderson made a strong case for reactivation on Monday, April 20, 1987, at Sec Taylor Stadium. The six-foot-five right-hander allowed three runs and six hits in eight innings as the exhibition with the I-

Cubs ended in a 5-5 tie. The game was called after ten innings so Chicago could catch a plane in time for a game the next night in St. Louis. "I'm not surprised [at the results], and they're [management] not, either," Sanderson said, after throwing 110 pitches. "I'm not running the team. I want to pitch against competition where it counts. Period."42

1986 Iowa Cubs (Courtesy: John Liepa)

Chicago scored five runs in the third inning, which included a triple with the bases loaded by Keith Moreland, who was hitting only .175 at the time. The I-Cubs tied the score with two runs off reliever Ron Davis in their half of the ninth. The I-Cubs came in sixth in the American Association at 64-74 under skipper Larry Cox. Wade Rowdon had 113 runs-batted-in to lead the AA. Catcher Damon Berryhill was named to the all-star team.

The I-Cubs beat the parent club for the third consecutive year on Monday, April 18, 1988. Outfielder Gary Varsho collected a home run, two doubles, and four runs-batted-in to lead Iowa to a 9-3 win before 8,131 spectators at Sec Taylor Stadium.

Iowa put the game away with five runs in the seventh inning. Doug Dascenzo started the scoring spree by reaching first base on Leon "Bull" Durham's error and advancing to second on a double by Greg Tabor. Soon afterwards, Dascenzo scored on a passed ball and Tabor crossed the plate on a double by Mark Grace. Bill Bathe's single drove in Grace, and then Bathe scored on Varsha's two-run homer.

Chicago scored twice in the first on a two-run double by former I-Cub Rafael Palmeiro. Ryne Sandberg's solo shot in the fifth accounted for the visitors' other run. Dave Masters, the tallest pitcher in baseball at six-feet-nine, gave up only four Chicago hits in seven innings. In 1988, the I-Cubs' pitching staff was the youngest in baseball with an average age of twenty-three. Besides the twenty-three-year-old Masters, Iowa's rotation included Len Damian, twenty-one; Jeff Pico, twenty-one; Roger Williams, twenty-four; and Bob Tewksbury, twenty-seven.

Eight former I-Cubs accompanied Chicago to the exhibition game that night: Palmeiro, Dave Martinez, Greg Maddux, and five others. *Baseball America* rated the Chicago Cubs' farm system the second best in baseball in 1988. "I had fun in the minor leagues. I had fun in [Class A] Peoria and here [Des Moines]," Maddux said on his way to an 18-8 season. "I made the best of it, and I had a good time."[43] The I-Cubs came in second in the Western Division of the American Association at 78-64, three games behind first-place Omaha. Outfielder Rolando Roomes and catcher Bill Bathe were selected to join the all-star team.

The I-Cubs collected only three hits, but it was enough to edge the parent club, 2-1, on Thursday, May 25, 1989. The crowd of 8,115 was the tenth largest since triple-A baseball came to Des Moines in 1969. "The only people who took the game seriously were those in the Iowa Cub front office," the *Des Moines Register's* Randy Peterson wrote. "General manager Sam Bernabe and ticket manager Todd Guske were last seen smiling ear-to-ear as an armored truck left long after the Iowa Cubs defeated the Chicago Cubs, 2-1."[44]

All three runs in the exhibition game were scored on sacrifice flies. Chicago scored early, thanks to a sacrifice fly by Ryne Sandberg in the first inning that scored Doug Dascenzo. Dascenzo led off the game with a single, advanced to second on a balk by pitcher Gabriel Rodriguez, and then moved to third on a groundout before scoring the first run. Rodriguez had been called up from double-A Charlotte to start for the I-Cubs. Iowa answered with a run of its own in the bottom of the first. Bryan House singled and eventually scored on a sacrifice fly by Hector Villaneuva. The I-Cubs' winning run in the fourth was unearned. Shortstop Domingo Ramos was unable to handle Butch Garcia's grounder. Moments later, Garcia crossed the plate on a sacrifice fly by Jeff Small.

"I'm sure this game wasn't real high on a lot of the players' priority lists, but it's something that has to be done," said Chicago first baseman Mark Grace, one of fourteen former Iowa players on the big Cubs' roster that night. "The people in Des Moines were good to me when I played here. It's nice to be able to pay them back a little."[45]

House, Small, and Brian Guinn had the only hits for the winners. Dascenzo and outfielder Mitch Webster garnered Chicago's only safeties. Webster played despite being on the injured list with a pulled quadriceps muscle. Kevin Coffman, Mike Capel, and Roger Williams pitched four innings of scoreless, hitless relief for the I-Cubs. Another Chicago player on the injured list, outfielder Andre Dawson, did not play.

The I-Cubs ended in third place in the Western Division of the American Association with a 62-82 record under skipper Pete Mackanin in 1989. Pitcher Kevin Blankenship tied for the league lead with thirteen wins.

Chapter 11

I-Cubs capture AA title;
Des Moines hosts all-star game;
Gartner group buys club

The continuation of triple-A baseball in Des Moines was assured on Tuesday, August 7, 1990, when voters approved a $12.5 million bond issue to rebuild Sec Taylor Stadium and to upgrade the city's parks and pools. "I'm about the happiest guy in the city of Des Moines," said I-Cub president Ken Grandquist after hearing the news.[1] "This is a real victory for fans of the Iowa Cubs," majority stockholder Dick Easter added.[2] The measure passed 12,497 to 9,415, or 57 to 43 percent. Voters in sixty of the city's ninety-nine precincts supported the issue.

A week before the referendum passed, the *Des Moines Register's* Randy Peterson put the issue this way: "It's simple, if the referendum proposal is approved, the team stays . . . If it is defeated, strike three. No more Triple-A baseball for Des Moines, at least under current ownership, without a new stadium."[3]

Mark Grace
(Courtesy: Scott
Sailor/Iowa Cubs)

The city planned to use lodging taxes rather than property taxes to repay the bonds. About $6.6 million of the bond issue was earmarked for the $7.5 million stadium renovation and expansion. Team owners were to pay $875,000 to increase grandstand seating from 7,819 to 10,266 and to add skyboxes and elevators. The project also called for increasing the concession stands from five to nine and bathrooms from three to six for women and five for men. Sixteen new skyboxes and a bigger press box with a restroom were also part of the plan. "When we get it done, it's going to be fantastic," said Grandquist, adding the team wanted to increase season ticket sales from 1,300 to 3,000 with a variety of new packages.[4]

Demolition of the old stadium started on September 10, 1991. Construction of the new stadium began on the same site in October of that year. The first game in the new Sec Taylor Stadium was played on April 16, 1992. With a then record 10,749 in attendance the I-Cubs beat Louisville, 3-2.

"Most of the noisy crowd of 10,749—far eclipsing the record of 9,167 set in 1986— was still around for the conclusion, despite 48-degree cold," the *Register's* Randy Peterson reported. "They liked what they saw."[5]

Converted shortstop Jim Bullinger replaced relief pitcher Jeff Robinson at the start of the ninth and retired the side in order for his fifth save. Bullinger induced Rod Brewer to ground out to first baseman Scott Bryant. Then Bullinger struck out the final two Louisville hitters, Ozzie Canseco and Jose Fernandez. The I-Cubs improved to 5-2 and moved within a half-game of first place Oklahoma City.

"It was nice to come into a ballgame up a run and everybody in the stands on their feet screaming," Bullinger said afterwards. "It was just a tremendous feeling. They gave that extra shot of adrenaline. But I wouldn't have been in that situation if the hitters didn't provide that one-run lead."[6]

Bryant started the decisive seventh inning with a double to the right-field corner. He scored when a ground ball hit by Mike Knapp rolled through the legs of shortstop Greg Carmona. "I just took off because I knew I could beat the ball to third base," Bryant explained.[7] Then Bryant heard a lot of yelling and saw manager Brad Mills waving. "I didn't even see the ball," Bryant said. "I was just watching Brad."[8]

Bryant and Derrick May had two hits each for the I-Cubs. Teammate Pedro Castellano extended his hitting streak with a single in the first inning that drove in a run. Besides May's run-scoring single, Rey Sanchez walked and stole second and third in the first inning. After the first inning, however, the I-Cubs did not get a runner past first base until Bryant's double in the seventh. Louisville tied the score at 2-2 when Canseco sent a two-run blast off the right-field scoreboard against starter Jeff Hartsock in the fourth inning.

The new Sec Taylor Stadium drew kudos from players and baseball authorities alike. "It was loud. Louder than it's ever been before," Derrick May said. "I think the way the ballpark's built has something to do with it."[9] Chicago Cub general manager Larry Himes said, "It's a nice place in a great setting with the [state] Capitol out there. I walked up the steps today. You don't realize how high you are."[10] American Association president Branch Rickey III was impressed, too. "Having spent most of my life in ballparks, I wasn't expecting this," Rickey said. "It's a great blend of the traditional and the modern."[11]

Referring to the remodeled stadium's thirty-two skyboxes, *Des Moines Register* columnist Mark Hansen compared Box 309 to a bachelor pad, because it had a mirror covering an entire wall and a foldout bed. A Shrimp Louis salad costing $8.95, excluding a 15 percent tip and 4 percent sales tax, was the most expensive item on the menu.

The businesses and individuals who sat in the thirty-two new skyboxes and the number of seats allotted to each skybox were the following: Ringland-Johnson-Crowley, ten; Pepsi-Cola, eight; Miller Beer / Iowa Retail Beverage, eight; Bankers Trust, eight; Principal Financial, eight; Denman & Co., eight; New England Financial Group, eight; Gamble Law Firm, eight.

Also, Parker Oil / Deshong & Assoc., eight; Bob Homer, eight; Dick Easter, eight; Bill Knapp, eight; KVI, eight; Gordon's Wholesale, eight; Emco Industries, eight; Nightly Rental Skybox, eight.

Others included Atlantic Bottling Co., twelve; Ken Grandquist / Iowa Cubs, twelve; Norwest Banks, twelve; Precision Sewing, eight; The Weitz Co. / Holmes-Murphy, eight; Mid-America Group, eight; Commtron, eight.

The last group included Whitfield Law Firm, eight; Ernst & Young, eight; American Cyanamid, eight; Casey's, eight; Boatmen's Banks, eight; IGF Insurance Co., eight; Budweiser / Nesbit Dist., eight; and John Deere, ten.[12] Six hundred parking places were lost due to the stadium's larger footprint and landscaping.

A walk-off home run by Karl "Tuffy" Rhodes in the eleventh inning lifted the I-Cubs to their first (and only) American Association championship on Wednesday, September 15, 1993. The I-Cubs took two of the first three games at the Nashville Sounds; then lost two of the next three contests at Sec Taylor Stadium. Rhodes also homered in the third and fifth games. "It's almost like someone scripted it," first-year manager Marv Foley said. "These guys have never given up. They're never out of a game."[13] Indeed, twenty-eight of the club's record eighty-nine victories came in the last at-bat.

"Rhodes knew it was a home run the second he hit it," the *Des Moines Register's* Mark Hansen said in a front page column the next day. "He'd barely completed his follow through when he lifted an index finger to the heavens and watched the ball clear the [left-field] fence."[14] Rhodes joined the I-Cubs on July 30 in a three-way trade with the Omaha Royals. His game-winning home run came off James Baldwin on a no-ball, one-strike pitch. The club had led the Western Division of the American Association since April 19. "With one swing of the bat, Des Moines became the center of the universe for twenty-five players who dream of Chicago . . . and you would have thought the World Series champion had been anointed in the sparkly little ballpark by the swollen [Des Moines and Raccoon] rivers," Hansen observed.[15]

Jim Bullinger pitched three innings of scoreless relief to pick up the win, and was named the playoff's Most Valuable Player. He allowed two hits, struck out five, and got superb support from his fielders. In the eleventh inning, Bullinger walked Joe Hall and then struck out Drew Denson and Chris Cron. Sensing a stolen base attempt, Foley called for a pitchout. With Hall on the move, second baseman Greg Smith fielded catcher Matt Walbeck's one-bounce throw and applied the tag for the last out of the inning. In the eighth inning, Denson led off with a double. The next batter, Cron, hit a line drive to I-Cub first baseman Matt Franco, who leaped and caught the ball in the webbing of his glove. The fielding gem saved another extra-base hit and the go-ahead run.

The I-Cubs scored in the first inning when Fernando Ramsey walked, moved to second on Smith's sacrifice bunt, and eventually scored on Eddie Zambrano's fly to center field. Nashville took the lead in the third on Norberto Martin's two-run home run. Iowa tied the game in the seventh when Doug Jennings doubled, advanced to third on Tommy Shields's single, and scored on Franco's fly to center.

The year ended on another positive note when president and general manager Sam Bernabe was named the American Association Executive of the Year.

In 1995, a $2 million clubhouse expansion was completed. The project included new offices for the manager and coaches, an expanded training room, an indoor batting cage, a new weight room and family lounge, and laundry and storage facilities, plus twelve skyboxes in left field. Five years later, eighty-eight new Home Plate Club seats were put behind home plate, and a $100,000 sound system was installed. In addition, the Cub Club was remodeled extensively and Principal Park was designated smoke free.

A standing-room-only crowd of 11,183 turned out on Wednesday, July 9, 1997, to see the only triple-A all-star game ever played in Des Moines. The contest featured the best players in the American Association, International League, and Pacific Coast League. The I-Cubs were represented by outfielder Robin Jennings and pitcher Dave Swartzbaugh, the losing pitcher. The all-stars representing the American League affiliates defeated their National League counterparts, 5-3.

Frank Catalanotto, a twenty-three-year-old second baseman for Toledo, was chosen a "star of stars" after hitting a home run and double, driving in two runs, and scoring once. "This was great, because I did it in an all-star game and a lot of my family was here," he said. "By far, it's the highlight of my season."[16] Other MVPs included Magglio Ordonez of Nashville and Nate Minchey of Colorado Springs.

Tuffy Rhodes (Courtesy: Steve Dunn)

From the start of the game, fans could tell it wasn't an ordinary regular season contest. The Canadian flag, representing the teams from Calgary, Edmonton, Ottawa, and Vancouver, flew above the center-field fence. Des Moines mayor Bob Ray and Iowa governor Terry Branstad threw out the ceremonial first pitches. The six-man umpiring crew included two Iowans: Bruce Dreckman of Marcus behind home plate and Pat Connors of Perry at second base.

Iowan Bill Fischer, the Richmond Braves' pitching coach, was honored before the game with a group of fifty from Council Bluffs cheering him on. "Bill goes to the Railway Tavern in the winter when he's off duty," a woman said. "He drinks a glass of water and visits with us."[17]

The triple-A all-star luncheon earlier in the day featured Sharon Robinson, daughter of Jackie Robinson, the first Black to play in the major leagues. She was introduced by Branch Rickey III, grandson of Brooklyn Dodgers owner Branch Rickey, who had brought Jackie Robinson to the major leagues. "I believe Mr. Rickey selected my father because of his character as well as because of his talent," Sharon Robinson said. "[Rickey] saw a person who was committed to something beyond himself, someone who was committed to social change."[18]

On Tuesday, July 8, Todd Helton of Colorado Springs won the twelve-man home run contest and received $1,000 and a contract from Louisville Slugger for his efforts. A crowd of 2,492 people watched Helton smash five home runs in the final round. Ivan Cruz of Columbus belted three; Paul Konerko of Albuquerque had two; and Aaron Boone of Indianapolis hit two pitches over the fence in the first round, but he was shut out in the final round.

The 350 or so dignitaries at the two-day festivities included former Dodgers manager Tommy Lasorda. The only previous connection Lasorda had to Des Moines was I-Cubs manager Tim Johnson. Lasorda managed Johnson in Albuquerque, the Dodgers' triple-A affiliate, in 1972. "I've been in some bigger cities, but never have I been in a place for an extended period of time where I felt as comfortable as I do here in Des Moines," Johnson said.[19]

The triple-A all-star game was not the only big news that day. In the afternoon, it was announced triple-A baseball would be realigned for next season, eliminating the American Association and putting the I-Cubs in the Pacific Coast League. The thirty major-league affiliates would be split into two leagues—sixteen in one league and fourteen in the other. Thus, the I-Cubs would have to travel no further than 135 miles to Omaha, Nebraska, but as many as 1,955 miles to Calgary, Canada.

Des Moines area baseball fans got a first-hand look at the home run hoopla surrounding Chicago Cub slugger Sammy Sosa in 1998. Sosa and seven other players for Chicago and the Iowa Cubs sent the ball out of Sec Taylor Stadium during an exhibition game on Thursday, August 13, 1998. The two teams were tied, 10-10, when the game was stopped after six innings. The total of twenty runs set a franchise record, breaking the old mark of nineteen when the Chicago White Sox beat Iowa, 12-7, in 1977.

The teams combined for eight home runs, and each club went back-to-back-to back. In the first inning, Mark Grace, Sosa, and

Henry Rodriguez put Chicago ahead with consecutive blasts off I-Cubs starter Kevin Foster. Mickey Morandini added to the visiting team's lead with a solo shot in the third. Iowa countered with three straight homers by Jason Maxwell, Robin Jennings, and Micah Franklin in the bottom of the third. Jason Hardtke homered for the I-Cubs in the fourth. Chicago added three runs in the fourth, one run in the fifth, and two runs in the sixth. The I-Cubs scored three times in each of the fourth and fifth innings.

Sosa was ejected in the fifth inning after kicking dirt on the shoes of home plate umpire Fred Cannon. The dust up started when Sosa jumped out of the dugout to protest Tyler Houston being called out at third base. After the ejection, Sosa tipped his cap, patted his chest a couple times, and ran to the clubhouse.[20] At the time, Sosa had forty-six homers in his pursuit of the major-league record set by Babe Ruth in 1927. When interviewed before the game by ESPN, the native of the Dominican Republic claimed he did not feel any pressure. "This isn't pressure. Pressure is what we went through back home," he said. "This is fun. It'll always be fun. Back home growing up . . . that was pressure."[21] As a lad in the Dominican Republic, Sosa shined shoes to earn spending money.

The I-Cubs had ten hits, including two each by Franklin and Matt Mieske, who drove in two runs. Chicago pounded out thirteen hits, including two each by Scott Servais and Jose Hernandez. The clubs collected five doubles; one each by Servais and Pedro Valdes of Chicago plus one by Franklin and two by Mieske of Iowa. Neither starting pitcher was effective. Foster was tagged for eight hits and seven runs (all earned) in four innings. He walked two and struck out six batters. Chicago starter Phil Norton gave up the same number of hits and runs in four innings. Norton issued one walk and struck out four.

In 1998, the I-Cubs hit a franchise-record 216 home runs. Ten players hit at least ten homers apiece: Rod McCall, thirty; Franklin, twenty-nine; Alan Zinter, twenty-three; Derrick White, eighteen; Pedro Valdes, seventeen; Robin Jennings, sixteen; Jason Maxwell, fifteen; Pat Cline, thirteen; Terrell Lowery; twelve; and Hardtke, eleven. Iowa pitchers Kurt Miller and Dave Swartzbaugh each recorded fourteen wins to lead the circuit. Miller and White were among the PCL's all-stars. Kennedy was chosen minor league manager of the year by *Baseball America* after the season.

The I-Cubs finished 85-59 and won the Central Division during their first year in the Pacific Coast League. Kennedy's club also tied the franchise record for regular season victories. However, the New Orleans Zephyrs beat Iowa two games to one in the PCL semifinals and eventually won the triple-A World Series. In 1997, Kennedy led Chicago's entry in Mesa to the championship of the Arizona Fall League and was manager of the year. His father, Bob, had guided the Chicago Cubs from 1963 to 1965 and was Chicago's general manager from 1977 to 1981. One of the elder Kennedy's last moves as general manager was to recommend switching the Cubs' triple-A affiliate from Wichita, Kansas, to Des Moines. "It just seemed to me like Des Moines was a natural," Bob Kennedy told the *Des Moines Register*.[22]

On October 1, 1999, ownership of the Iowa Cubs was transferred from a group led by Ken Grandquist to Raccoon Baseball Incorporated. Headed by former news executive Michael Gartner, RBI also included president/general manager Sam Bernabe, attorney/I-Cubs corporate secretary Michael Giudicessi, and Dr. Doug Dorner, a vascular surgeon. Gartner's son, Mike, was added to the investment group in 2010.

Chapter 12

Before the 2000 season, Home Plate Club seats were added behind home plate, a $100,000 sound system was installed, and Sec Taylor Stadium was designated a smoke-free facility.

"Priormania" swept through Sec Taylor Stadium when Chicago Cubs pitching prospect Mark Prior struck out ten batters and hit two home runs in his triple-A debut on Tuesday, May 7, 2002. Prior's 111-pitch performance carried the I-Cubs to a 6-1 win over Tucson with 8,243 on hand. Seventy-three of his first pitches were strikes.

"I was happy I struck out the side in the first inning; I did it in my first start at Double A, too," he said. "After that, I just wanted to make quality pitches."[1]

The twenty-one-year-old California native struck out the side in the first and third innings and homered in the fifth and seventh innings. Nine of his ten pitches in the opening frame were strikes. "God opened up a nice wind stream, I guess," he said, referring to his two blasts over the left-field fence. "I don't know where the home runs came from."[2] His curtain calls after hitting the home runs were a first for him, he added. "Everybody kept trying to push me out there," he said. "That was interesting."[3]

Making only his seventh minor league start, Prior threw fastballs, curves, and a few changeups. "I wasn't in a situation where I felt I had to throw it [the changeup] a whole lot," he explained.[4]

"It looks like the [Chicago] Cubs have another Kerry Wood," Tucson outfielder Micah Franklin said after the game that drew

8,243, twice the usual weeknight crowd in May. "He was throwing so easy that it looked like he was throwing an off-speed pitch, but every time it would be a fastball."[5]

Prior compiled a 5-2 record and 2.29 earned run average in nine minor league starts with seventy-nine strikeouts and only eighteen walks that season. He made his major-league debut on Wednesday, May 22, 2002, against the Pittsburgh Pirates at Wrigley Field. He pitched the Cubs to a 7-4 victory, giving up four hits and two earned runs in six innings. He struck out ten and issued two bases on balls. He finished his big-league rookie season with a 6-6 record and a 3.32 earned run average. He struck out 147 and walked thirty-eight batters in 116 and two-thirds innings.

After an 18-6 season, in which he struck out 245 batters in 211 and one-third innings the next year, Prior's career was cut short by injuries. He was out of baseball in 2007, 2008, and 2009. He tried to make a comeback with the Texas Rangers in 2010, the New York Yankees in 2011, the Boston Red Sox in 2012, and the Cincinnati Reds in 2013, reaching as high as Triple A. Prior now serves as the pitching coach for the Los Angeles Dodgers.

After the 2002 season, the playing surface was replaced with the same type of grass as Wrigley Field in Chicago. The project lasted three months and cost nearly $1 million. The clubhouse was improved again before the 2013 season. The locker, shower, and restroom areas for both the I-Cubs and visitors were enlarged along with the I-Cub fitness room. The indoor batting cage also was expanded.

On Thursday, August 5, 2004, Sec Taylor Stadium was renamed Principal Park in recognition of Principal Financial Group Inc.'s $2.5 million donation for major ballpark improvements. The move coincided with the $26.5 million Principal Riverwalk slated for downtown Des Moines. (Principal Park is on the south end of the Riverwalk.) The improvements included a new entrance and an elevated water fountain outside the right-field fence and the addition of a right-field seating area. Also added was a twenty-foot-wide path allowing fans to walk around the outfield or watch the action from outside the outfield fence, and a new façade on the stadium's north side to match the one on the west side. The playing field at Principal Park is named after the iconic *Des Moines Register* sports editor, Sec Taylor.

Michael Gartner, majority owner of the I-Cubs, said his ownership group, Raccoon Baseball Inc., would spend $1 million for two new scoreboards—a video message board and a vintage scoreboard with numbers hung by hand after half innings. The city was also asked to spend $1 million on new seats for the 11,500-seat ballpark. Des Moines city manager Eric Anderson said the city had already allocated $2 million in the next year's fiscal budget for stadium upgrades, such as new seats.[6] The city council could decide to move those projects up, he added.

The revenue from the stadium naming rights could have gone to the team's owners. Instead, Des Moines received the money from the Principal Foundation. "We thought that as good citizens in a downtown area that is changing dramatically, that having the money go directly back into the stadium would be the appropriate thing to do," Gartner said. "It's a way to get the city-owned stadium completed and guarantee that professional baseball will stay in Des Moines until at least 2022."[7]

Making his third and final rehab appearance, Chicago Cubs hurler Kerry Wood struck out nine batters in five and two-thirds innings in a 2-1 victory over Oklahoma City on Friday, June 24, 2005. A then record Principal Park crowd of 13,669 saw Wood give up a homer to Jason Botts in the fourth inning. "Today was a key for me," Wood said. "During the last couple starts, I wasn't locating the fastball the way I wanted to. My breaking balls had been good, my velocity was good on my fastball, but the location wasn't where it needed to be."[8]

Wood's eighty-four pitches included fifty-eight strikes. He threw a mixture of pitches to the twenty-two batters he faced. At times his fastball was clocked at ninety-seven miles per hour on the radar gun. When he left the game in the sixth inning, he received a standing ovation on his way to the dugout and another when he walked to the clubhouse down the left-field line.

In 2005, the week-long Iowa high school baseball tournament was held at Principal Park for the first time. The event drew 33,699 spectators, which broke the old record of 22,138 set three years earlier. Valley High School of West Des Moines captured its third straight Class-4A title and fifth overall. Sioux City Bishop Heelan won the Class-3A championship. Wilton claimed the Class-2A title and finished 42-0. Kee earned its ninth state title in Class 1A in sixteen tournament appearances. "I really like this place," Wilton right fielder Curtis Fry said. "I just love the atmosphere here . . . Playing here has definitely made my high school experience special."[9]

In January 2006, *At The Yard* magazine picked the cover of the *Iowa Cubs 2005 Yearbook* as runner-up in the best cover category. First place went to the Tulsa Drillers and their *100th Anniversary Edition*. The award-winning Iowa Cubs program was designed by Jeff Lantz and Matt Norby and created by Jon Pugh.

However, the ball team did not fare as well, and finished last in the North Division of the Pacific Coast League after starting 1-8. The I-Cubs never had a .500 or better record after that. Despite finishing 64-75, the ballclub attracted 529,354 fans to Principal Park, the second highest single-season total in franchise history at that point.

Relief pitcher Jermaine Van Buren set a club record with twenty-five saves and was named to the PCL post-season all-star team. Blake Parker tied Van Buren's saves record in 2014. Van Buren broke the former record of twenty-two saves by Marc Pisciotta in 1997.

The I-Cubs celebrated their twenty-fifth anniversary in 2006 and saluted the fans for their support throughout the years. "Everything we do is driven by our fans," president and general manager Sam Bernabe said. "If it wasn't for our fans and corporate support, there would have been no renovations in 1992 and no renovations for the 2006 season. Everything we do is for the fans . . . from the new scoreboard to the new videoboard to the fountain in right field. If we don't have their support, we don't even exist."[10]

I-Cubs majority owner Michael Gartner echoed Bernabe's sentiment. "Your support of baseball is phenomenal. Des Moines is the smallest of the thirty markets with triple-A baseball, yet we always rank high in attendance," he said, in reference to the fans. "We're the only triple-A market where the annual attendance exceeds the area's population."[11]

Principal Park hosted one of the more unique games in minor league history on Saturday, June 14, 2008. With widespread flooding in central Iowa, the Iowa Cubs and Nashville Sounds played a triple-A Pacific Coast League game that drew an official attendance of zero. "The only other time I can remember that a game was purposely played in front of an official crowd of zero was about three years ago in an Independent League," then Pacific Coast League commissioner Branch Rickey said at the time. "They did it for the publicity. As far as it being done out of necessity, like in Des Moines, I can't recall that ever being done."[12]

Club officials were forced to postpone the previous night's game when floodwaters started creeping onto the playing field from the outfield area that morning, eventually filling the visitors' dugout. The next day the I-Cubs received permission from the City of Des Moines to play baseball as long as no spectators were on hand. "The threat of flooding had subsided and it was a beautiful day. I said [to the city], 'Listen, I'll do a game. We don't have to have anyone here, but I have to get these games in,'" I-Cub president and general manager Sam Bernabe recalled eight years later. "They said, 'You can play as long as the only people there are the participants. You can't have anybody else in the stadium. You can't turn the scoreboard on. You can't do any PA. You can't do any [National] Anthem. You can't play any music. And you can't have any staff there.' So, there were basically six of us here with the two teams and the umpires."[13]

I-Cubs starting pitcher Sean Marshall compared the ballpark's atmosphere to an intrasquad game. Teammate Matt Murton, who had one of his team's seven hits, likened the experience to playing catch in the backyard. And I-Cub Josh Kroeger, who had a game-winning homer in the home team's 5-4 victory, said the only other time he played in front of a crowd of zero was in rookie ball.

During the next day's doubleheader, season ticket holder Grace Ann Powers expressed relief that Principal Park was open to the public for the first time in fifteen days. "We need something like this to take our minds off the flood, if just for a few hours," she said.[14]

After spending the final ninety-three days of the regular season in first place in 2008, the I-Cubs under manager Pat Listach won its first division title in the Pacific Coast League since 2004. The Oklahoma City RedHawks then defeated the I-Cubs three games to two in the first round of the playoffs.

Despite losing the playoffs, the I-Cubs had several memorable individual performances in 2008. President and general manager Sam Bernabe received the Pacific Coast League Executive of the Year Award. Listach was named the PCL Manager of the Year. First baseman Micah Hoffpauir slugged twenty-five home runs and drove in one hundred runs in only seventy-one games with the Des Moines ballclub, and was named the Minor League Player of the Year in the Chicago Cubs' organization. Pitcher Mitch Atkins won eight games and lost only one in ten starts for the I-Cubs. Between Double A and Triple A, Atkins won seventeen of twenty-four decisions. As a result, Atkins was chosen Chicago's Minor League Pitcher of the Year.

Two former Iowa players—catcher Geovany Soto and pitcher Rich "Goose" Gossage—also were honored in 2008. Soto, who played for the I-Cubs from 2005 to 2007, was the Rookie of the Year in the National League. The Puerto Rico native hit .285 with twenty-three home runs and eighty-six runs-batted-in for the Chicago Cubs. Gossage, who played for the Iowa Oaks in 1973, was inducted into the Baseball Hall of Fame in Cooperstown, New York.

The year 2009 marked the forty-first straight year of triple-A baseball in Des Moines and the 102nd year of professional baseball in the city. The ownership partnership of Gartner, Giudicessi, Bernabe, and Dorner also observed its tenth anniversary.

On August 9, the I-Cubs beat the Las Vegas 51s, 5-4, at Wrigley Field in Chicago. A franchise record 16,280 people saw a minor league game played on a major-league field.

"Any time you're at a place like Wrigley Field," manager Bobby Dickerson said, "I mean, I'd hate to think that someone doesn't get [goose] bumps just to be here."[15] Unlike the I-Cub players, Dickerson had access to a locker in the major-league Cubs clubhouse—Chicago manager Lou Piniella's locker. When they got inside the clubhouse, the players discovered that the lockers for the Chicago players had been covered with clear, protective plastic. So the I-Cubs had to change in the middle of the clubhouse and put their street clothes on a large set of metal rods.

Infielder Bobby Scales had been up with Chicago as late as mid-June. He called Sunday morning's wake-up call after a night game the preceding night "tough."[16] [Iowa and Las Vegas took separate charter flights from Des Moines that morning to get to Chicago in time for the afternoon contest.] "It seemed like a lot of people had a lot of people in town this homestand— I know my parents were in town. Sure, you want the opportunity to play here, but you could do without the travel."[17]

Micah Hoffpauir (Courtesy: Steve Dunn)

Iowa's Brad Snyder extended his hitting streak to seventeen games with a hit in the second inning. Jason Berg pitched one inning of scoreless relief to record his sixth win in seven decisions. John Ford-Griffin hit a two-run home run in the sixth inning that gave the I-Cubs a 3-2 lead. "It makes you want to come back and play harder and [have that] chance to get called up at the end of the year," Ford-Griffin said about his experience playing at Wrigley Field.[18]

On September 4, 2009, thirty-four men and women from fifteen countries were sworn in as U.S. citizens before the I-Cubs' game against the Albuquerque Isotopes at Principal Park. After a short speech by federal judge Robert Pratt, the name and homeland of each of the nearly-new citizens were announced from the press box while they lined up along the third-base line. Pratt then administered the oath of allegiance. Afterwards, the new Americans were joined by other members of their families as guests of the I-Cubs. The ceremony has been held every year since then.

The I-Cubs finished 72-72 under Dickerson and drew 536,872 fans to the ballpark, the fourth highest total in the Pacific Coast League. The team had a .271 batting average and 4.14 earned run average, second lowest in the PCL.

Music, not baseball, was the reason a record 18,158 people came to hear the Dave Matthews Band at Principal Park on Friday, September 25, 2009. It was the band's first performance in Iowa in five years. "When the first menacing guitar strums of 'Rhyme and Reason' hit the cool autumn air, the crowd erupted," the *Des Moines Register's* Sophia Ahmad said. "The song is from the band's first solo album, 'Under the Table and Dreaming.' But on Friday at Principal Park, it was under the night sky and screaming."[19]

Lexi Short, twenty-four, of Des Moines got hooked on the band in high school. "I went to a live show and I was a fan ever since," Short said, during her seventh DMB show.[20]

Apparently, the concert didn't damage the playing surface. "It's not ideal [for the playing surface], but it's something that can be fixed," I-Cub president and general manager Sam Bernabe said six and a half years later. "We didn't have any damage with the Dave Matthews show. In fact, you hardly knew there was a show."[21] The single-game attendance record for a baseball game at Principal Park is 15,188 on June 8, 2007, when the I-Cubs hosted the New Orleans Zephyrs and a post-game fireworks show.

The Kiwanis Miracle League conducted its first full season on a state-of-the-art field just west of Principal Park in 2009. The organization is designed for youth with physical and mental challenges. The all-handicapped facility features a flat, cushioned, rubberized surface that helps prevent injuries and makes it easier for players in wheelchairs and walkers to participate. The Iowa Cubs, Kiwanis Clubs of Des Moines, and Greater Des Moines Leadership Institute Class of 2007-2008 sponsored the $1.3 million project. In 2009, more than eighty Miracle Leagues in the U.S. served more than 80,000 children.

Chapter 13

Sandberg at helm;
Pevey reaches milestone;
I-Cubs make playoffs

Hall of Fame second baseman Ryne Sandberg succeeded Dickerson as the Iowa Cubs' manager in 2010. The native of Spokane, Washington, played in ten All-Star Games and received nine Gold Gloves during his sixteen-year major-league career that ended in 1997.

"It's a step in the right direction for what I'm doing [pursuing a major league managerial position]," he said before the season started. "This is something I really have taken to, I really enjoy. My goal is to do this at the major-league level, so this is obviously a real nice stepping stone."[1]

I-Cub fans could expect him to manage like he played for the Chicago Cubs. "I ask the guys to play hard, give it all they can, but also play the game and have fun," he said. "It is a game. I like the guys to enjoy it, and I think that brings out the most in their abilities."[2]

After never considering a major-league managerial career during his playing days, Sandberg changed his mind after the Hall of Fame inducted him and the Chicago Cubs retired his uniform number 23 in 2005. Sandberg managed the Peoria Chiefs in the low-A Midwest League during 2007 and 2008. The next year, he guided the Tennessee Smokies in the double-A Southern League. His first Peoria team shared a division title, and Tennessee advanced to the Southern League finals.

At the triple-A level, "you're not only filling out reports about your guys each night after games, you're [also] helping out the scouting department with the guys you're playing against," he said about his expanded duties.[3]

Known for his calm demeanor as a player, Sandberg explained that action and energy were keys to his managerial style. "I like action on the field; I like energy," he said. "I really enjoy the National League style of play, using guys on the bench and having some strategy in trying to win a game."[4]

Under Sandberg's guidance, the I-Cubs finished twenty games over .500 at 82-62, which tied for first place in the division. He was also named PCL Manager of the Year. In addition, outfielder Brad Snyder was selected a TOPPS/MiLB triple-A all-star after hitting .308 with twenty-five home runs and 106 runs-batted-in in 132 games.

Iowa Sports Turf Management headed by Chris Schlosser was named the top grounds crew in the Pacific Coast League in 2010. The company was founded in 2006 by the I-Cubs ownership group and started to maintain athletic facilities in Des Moines by contract. The company also began to offer maintenance services in central Iowa, using some of its equipment at Principal Park.

"The number of maintenance services offered grew quickly and led the company to start offering athletic field construction and renovation services in 2009," the firm's website says. "The company's services, clients and projects have grown each year since."[5] Originally known as Iowa Cubs Sports Turf Management, the word "Cubs" was dropped from the corporate name on January 1, 2019.

While having a 40-31 record at home, Iowa finished in the cellar of the Pacific Coast League's American Conference Northern Division in 2011. Manager Bill Dancy's club compiled a 66-77 regular season record, thirteen-and-a-half games in back of the first-place and PCL champion Omaha Storm Chasers. However, the I-Cubs had a paid attendance of 500,675 at home.

Despite the team's adversity, several individual achievements stood out. First baseman Bryan LaHair was named the PCL most valuable player, based on his .331 batting average, thirty-eight home runs, and 109 runs-batted-in in 129 games. LaHair's thirty-eight homers broke the club record of thirty-seven set by Joe Hicks in 1984. LaHair also led the league with a .664 slugging percentage, seventy-eight extra-base hits, 303 total bases, and nine intentional walks. He tied for the league lead in runs-batted-in, was fourth in doubles with thirty-eight, and tied for fifth in batting and runs scored with ninety-one.

LaHair and catcher Wellington Castillo hit back-to-back home runs three times. Lou Montgomery, Bobby Scales, and Matt Spencer contributed grand slam home runs. Outfielder Brett Jackson clubbed six leadoff homers—a franchise record.

In addition, three Iowa pitchers struck out nineteen Albuquerque batters in a 6-5 victory in fifteen innings at Principal Park on June 27. Starter Jay Jackson recorded five of the nineteen punchouts. Relievers Scott Maine and John Gaub added seven apiece. Pitcher J.R. Mathes finished the season with forty-two wins in his I-Cubs' career— another franchise record.

Once again, the I-Cubs ended up in last place in the American Conference Northern Division of the Pacific Coast League in 2012, this time with a 53-87 record under manager Dave Bialas. They finished twenty-eight games behind first-place Omaha. Their fifty-three wins were the fewest since 1992. Nevertheless, the I-Cubs drew 509,798 to Principal Park, their fourth straight season of 500,000-plus attendance.

First baseman Anthony Rizzo led the club with a .342 batting average and twenty-three home runs in seventy games. Rizzo was promoted to the Chicago Cubs after hitting a game-winning home run on Father's Day. He is best known perhaps for catching the final out in the seventh game of the 2016 World Series, the Chicago Cubs' first world championship since 1908.

Relief pitcher Blake Parker notched six saves for thirty-four in his I-Cubs career, tying the record shared by Jim Bullinger and Michael Wuertz. Twenty-five ceremonial first pitches were thrown before the game on May 18 that season, "[A] franchise record we hope never to break," the team said in its 2013 yearbook.[6] In July, the average actual temperature at game time was 96.3 degrees, and the average heat index was in the triple digits.

In 2013, the I-Cubs had the best home record—44-28—in the PCL. However, they had the worst road mark for the third straight year, giving them a 66-78 record overall in manager Marty Pevey's first season. Despite playing under .500, the ballclub remained in playoff contention until the final weekend of the season. There were 172 transactions and sixty-two different players that season, both franchise records at the time.

The I-Cubs lost two home dates when more than three inches of snow fell on May 2 and again on May 3, and temperatures dropped to record lows of forty-one and thirty-five degrees. In fact, six of the team's first twenty-one home games were postponed due to inclement weather.

Six I-Cub hurlers struck out a combined twenty-one New Orleans batters on June 1, which set a franchise record. Ian Stewart hit three home runs and tied a franchise record with eight runs-batted-in on June 8 against Round Rock. Edgar Gonzalez also hit three round-trippers on August 6 at Tacoma. Blake Parker collected seven saves and set the franchise career record at forty-one. On May 13, the I-Cubs turned five double plays at Reno, which tied a franchise record.

For the first time in five years, the I-Cubs finished above .500 in 2014. Minor league player of the year Kris Bryant contributed mightily to Iowa's 74-70 record. The Las Vegas native joined the I-Cubs on June 19 after his promotion from double-A Tennessee. His first five hits in Triple A were home runs—a franchise record. He led the minor leagues with forty-three home runs, including twenty-one for Iowa. He also was the minor league leader in extra-base hits with seventy-eight; total bases, 325; slugging, .661; and on-base plus slugging percentage, 1.098.

In addition, Bryant and teammate Javier Baez were chosen to play in the All-Star Futures Game at Minneapolis, Minnesota, on July 13. Bryant played for the U.S. team that rallied and won, 3-2. Baez's two-run home run accounted for the U.S. world team's runs. The twenty-one-year-old Baez led the I-Cubs in home runs with twenty-three; runs-batted-in, eighty; runs scored, sixty-four; multi-RBI games, twenty-four; and strikeouts, 130.

Relief pitcher Blake Parker saved twenty-five games to lead the PCL and tie an Iowa single-season record. He remains the all-time franchise leader in saves with sixty-six.

Chris Rusin tossed the first Iowa no-hitter in thirty years at New Orleans on May 7, 2014. The left-hander allowed only three baserunners and collected two hits and two runs-batted-in in the 3-0 victory. Iowa pitchers produced seven no-hitters in the Western League and Three-I League from 1947 to 1960. Nine more no-hitters have been recorded since 1960, including combined gems on September 1, 1977; May 9, 2021; and July 11, 2021. The I-Cubs' pitching staff turned in a PCL-leading fifteen shutouts—a new franchise record.

For the first time in franchise history, three I-Cubs were named to the All-PCL all-star team in 2014: Arismendy Alcantara, Tsuyoshi Wada, and Parker. Those three plus pitcher Kyle Hendricks were chosen to play in the triple-A All-Star Game in July. Led by Matt Szczur's thirty stolen bases, the I-Cubs finished second in the PCL in that department with 135.

In December 2014, I-Cub president and general manager Sam Bernabe was honored as Baseball America's Minor League Executive of the Year during the baseball winter meetings in San Diego, California. "I'm very honored and humbled to receive this award. With the Iowa Cubs, I have great partners and appreciate the hard work of my staff over the years to build and maintain the great relationships we have with the City of Des Moines, our business community, our great fans, and the Chicago Cubs," Bernabe said. "I also really enjoy being part of minor-league baseball on a national level. It's a role that has allowed me to work alongside some terrific people and contribute to growing and promoting the great game of baseball."[7]

At the time, Bernabe served as chairman of the Board of Trustees of Minor League Baseball and as the Pacific Coast League's representative. He was also a member of the joint triple-A Marketing Committee, National Association of Professional Baseball Marketing Committee, and Professional Baseball Playing Rules Committee.

Principal Park video board
(Courtesy: Steve Dunn)

A new state-of-the-art video board was installed in right field before the 2015 season. "The response to the new video board has been great. We're thinking about putting another one in," Bernabe said in early 2016. "We put a lot of replays on the video board—as long as they're not controversial. The league office asks us not to show replays of controversial calls. Those guys [umpires] out there are doing the best job they can. So, we don't want to throw gas on a fire that doesn't need to burn."[8] The new all-digital video board and ancillary equipment cost nearly $1 million.

A second elevator near the main entrance to Principal Park was added for the mezzanine and skybox levels in 2015, too. "This should greatly help our disabled friends and fans, as well as the folks who go to the skyboxes and don't like climbing the equivalent of four flights of stairs," majority owner Michael Gartner said in the team's annual yearbook. "When the park was built nearly twenty-five years ago, the builders put in that second shaft—but forgot the elevator."[9]

Principal Park also got a new cooling system for the skyboxes in 2015. "It also will help the fans along the third-base line; the new chiller will be much quieter than the old one," Gartner pointed out before the season started.[10] In addition, the press box windows were replaced and the offices on the first floor were remodeled.

The field itself was replaced in the fall of 2014. The grounds crew put down 265 tons of sand and then brought in two-and-a-half acres of a newly developed type of sod from a sod farm in Colorado for the new field.

On December 11, 2015, the I-Cubs announced they would extend the backstop netting to the far ends of each dugout to improve fan safety at Principal Park. The decision was in line with Major League Baseball's recommendation that all stadiums of major-league teams and their affiliates have extended netting by Opening Day 2017. "For years, about a third of our fans have been watching games from behind netting, and it's clear the netting does not interfere with the enjoyment of the game," Bernabe said in the announcement. "In fact, most people forget the net is even there."[11]

The engineering for the backstop netting extension was complex and expensive, according to Gartner. "Two new poles are anchored thirty or forty feet into the ground just outside the stadium, one down each foul line, to support the guy wires that hold the screen and let it withstand the terrific pressure of holding up the additional 8,200 square feet of mesh extending the one hundred feet to the ends of the dugouts," Gartner explained.[12]

In 2016, Iowa fans had their eyes on the Chicago Cubs as well as their own team in the Pacific Coast League.

Nineteen players on Chicago's postseason roster played for the I-Cubs. (The list included Albert Almora Jr., Jake Arrieta, Javier Baez, Kris Bryant, Willson Contreras, Carl Edwards Jr., Dexter Fowler, Kyle Hendricks, Anthony Rizzo, Addison Russell, and Kyle Schwarber.) Eight of the team's ten starters in the deciding game of the World Series were former Iowa players. "We've always been proud of the great young men who have played for us—but we've never been prouder than we were last year," I-Cubs majority owner Michael Gartner said in his introduction in the *2017 Iowa Cubs Yearbook*.[13]

A total of 3,487 fans turned out for a watch party open house at Principal Park for Game 3 of the World Series. In fact, ten postseason open house events drew a total of more than 10,000 fans to the ballpark at the confluence of the Des Moines and Raccoon Rivers.

More than 1,300 fans had an opportunity to see and take a photo with Chicago's World Series trophy on February 1, 2017, at Principal Park. The much-anticipated event lasted longer than its scheduled ninety minutes. A few fans even arrived at Principal Park the night before the photo opportunity.

The I-Cubs won twenty of their last thirty-one games to finish 67-76 in Chicago's historic year. Iowa used a franchise record seventy-three players, breaking the old record of sixty-seven in 2004. Almora Jr. and Contreras were among a half dozen players who made their major league debuts. Pitcher Joe Nathan, forty-one-years-old, became the franchise's oldest player ever when he rehabbed at Iowa.

The longest game in 2016 on Saturday, April 23, took thirteen innings and four hours and six minutes to complete. Oklahoma City beat the I-Cubs, 6-4, in a game that did not end until 11:18 p.m. Despite finishing under .500, the team drew 504,160 to Principal Park. It could have been worse. In 1908, the Des Moines Boosters were last in the Western League, thirty-five-and-a-half games behind the first-place Sioux City Soos.

The second annual Iowa Baseball Camp for the Deaf was held in June at Principal Park and the Johnston Little League Park. Two I-Cubs players, outfielder John Andreoli and pitcher Rob Zastryzny, worked with twenty-six boys and girls from throughout the Midwest. The campers also signed the national anthem and "Take Me Out to the Ballgame" at an I-Cub game.

A new HD ribbon video board atop the left-field suites and state-of-the-art LED lighting from Musco were added in 2017. The new 130-foot-wide video board provides more stats and information for fans and players, while the new lights provide brighter lighting for the playing field. The energy efficient lights also can "dance" to the music. In addition, free wi-fi was added throughout the ballpark, and space for the merchandise store was expanded into the concourse.

A new batting cage beyond the left-field wall was added before the start of the 2018 season. Coupled with the existing batting cage in the home clubhouse, the improved facilities help player development. On April 7 of that year, the *Des Moines Register* published an article about the greatest team in Iowa Cubs and Oaks history in conjunction with the franchise's fiftieth year of triple-A baseball. The twenty-six member squad was selected by I-Cubs chairman and majority owner Michael Gartner, president and general manager Sam Bernabe, vice president and assistant general manager Randy Wehofer, and Randy Peterson who previously covered the teams for the *Register*.

Their choices were manager, Ryne Sandberg; catcher, Joe Girardi; first base, Rafael Palmeiro; second base, Tony LaRussa; shortstop, Shawon Dunston; third base, Kris Bryant; outfield, Joe Carter, Manny Ramirez, and Harold Baines; and pitcher, Greg Maddux. Kerry Wood, Vida Blue, Jake Arrieta, and Hideo Nomo rounded out the starting pitching staff. The panel picked Goose Gossage as the closer in a bullpen that also included Mark Prior, Rod Beck, Carlos Zambrano, and Jamie Moyer. Seven players were chosen for the bench: first basemen Mark Grace and Anthony

Rizzo, shortstop Bucky Dent, outfielders Tuffy Rhodes, Shane Victorino, and Terry Francona, and catcher Geovany Soto, the first player in Des Moines/Iowa franchise history to win the Pacific Coast League's Most Valuable Player Award. Judging by each player's statistics, the panelists put more emphasis on their accomplishments in the major leagues than in the minor leagues at Iowa. For example, first baseman Micah Hoffpauir, who played seven seasons with the I-Cubs and is the club's all-time leader in seven offensive categories, is not on the list.

On Thursday, April 12, manager Marty Pevey earned his 1,000th win as a manager and 356th as the I-Cubs skipper. Thus, he became the Iowa franchise's all-time leader in managerial wins with his team's 6-3 victory in eleven innings over the Nashville Sounds. "I'm just honored to have been given the opportunity to be put in this position and make an impact on so many players," he said.[14] Joe Sparks had held the franchise record for managerial wins with 355.

In May 2019, the I-Cubs announced they planned to extend the netting from the end of each dugout to both foul poles for the start of the 2020 season. President and general manager Sam Bernabe said the move had been contemplated for quite some time. "I remember having a conversation with Andy MacPhail when he was the president of the [Chicago] Cubs—that far back—about running nets down," Bernabe told *Register* sportswriter Tommy Birch. "So, we've been giving it consideration. It's been on my radar for a long time."[15]

Iowa clinched a berth in the Pacific Coast League playoffs for the first time since 2008, by defeating the Memphis Redbirds, 5-1, at Principal Park on Friday, August 30, 2019. It marked a complete turnaround from the previous season when the I-Cubs finished last in the PCL's American Northern Division with a 50-88 record. "Last year, we knew we were a little short," manager Marty Pevey said. "We lost a lot of games by one run. We were short a position player-wise and organizations go through that at times. We battled every game. The guys played hard. We just didn't have those big boppers in the lineup—guys that could drive the ball and hit the three-run homer and make you look smart."[16]

Not only did the I-Cubs have seven players with at least ten home runs, but also they had the PCL's Pitcher of the Year in Colin Rea, who had a 14-4 record and 3.95 earned run average going into the playoffs. Robel Garcia displayed some of the team's power when he smacked a grand slam in the victory over Memphis. The Redbirds got back into the playoff picture by winning seventeen of their last twenty games entering the decisive contest on August 30. Iowa just needed to win one game in the four-game series to clinch a berth in the playoffs.

After losing the first two semifinal games at Round Rock, the I-Cubs returned home and won two games by one run each to even the best-of-five series. However, they lost the decisive fifth game, 10-5, to the Express. "It [the season] was awesome," manager Pevey said afterwards. "I told them [the players] in there, I appreciated everything they did. They brought it every day. A lot of intensity. And they prepared well."[17] The I-Cubs jumped out to an early 3-0 lead, but the Express put the game away with a seven-run third inning. Round Rock sent eleven batters to the plate in the inning, which featured a three-run home run by Alex De Goti that gave his team a 6-3 lead.

Three of the five games were decided in extra innings, including Game 4 in Des Moines that ended on Phillip Evans' walk-off sacrifice fly. The I-Cubs also won Game 3 in Des Moines, 3-2. "Every game was close until the last half of this one," Iowa first baseman Jim Adduci said. "That's what baseball is right here. It's good for these guys here that are a little bit younger and haven't been to the big leagues. That's what it's like every day."[18]

Chapter 14

Pandemic shuts down season;
staff tosses two no-hitters;
Gartner group sells team

Principal Park remained silent throughout the 2020 season due to the worldwide Coronavirus pandemic that shut down major-league spring training camps in Arizona and Florida before the end of spring training. Although the major leagues were able to play a shortened sixty-game schedule plus expanded playoffs and the World Series, minor league baseball was shut down entirely.

While the I-Cubs were not one of the forty minor league teams eliminated under MLB's minor league contraction, they were part of a new triple-A league known as Triple-A East in 2021. Their division also included the Columbus Clippers, Indianapolis Indians, Louisville Bats, Omaha Storm Chasers, St. Paul Saints, and Toledo Mud Hens. The I-Cubs and Storm Chasers previously were members of the Pacific Coast League; the others, the International League. Due to ongoing COVID-19 concerns in 2021, the triple-A season didn't start until May 4. However, the triple-A season did not end until October 3, about a month later than normal.

I-Cubs announcer Alex Cohen and his girlfriend Tessa Chen were the subjects of a new episode of *House Hunters* on March 30. The pair got the idea to apply for the show when Chen decided to move from San Francisco to Des Moines during the pandemic. After adopting a dog, they sought more space than Cohen's one-bedroom apartment. "I'm used to being able to talk behind the lens of a camera for three hours and not have the lights, camera and action part of it," Cohen said. "Just having everything front and center on me, it was kind of vulnerable. It was kind of a liberating feeling. You put yourself out there."[1] The couple moved to their new home in the fall of 2020. They did not see the episode until the night of March 30 like everyone else.

After 604 days without baseball, Principal Park hosted minor league baseball again on Tuesday night, May 4, 2021. "It's been brutal," president and general manager Sam Bernabe said, referring to the historic absence of games.[2] A minor league game had not been played in Des Moines since September 8, 2019. However, there were signs the I-Cubs' management was taking precautions against a disease that had claimed approximately 375,000 lives in the U.S. in 2020.[3] Seats along the first- and third-base lines were blocked to prevent fans from getting close to the dugouts and bullpens. Fans had to wear face masks and social distancing was observed. The national anthem was sung on the concourse rather than on the field. On-field promotions were cut, and employees fired hot dogs and T-shirts from the tops of the dugouts instead of from a cart driven around the field. Without bat boys, players and coaches picked up equipment.

The Indianapolis Indians jumped out to a quick start when leadoff hitter Travis Swaggerty sent one of starter Joe Biagini's pitches over the fence. Indians starter Chase DeJong then held the I-Cubs hitless for five innings as the visitors won, 3-0. Still, most of the announced crowd of 3,656 were just happy professional baseball had returned to Principal Park. They cheered when vendor Alejandro Gomez shouted "Yummy, yummy," and rejoiced when Sergio Alcantara broke up DeJong's no-hitter.[4]

Starting in May, Iowa fans could watch the team on Marquee Sports, a regional TV network specializing in Chicago Cubs coverage. "Our game was on at a sports bar in Des Moines for the first time ever last night," said Randy Wehofer, vice president and assistant general manager of the I-Cubs.[5] I-Cubs president and general manager Sam Bernabe compared the deal with Marquee to the Chicago Cubs' relationship with WGN, which started in 1948. Despite the Cubs' lack of success, they were on cable TV across the country, which spread the Cubs' brand. "Well, Marquee Sports now is going to end up doing that same kind of thing," Bernabe said.[6] A fourteen-game schedule was set for 2021, starting with Omaha on May 19 and ending with Toledo on September 9.

In 2021, the Betfred Sports Left Field Lounge replaced the Cub Club restaurant in left field. The new area for those twenty-one and older offers upscale food and beverages plus big screen TVs. In addition, several new security-related measures were adopted, in part due to the pandemic. Fans now pass through metal detectors when they enter the ballpark. No weapons are allowed inside Principal Park, even with a permit. Cash is no longer accepted, either. Only credit or debit cards are accepted. Two reverse ATM machines that take bills and dispense cards are located near the Fan Services Center behind home plate. Game programs have gone digital, too. Fans can look for the QR code outside and inside Principal Park to download the program for free.

On Sunday, May 9, 2021, four I-Cub pitchers, including former major leaguer Shelby Miller, combined for a nine-inning no-hitter against the visiting Indianapolis Indians. Miller, who opted out of the 2020 COVID-19 season, struck out five and walked one batter in his opening three innings of work. Right-hander Tommy Nance repeated Miller's performance in the fourth, fifth, and sixth innings and was credited with his first win of the season. Left-hander Brad Wieck fanned five batters in the seventh and eighth innings before giving way to Ryan Meisinger, who walked a batter in the ninth inning. Meisinger picked up his first save of the season.

The I-Cubs got the only run they needed in the fifth inning when Andrew Romine scored on Nance's sacrifice fly to center field. They added an insurance run in the bottom of the eighth inning on Abiatal Avelino's single that scored D.J. Artis. After Meisinger walked Chris Sharpe in the top of the ninth inning, Travis Swaggerty grounded out sharply to first baseman Taylor Gushue, with Sharpe reaching second base. The next batter, Cole Tucker, lined out to left fielder Cameron Maybin. The last hitter, Kevin Kramer, lined out to right fielder Rafael Ortega to preserve the no-hitter.

Four umpires were on hand instead of the usual three: John Tumpane behind home plate, Matt Winter at first base, Jose Matamoros at second base, and Alex Tosi at third base. The two-hour-and-twenty-eight-minute game was played under cloudy skies with a game-time temperature of fifty-five degrees. The game drew 3,318 fans.

Three I-Cub pitchers held the St. Paul Saints hitless in the seven-inning first game of a doubleheader on Sunday, July 11, 2021, at Principal Park. Left-handed starter Justin Steele struck out five and walked two Saints in three and two-thirds innings of work. Right-hander Scott Effross fanned three of the four batters he faced. Right-hander Dillon Maples struck out two and issued two walks in the sixth and seventh innings. Steele, who originally started the season in the Chicago Cubs' bullpen, was sent down to Iowa to become a starter later in the season.

The I-Cubs broke a 0-0 tie in the seventh inning when Tyler Ladendorf scored from third on Trent Giambrone's sacrifice fly. With one out, Ladendorf walked and advanced to third base on Ian Miller's single before coming home on Giambrone's fly to right field. The I-Cubs got out of a jam in the top of the seventh inning thanks to second baseman Giambrone, who turned a bunt popup into an unassisted double play.

The I-Cubs won the second game, 3-2, holding the visitors to three hits. The doubleheader drew one of the biggest crowds of the season at 8,575. The two-hour-and-four-minute game was played under overcast skies at sixty-eight degrees and a thirteen-mile-per-hour wind blowing in from left field.

After hosting the Iowa High School Athletic Association state baseball tournament since 2005, Principal Park was the site of triple-A baseball games rather than high school games during the last week of July 2021. The restructuring of minor league baseball and scheduling changes forced officials to move the state tournament games to Carroll and Iowa City in 2021. Over sixteen years, the high school state baseball championship tournament drew 483,254 fans, including 29,904 in the pandemic year 2020.

On December 8, 2021, the sale of the I-Cubs to Diamond Baseball Holdings (DBH) was announced. DBH is a subsidiary of Endeavor, a global sports and entertainment company. "My partners and I wish the new owners well, and we're particularly pleased that Sam Bernabe will remain as president and general manager of the team," said Michael Gartner, chairman and principal owner of the team since October 1, 1999. "We hope Sam and his new colleagues have as much fun running the team as we have had."[7] "Diamond Baseball Holdings will be global in our ambitions and hyper-local in our approach, and creating incredible fan experiences will remain our number one priority," said DBH executive chairman Pat Battle and CEO Peter Freund. "Additionally, we look forward to providing opportunities for growth to the employees of PDL Clubs whose passion and ingenuity have built the sport through the decades."[8]

In a letter to fans, Gartner noted that paid attendance at home surpassed 500,000 in twelve years of his group's ownership. Another 483,254 fans came to Principal Park during the sixteen years his group hosted the Iowa High School Baseball Tournament. "We were the first baseball park to hold swearing-in ceremonies for new citizens before a game, which we have done annually since 2009," Gartner said. "In all, 419 men and women have become citizens in park ceremonies."[9]

Gartner also expressed satisfaction that Bernabe had agreed to remain as general manager. "He has worked here his entire life, and he knows Minor League Baseball better than probably anyone else in America," Gartner said. "He long served as head of the Minor League Board of Trustees, was named minor league executive of the year, and has long been a force for good in baseball."[10]

Eleven days after the sale was announced, the *Des Moines Register* weighed in on the subject. "In the best scenario, Endeavor will use its ownership of multiple teams to produce an influential, independent voice with a better chance of bending Major League Baseball's ear than the cities and franchises who lost their affiliated professional teams last year or will struggle to meet league-imposed facilities requirements," the newspaper wrote. "Perhaps Endeavor can help persuade MLB to recognize the value to the big leagues of nurturing old and new fans through affordable visits to relaxing parks with compelling players on their way up. In the worst scenario, far-off owners eventually will try to hold Des Moines hostage with the threat of seeking greener pastures."[11] The agreement between the franchise and city that transferred to the new owners keeps the I-Cubs at Principal Park through at least 2027, the newspaper noted.

Five days after the franchise's sale was finalized, Gartner and the rest of the ownership group had a big surprise for the club's twenty-three full-time employees. After gathering the employees in the Betfred Sports Lounge at Principal Park and on zoom, Gartner thanked them and said he was going to hand out new business cards. "Everybody kind of laughed and at that point just with his tone, we knew there was going to be more than just business cards," said Alex Cohen, the team's broadcaster.[12]

Each employee received an envelope with a payroll check—not a business card. Everyone—even the custodian—got a check based on the number of years of their employment with the team from the proceeds of the sale of the ballclub. The longest-tenured employee received $70,000. "It was pretty crazy," Cohen said. "People were crying and shaking."[13]

Scott Sailor, the club's former director of communications, said the move was "a fantastic gesture, no matter what business you're in, but to be in minor league baseball with a lot of long days, a lot of long hours and a lot of hard work, it was really nice and appreciated."[14]

A Pulitzer Prize-winning journalist, Gartner epitomized a fan- and staff-friendly owner. During I-Cubs games, he walked around the ballpark and talked with fans. When the COVID-19 pandemic canceled the 2020 minor league season, he kept his staff employed instead of imposing layoffs or furloughs so the employees could get by.

Gartner presented his idea to Bernabe on his last day at Principal Park. Not only did Bernabe "love it," but also the other owners did as well.[15] "Those people really, really could use the money," Gartner said. "They've got mortgages. They've got little kids. Some of them probably have college debt and car payments. It helps them over the humps."[16]

Sailor, who had worked for Gartner at the *Ames Tribune* and *Des Moines Register,* was not surprised by Gartner's gesture. "That's the kind of guy he is," Sailor explained. "It might have surprised some of the others."[17] Sailor's tweet about the sharing of the sale's proceeds got more than 1,000 likes, and was noticed by *The New York Times* and Yahoo.

The I-Cubs joined the twenty-team triple-A International League in 2022. In 2021, leagues had regional names while major league baseball was in the process of acquiring the rights to use the historical names, such as International League, Pacific Coast League, and Midwest League. The I-Cubs are now only one of three minor league franchises to play in all three historic triple-A leagues: American Association, International League, and Pacific Coast League. Nashville and Omaha also have belonged to three triple-A leagues.

On August 8, 2022, the Des Moines City Council agreed to spend $5.8 million on Phase 1 of upgrades to Principal Park. The "batter's eye" in centerfield was modified in response to new major-league facility guidelines. The "batter's eye" is the blank space on the outfield wall the hitter sees when the pitcher throws the ball from the mound. The new taller wall is positioned just behind the outfield wall. It blocks the view of the Iowa Capitol and its shiny dome that can blind the hitter. About twenty percent of the fans in the stands are not be able to see the Capitol either.[18]

"Our bigger problem is behind the outfield wall, the Capitol included," president and general manager Sam Bernabe explained. "Sunny days, the pitcher, the left-handed batter, the sun is shining, and they're blinded. So, it's an adjustment we need to make."[19] The Des Moines City Council approved the change as well as other less visible modifications to Principal Park. The other renovations, including new clubhouses beyond the left-field fence and possibly new parking for players, started in the fall of 2022 after the season ended. Construction is scheduled for completion in the spring of 2024.

A day after the city council's action, Endeavor Group Holdings announced that it sold the I-Cubs and nine other minor league clubs to one of its largest investors, Silver Lake Partners, due to a perceived conflict of interest. Diamond Baseball Holdings, which had been managing the Iowa team and the others for Endeavor, remained in place. "Coming off several months of invaluable support and guidance from Endeavor in establishing this organization, and now moving into Silver Lake's proven portfolio, the entire DBH organization is enthusiastically focused on this next phase of aggressively growing the business," said DBH executive chairman Pat Battle and CEO Peter Freund.[20]

The minor league purchases by Endeavor created a situation in which one company employed sports agents while owning teams expected to develop players for major-league baseball. Before the sale by Endeavor, the Major League Baseball Players Association said it would decertify Endeavor's talent agency group, William Morris Endeavor, as an agent for MLB players if Endeavor continued to own the teams.[21] Silver Lake paid $280 million for the I-Cubs and nine other teams, reported *Deadline,* a website that covers the entertainment business.[22] The other clubs were the Memphis Redbirds, Scranton/Wilkes Barre RailRiders, Hudson Valley Renegades, San Jose Giants, Gwinnet Stripers, Mississippi Braves, Rome Braves, Augusta Green Jackets, and Oklahoma City Dodgers.

The ongoing upgrades to Principal Park are part of a master plan unveiled on December 10, 2021. The plan provides "an overall vision to provide a unique fan experience that will sustainably extend the life of Principal Park for the next 30 to 50 years."[23] The five-phase plan would cost approximately $38 million to $45.5 million to implement, using 2022 dollars. The plan also included another $32.5 million to $35 million of off-site economic development opportunities, such as a parking garage on the parking lot west of the ballpark plus retail, restaurants, or bars. The 129-page plan offers a road map to an even greater fan-friendly experience inside and outside thirty-one-year-old Principal Park.

Major League Baseball's new facility standards require ballclubs to be in full compliance by April 2025. Besides the batter's eye, which has been addressed, Principal Park's greatest facility deficiencies concern space for female staff, shower and toilet amenities in the home and visitor clubhouses, secure parking for players, and space for food preparation and consumption for the visiting team, the master plan says. The existing clubhouse would get a small addition for a new weight room and family waiting area. The clubhouse upgrades are expected to cost approximately $6.4 million.

As for the ballpark's infrastructure itself, the master plan cites the facility's stained and damaged ceiling tiles, flooring, and walls due to water infiltration; aging mechanical and electrical systems; parking and lighting issues; and "worn, dated" interior and exterior.[24] New LED lighting and mechanical/electrical equipment would increase the staff's and fans' comfort, cut energy use, and increase the ballpark's lifespan, the master plan adds.

In addition, the parking lots, which need to be rebuilt, do not have lighting that would increase fans' "comfort, safety, and security."[25] The water infiltration problems could be solved by replacing the roof and providing new cladding (covering or coating). The interior of the ballpark needs new carpet, ceiling tile, millwork, and countertops, "which are worn and dated."[26] The estimated cost of getting Principal Park back to its prime operational condition is $8.7 million.

A survey of 2,300 people led to twenty-six opportunities to enhance the ballpark "and better integrate the entire complex into the surrounding context of downtown Des Moines. These improvements would benefit people year-around whether passing by on their bikes or enjoying a meal prior to attending a ballgame. Additional consideration was given to ways to provide space for events not directly related to baseball."[27]

Some of those improvements include a new main entrance on the northwest corner of Principal Park to better connect the ballpark to downtown and enhance the facility's presence and identity. The master plan proposes a park at the confluence of the Des Moines and Raccoon Rivers with a trail for walking, biking, and passive play as well as opportunities for fishing near public art at the rivers' confluence. A large green space could hold concerts, farmers' markets, and festivals. The total estimated cost, including player parking upgrades, is estimated at $13.5 million to $15.5 million.

The master plan also calls for a Raccoon River Park, costing an estimated $3.5 million to $5 million at the southwest corner of Principal Park with a Wiffle ball field, large video screen, improved tailgate area, and new playground equipment.

Upgraded premium amenities costing approximately $12.5 million to $14.5 million could include a new VIP entry, mezzanine club space, as many as eight new mezzanine level suites, and two more open-air party decks.

In general, "once these improvements are realized, they would ensure the longevity of AAA baseball in Des Moines, preserve a valued asset for the community, and create new and exciting opportunities for the city and its residents long into the future," the master plan says.[28] The I-Cubs' current Professional Development League agreement with the Chicago Cubs runs through 2030.

View from ballpark suites (Courtesy: Steve Dunn)

Marty Pevey finished the 2023 season as the I-Cubs' longest-tenured manager in franchise history. He has a 680-737 record with the team dating back to 2013 when he replaced Dave Bialas as manager. Overall, he has 1,324 wins in twenty-one seasons as a minor league manager. Pevey started in the Chicago Cubs organization in 2009 as manager of the Peoria Chiefs in the Midwest League. He was selected the Midwest League's co-Manager of the Year after the Chiefs finished 81-57. He also served as Chicago's catching coordinator from 2010 to 2012. Pevey has accumulated forty-one seasons in professional baseball—thirteen as a player and twenty-eight as a coach.

The female athlete of the year helped draw the biggest crowd to an I-Cubs home game in three years and ten months on Saturday, June 3, 2023. West Des Moines native Caitlin Clark met fans and signed autographs before the I-Cubs' game against the Columbus Clippers. Fans started lining up outside the ballpark as early as 6 a.m. Saturday for a chance to see Clark and get an autograph. The University of Iowa star also threw out the ceremonial first pitch before the start of the game. The official attendance was 10,692, the biggest crowd since Friday, August 30, 2019, when 10,724 saw the PCL playoff-bound I-Cubs beat the Memphis Redbirds, 5-1.

I-Cubs starting pitcher Caleb Killian turned in his first quality start of the season but was tagged with the loss. In six innings of work, Killian gave up three runs on four hits and one walk and struck out three. His replacement, Codi Heuer, served up a two-run home run by Columbus' Chris' Roller, which gave the Clippers a 5-1 lead. The I-Cubs tried to come back in the ninth with two runs on Yonathan Perlaza's double and Nelson Velazquez's single.

A sacrifice fly by Bryce Windham in the second inning gave the I-Cubs a short-lived 1-0 lead. The Clippers took a 2-1 lead in the third on a double by Bo Naylor. Columbus added a run in the sixth inning on a balk by Killian. With the loss, the I-Cubs fell to 31-22, a half-game ahead of second-place St. Paul.

Yonathan Perlaza's three-run walk-off home run lifted the I-Cubs to a 7-5 victory over the Memphis Redbirds at Principal Park on Friday, June 23, 2023. The biggest home crowd in four years saw

Iowa move thirteen games over .500 at 42-29. Down 5-3 at the start of the ninth inning, catcher Bryce Windham's single drove in the fourth run. Then Perlaza warmed up the fans waiting for a postgame fireworks show by launching a pitch over the right-field wall with two runners on base. It was the I-Cubs' first walk-off home run since Jared Young's in the final game of last season on September 28 against Toledo.[29]

Richard Palacios gave Memphis a 1-0 lead with a solo home run in the first inning. The I-Cubs tied the score on David Bote's groundout in the bottom of the first. The Redbirds regained the lead on Matt Koperniak's run-scoring triple in the third. Young's twelfth home run of the year in the bottom of the third tied the game at two.

Memphis forged ahead with three runs in the seventh on doubles by Palacios and Juan Yepez as well as a sacrifice fly from Chad Pinder. Another run-scoring groundout by Bote in the eighth cut the deficit to two runs.

Young went three-for-four at the plate with a home run, triple, a run batted in, and two runs scored. At that point, he was hitting .327 in the last fifty games and ranked ninth in the International League. The twenty-seven-year-old Canadian native had twelve home runs and forty-one runs-batted-in, too. In fifty-three games, the twenty-four-year-old Perlaza was batting .300 with eight home runs, twenty-one doubles, three triples, and thirty-nine runs-batted-in.

Starter Chris Clarke went five innings for Iowa—his longest outing of the season. The right-hander gave up two runs and two hits, struck out two, and walked four. Cam Sanders struck out the side in the ninth and got his fourth win of the season against no losses. The official attendance was 11,268.

For the second night in a row, the I-Cubs posted a walk-off victory thanks to Jared Young's two-run home run over the center-field fence on Saturday, June 24, 2023. Iowa gave up three runs in the top of the ninth inning and trailed Memphis 5-2 at that point.

Jake Slaughter started the comeback with a solo homer in the bottom of the ninth. After a strikeout and a walk, Bryce Windham drove in a run with a double into the right-field gap. Following a flyout, Darius Hill singled up the middle to bring in the tying run. Young then smacked his game-winning round tripper, giving Iowa back-to-back walk-off wins for the first time since July 11, 2021.

That night's heroics gave the I-Cubs five walk-off wins for the season. The previous three came on two sacrifice flies and a fielder's choice. The I-Cubs also improved their record to 43-29.

Nick Neidert started for Iowa, pitched six innings, and gave up only three hits and one run, the latter coming on Masyn Winn's solo shot in the fourth inning. Reliever Bailey Horn was charged with a blown save after giving up three hits including Luken Baker's homer in the seventh. Rowan Wick followed Horn and pitched a scoreless eighth. Daniel Palencia started the ninth and was touched for three runs, three hits, and one walk. Riley Martin retired the last two Memphis hitters in order in the ninth and earned his first win of the season. Kodi Whitley was charged with the loss, his fourth of the season, after surrendering the five runs and four hits in the decisive ninth inning. A total of 6,473 were on hand.

A month later, a three-run walk-off home run in the ninth by Edwin Rios made the difference in a 5-3 win over the Indianapolis Indians. The 450-foot blast was Rios' ninth of the season for the I-Cubs, who improved their record to 55-38 in the Western Division of the International League. Rios was two-for-five at the plate.

Hayden Wesneski, who started the season in Chicago, hurled five shutout innings, giving up four hits and striking out eight. He walked only one hitter. Reliever Riley Martin got into trouble in the eighth when he gave up a two-run home run and the lead. Moments later, he was ejected. His replacement, Cam Sanders, retired the next six batters—four on strikeouts—and picked up the win.

Nick Madrigal played seven innings at third base for Iowa and went two-for-three and scored one run. Center fielder Alexander Canario singled in two runs in the fourth inning and finished one-for-four. Canario also got an assist when he threw out the Indians' Miguel Andujar at home. The game drew 6,524 to Principal Park.

The Chicago Cubs' top-rated prospect lived up to the hype by hitting a walk-off home run over the center-field fence to give the I-Cubs a come-from-behind 5-3 victory Tuesday, August 14, at Principal Park. In the bottom of the tenth inning, Pete Crow-Armstrong nailed a pitch by Louisville Bats reliever Silvino Bracho with Chase Strumpf on second and no outs. The twenty-one-year-old Crow-Armstong also got the first hit off Louisville starter Hunter Greene, who was making a rehab appearance.

The victory in the first of a six-game series extended Iowa's winning streak to six games and improved its record to 66-46. The I-Cubs came into the game a half-game behind first-place St. Paul in the second half standings of the Western Division of the International League.

The Bats pulled ahead 3-0 in the fourth inning on four hits, including Jason Vosler's two-run homer and a walk by I-Cubs starter Nick Neidert. The home team got a run back in the bottom of the fourth when Crow-Armstrong scored on a double play. A sacrifice fly by Chase Strumpf scored Miles Mastrobuoni in the seventh and cut Louisville's lead to 3-2. Yonathan Perlaza doubled to lead off the I-Cubs' eighth. Two batters later, a run-scoring single by Alexander Canario tied the score.

Iowa relievers Stephen Gonsalves, Nick Burdi, Brendon Little, and Chris Clarke, the winning pitcher, tossed six innings of hitless, scoreless ball. Crow-Armstrong's homer was his fourth in only two weeks with Iowa. Since joining the triple-A club, the Sherman Oaks, California, native was hitting .289 with three doubles, seven runs-batted-in, and eight walks in eleven games. In seventy-three games with double-A Tennessee, he hit .289 with nineteen doubles, five triples, fourteen homers, sixty runs-batted-in, and twenty-seven stolen bases. He had an on-base percentage of .371 and a slugging average of .527. His defense in center field is already considered Gold Glove level.

Yonathan Perlaza's two home runs and four runs-batted-in were the difference in the I-Cubs' 7-6 victory over the St. Paul Saints on Friday, September 15. Perlaza's first blast over the right-field video board in the third inning cut the Saints' lead to 3-2. Iowa pitchers Ben Brown, Cam Sanders, Brandon Hughes, and Nick Burdi held St. Paul scoreless in the next five innings. The I-Cubs forged ahead with five runs in the sixth inning, which included Perlaza's three-run homer. In the ninth inning, Iowa pitcher Tyler Duffey walked two batters after striking out Chris Williams. Duffey fanned the next hitter, Brooks Lee, but gave up a three-run homer to Trevor Larnach, which made the score 7-6 in Iowa's favor. Duffey recovered by striking out Kyle Garlick. The win on the last Friday night fireworks show of the season gave the I-Cubs a 34-32 record in the second half of the International League season and kept their playoff hopes alive.

Five Iowa pitchers combined for a six-hit shutout against St. Paul on Sunday, September 17, the final home game of the season. The 1-0 victory extended the I-Cubs' winning streak to five games over the Saints and improved their season record to 79-62 and second-half mark to 36-32.

The I-Cubs scored the only run of the game in the second inning when P.J. Higgins singled and crossed home plate three batters later on a throwing error by St. Paul shortstop Michael Hellman. Cole Roederer and designated hitter Nelson Maldonado also singled in the inning, but Darius Hill grounded out with the bases loaded and two outs. The Saints had scoring opportunities in the second, third, and ninth innings, but failed to capitalize. A third-to-second-to-first base double play by the I-Cubs in the seventh extinguished another potential St. Paul scoring opportunity.

Starter Shane Greene allowed four hits and struck out three in three innings of work. His replacement, Chris Clarke, pitched two innings of one-hit ball, struck out two, and picked up the win. Jeremiah Estrada fanned one batter in sixth inning. His successor, Keegan Thompson, walked one hitter in the seventh. Left-hander Bailey Horn earned the save after giving up one hit and striking out one batter in the last two innings. The game drew 7,027 fans and took two hours to complete.

The I-Cubs extended their winning streak to eight games with a 7-6 victory at Louisville Thursday, September 21. It marked Iowa's longest winning streak since May 4-11, 2007. P.J. Higgins gave the I-Cubs a short-lived lead with a solo home run in the ninth inning. In the bottom of the ninth, however, a double by Jhonny Pereda tied the score at 6-6. At first, it appeared Pereda had a walk-off home run for the Bats, but the umpires ruled the ball hit below the yellow line on the outfield wall.

In the tenth, Brennan Davis knocked in the winning run with a single through the right side of the infield. Reliever Tyler Duffy struck out the side in the bottom of the inning to earn his second save of the season.

Matt Mervis gave Iowa an early 1-0 lead in the first inning with his twenty-second home run of the season. Jose Barrero's solo homer in the second tied the score at 1-1. Louisville forged ahead with four runs in the bottom of the fourth thanks to run-scoring singles. In the sixth, the I-Cubs' Darius Hill drove in a run with a triple and scored himself when the throw to home landed in the Bats' dugout. Iowa scored twice in the seventh on singles by Higgins and Hill. Hill went three-for-five at the plate with a triple and two runs-batted-in.

Despite missing the playoffs, the I-Cubs finished 82-65 and set several franchise single-season records in 2023. Their pitching staff struck out 1,395 batters, breaking the one-year-old record of 1,367. On the other hand, the pitching staff had a WHIP (walks and hits per inning pitched) of 1.55, a franchise record. Offensively, the I-Cubs established new highs with 5,762 total plate appearances, 892 runs scored, 856 runs-batted-in, 729 walks, ninety hit by pitches, and 538 extra-base hits. Their on-base percentage of .368 tied a forty-nine-year-old record. Their 207 home runs were nine fewer than the record of 216 in 1998. Jonathan Perlaza had the best season individually. The minor league veteran led the team in runs scored, one hundred; hits, 131; doubles, forty; home runs, twenty-three; runs-batted-in, eighty-five; walks, seventy-six; strikeouts, 119 (tied); and total bases, 246. Caleb Killian led the pitching staff with eight wins.

The franchise has been blessed with owners and front office personnel, such as Charles Sherman, William Park, Tom Fairweather, Lee Keyser, Ray Johnston, Ken Grandquist, Michael Gartner, Sioux City native Salty Saltwell, John Holland, and Sam Bernabe. J.L. Wilkinson of Algona was ahead of his time with his multi-national team that was based in Des Moines before moving to Kansas City, where it became a power in the Negro Leagues.

New York Yankee sluggers Babe Ruth and Lou Gehrig brought their exciting brand of baseball to Des Moines during the Roaring Twenties. Lee Keyser put Des Moines on the national map with the first nationally broadcast professional baseball game under permanent lights. Negro Leagues stars such as Satchel Paige, Buck O'Neil, Willie Wells Sr., Willard Brown, and Turkey Stearns played in Des Moines before the major leagues were integrated. Central Iowa baseball fans also got to see one of their own, Bob Feller of Van Meter, pitch in two exhibition games.

Hall of Famers Ryne Sandberg, Tony LaRussa, Harold Baines, Goose Gossage, and Greg Maddux either managed or played at Sec Taylor Stadium or Principal Park. Des Moines holds the distinction of being one of the few cities with teams in three triple-A leagues at one time or another: American Association, Pacific Coast League, and International League. Even though the worldwide pandemic knocked out the 2020 season, the Iowa Cubs continue to entertain thousands of fans each year.

With the 2023 season in the books, central Iowa baseball fans can look forward to Opening Day on Friday, March 29, 2024, in Omaha.

ENDNOTES

CHAPTER 1

[1] "A League Nine For Des Moines," *Iowa State Register*, September 17, 1886: 7.

[2] John Liepa, "Professional Baseball Comes To Des Moines," *2014 Iowa Cubs Yearbook*, 43.

[3] "A League Nine For Des Moines," *Iowa State Register*.

[4] "Our Base Ball Boys," *Persinger's Saturday Times*, March 26, 1887: 1.

[5] "Our Base Ball Boys," *Persinger's Saturday Times*.

[6] "The New Des Moines Club," *The Sporting News*, December 31, 1886.

[7] "Our Base Ball Boys," *Persinger's Saturday Times*.

[8] "The Death Of Mr. W.A. Park," *Iowa State Register*, April 3, 1897: 3.

[9] "William Albert Park," *History of the City of Des Moines and Polk County*, 292.

[10] The two games against the Browns on March 30-31 were rained out. "Our Boys At Home," *Iowa State Register*, April 2, 1887: 8.

[11] The players' pictures also appeared in *The Sporting News* on Saturday, April 30, 1887. At the time, *The Sporting News* printed about 56,500 copies a week.

[12] Liepa, "Professional Baseball Comes To Des Moines," 43-44.

[13] "Our Base Ball Boys," *Persinger's Saturday Times*.

[14] "Our Base Ball Boys," *Persinger's Saturday Times*.

[15] "Our Base Ball Boys," *Persinger's Saturday Times*.

[16] "Our Base Ball Boys," *Persinger's Saturday Times*.

[17] "Our Base Ball Boys," *Persinger's Saturday Times*.

[18] "Our Base Ball Boys," *Persinger's Saturday Times*.

[19] "Our Base Ball Boys," *Persinger's Saturday Times*.

[20] "Our Base Ball Boys," *Persinger's Saturday Times*.

[21] "Our Base Ball Boys," *Persinger's Saturday Times*.

[22] "Our Base Ball Boys," *Persinger's Saturday Times*.

[23] "Our Base Ball Boys," *Persinger's Saturday Times*

[24] "Our Base Ball Boys," *Persinger's Saturday Times*.

[25] "Our Base Ball Boys," *Persinger's Saturday Times*.

[26] "Our Base Ball Boys," *Persinger's Saturday Times*.

[27] "A Banquet," *Iowa State Register*, April 15, 1887: 6.

[28] "A Banquet," *Iowa State Register*.

[29] "A Banquet," *Iowa State Register*.

[30] "North Western," *The Sporting News*, April 30, 1887: 3.

31 "North Western," *The Sporting News.*

32 "We Got 'Em," *Iowa State Register*, May 1, 1887: 16

33 Hutchinson, a 5-foot-9-inch, 175-pound righthander, compiled a 180-158 record over seven seasons for the Chicago White Stockings, who eventually became the Chicago Cubs. During that span, he completed 317 of 339 starts. He had records of 41-25 in 1890, 44-19 in 1891, and 36-36 in 1892. He completed sixty-five games in 1890, fifty-six games in 1891, and sixty-seven in 1892. He had a lifetime WAR (wins above replacement value) of 38.9. Baseball-reference.com, accessed June 14, 2023.

34 Lloyd Johnson and Miles Wolff, *Encyclopedia of Minor League Baseball*, Third Edition (Durham, N.C.: Baseball   America, 2007), 148.

35 The eight original members of the Western Association were Des Moines, Chicago, Milwaukee, Minneapolis, St. Paul, Omaha, Kansas City, and St. Louis. St. Louis disbanded on June 20, 1888, and was replaced by   Sioux   City. After playing its last game on August 18, 1888, Minneapolis sold its franchise to Davenport. "1888," *Encyclopedia of Minor League Baseball*, 152.

36 "Formation of the Western Association," *Chicago Tribune*, October 27, 1887: 6.

37 "Around the bases," *Iowa State Register*, January 22, 1888: 12.

38 "The National Game," *Iowa State Register*, February 5, 1888: 12.

39 "The National Game," *Iowa State Register.*

40 "Spring sports," *Iowa State Register*, April 8, 1888: 16.

41 "First victory," *Iowa State Register*, April 29, 1888: 23.

42 "First victory," *Iowa State Register.*

43 "The Des Moines Club," *The Sporting News*, June 2, 1888: 1.

44 "The Des Moines Club," *The Sporting News.*

45 "The Des Moines Club," *The Sporting News.*

46 "The Des Moines Club," *The Sporting News.*

47 "The Des Moines Club," *The Sporting News.*

48 "The Des Moines Club," *The Sporting News.*

49 "The Des Moines Club," *The Sporting News.*

50 "The Des Moines Club," *The Sporting News.*

51 "The Des Moines Club," *The Sporting News.*

52 "The Des Moines Club," *The Sporting News.*

53 "The Des Moines Club," *The Sporting News.*

54 "The Des Moines Club," *The Sporting News.*

55 "The Des Moines Club," *The Sporting News.*

56 Hutchison had a 180-158 record with a 3.56 earned run average with the Chicago White Stockings and Colts, the predecessors of the Chicago Cubs, from 1889 to 1895. In that seven-year span, he pitched in 358 games, started 339, completed 317, struck out 1,225, and walked 1,109. He also pitched in 3,022 1/3 innings and had twenty-one shutouts. In seventy-one games with the Colts in 1890, he had a 41-25 record, a 2.70 earned run average, and five shutouts. In 1891, he finished 44-19 with a 2.81 earned run average and four shutouts. www.baseball-reference.com/players/h/hutchbi01.shtml, accessed August 3, 2023.

57 Liepa, "Professional Baseball Comes To Des Moines," 44.

[58] Ralph Christian, "Memorable Moments in Des Moines Baseball," prepared for the Field of Dreams Chapter of the Society for American Baseball Research, 2002.

[59] "Base Ball News of the Week," *Des Moines Leader*, February 9, 1896: 15.

[60] "Base Ball News of the Week," *Des Moines Leader*.

[61] "Base Ball News of the Week," *Des Moines Leader*.

[62] "Base Ball News of the Week," *Des Moines Leader*.

[63] "Base Ball News of the Week," *Des Moines Leader*.

[64] "Base Ball News of the Week," *Des Moines Leader*.

[65] "Base Ball," *Des Moines Leader*, March 15, 1896: 20.

[66] "Base Ball," *Des Moines Leader*.

[67] "The Millers Defeated," *Des Moines Leader*, April 5, 1896: 8.

[68] "The Millers Defeated," *Des Moines Leader*.

[69] "May Lose the Champions," *Des Moines Leader*, June 23, 1896: 1.

[70] "May Lose the Champions," *Des Moines Leader*.

[71] "Base Ball Stock Company," *Des Moines Leader*, August 12, 1896: 4

[72] "Pennant Waves But Champions Lose To Omaha 11 To 2," *Des Moines Register and Leader*, June 2, 1910: 8.

[73] Johnson and Wolff, *Encyclopedia of Minor League Baseball*, 171.

[74] "Pennant Waves But Champions Lose To Omaha 11 To 2," *Des Moines Register and Leader*.

[75] "The Death of Mr. W.A. Park," *Iowa State Register*.

[76] "The Death of Mr. W.A. Park," *Iowa State Register*.

[77] *Iowa State Register*, April 10, 1897: 6.

[78] *Iowa State Register*, April 10, 1897.

[79] *Iowa State Register*, April 10, 1897.

[80] *Iowa State Register, April 10, 1897.*

[81] "Stops All Games on Sunday," *Iowa State Register*, April 13, 1897: 6.

[82] "Base Ball," *Des Moines Leader*, August 7, 1897: 15.

[83] "We Beat the Cherries Bad," *Iowa State Register*, June 19, 1897: 7.

[84] "Des Moines May Drop Out," *Iowa State Register*, August 10, 1897: 5.

[85] Ralph Christian, "Memorable Moments in Des Moines Baseball," prepared for the Field of Dreams Chapter of the Society for American Baseball Research, 2002.

[86] "No League Franchise," *Des Moines Leader*, January 28, 1898: 6.

[87] Christian, "Memorable Moments In Des Moines Baseball."

[88] "No League Franchise," *Des Moines Leader*, January 28, 1898: 6.

[89] "No League Franchise," *Des Moines Leader*.

[90] "No League Franchise," *Des Moines Leader*.

CHAPTER 2

[1] "Baseball A Go For 1900," *Des Moines Register*, February 13, 1900: 8.

[2] "Baseball Now Assured," *Des Moines Leader*, March 7, 1900: 4.

[3] "Baseball Now Assured," *Des Moines Leader*.

4 "Baseball A Go For 1900," *Des Moines Register*.

5 "Team Is Now Complete," *Des Moines Register*, March 27, 1900: 2.

6 "Team Is Now Complete," *Des Moines Register*.

7 "Team Is Now Complete," *Des Moines Register*.

8 "Team Is Now Complete," *Des Moines Register*.

9 "Team Is Now Complete," *Des Moines Register*.

10 "Team Is Now Complete," *Des Moines Register*.

11 "Team Is Now Complete," *Des Moines Register*.

12 "Team Is Now Complete," *Des Moines Register*.

13 "Baseball Now Assured," *Des Moines Leader*: 4

14 "Baseball Now Assured," Des Moines Leader.

15 A group of businessmen organized Highland Park College in 1899. The cornerstone was laid in the fall of 1899 and the college opened in September 1890. In 1920, it merged with Central College and Des Moines College to become Des Moines University. The school closed in 1929. The Park Fair Mall now occupies the site. Iowaheritage.org, accessed May 13, 2023. Notable alumni include architect and engineer Archie Alexander of Ottumwa; actor Conrad Nagel of Keokuk; railroad executive Ralph Budd of Waterloo; jurist William Christianson of Moody County, South Dakota; and U.S. Rep. Sydney Anderson of Zumbrota, Minnesota.

16 "Auditorium Dedicated," *Des Moines Leader*, August 29, 1899.

17 "Auditorium Dedicated," *Des Moines Leader*.

18 "Auditorium Dedicated," *Des Moines Leader*.

19 "Team Is Now Complete," *Des Moines Register*.

20 "Outlook At Des Moines," *The Sporting News*, October 31, 1903: 6.

21 "Outlook At Des Moines," *The Sporting News*.

22 "Outlook At Des Moines," *The Sporting News*.

23 "Name Ball Team The Politicians," *Des Moines Register and Leader*, April 10, 1904: 8.

24 "Name Ball Team The Politicians," *Des Moines Register and Leader*.

25 "Name Ball Team The Politicians," *Des Moines Register and Leader*.

26 "To Select Name For Local Club," *Des Moines Register and Leader*, April 7, 1904: 7.

27 "To Select Name For Local Club," *Des Moines Register and Leader*.

28 "Des Moines Weakness," *The Sporting News*, April 16, 1904: 5.

29 "Des Moines Weakness," *The Sporting News*.

30 *Des Moines Register*, April 11, 1904: 2.

31 *Des Moines Register*, April 11, 1904: 2.

32 *Des Moines Register*, April 11, 1904: 2.

33 *Des Moines Register*, April 11, 1904: 2.

34 "Callahan Out Of the Game," *Des Moines Register and Leader*, April 12, 1904: 9.

35 "Politicians Lose Opening Game," *Des Moines Register and Leader*, April 25, 1904: 2.

36 "Denver Club Makes It Four Straight," *Des Moines Register and Leader*, April 28, 1904: 7.

37 "Entire Change Of Baseball Officers," *Des Moines Register and Leader*, December 11, 1904: 9.

38 "Cantillon Talks On Hitting Proposition," *Des Moines Register and Leader*, December 17, 1904: 4.

39 "Bill Rourke In Des Moines," *Des Moines Register and Leader*, December 10, 1904: 7.

40 "Cantillon Talks On Hitting Proposition," *Des Moines Register and Leader*.

41 "Pennant Waves But Champions Lose To Omaha 11 To 2," *Des Moines Register and Leader*, June 2, 1910: 8.

42 "Des Moines Is Victor After Great Finish," *Des Moines Evening Tribune*, September 29, 1909: 1.

43 "Des Moines Is Victor After Great Finish," *Des Moines Evening Tribune*.

44 "Des Moines Is Victor After Great Finish," *Des Moines Evening Tribune*.

45 "Des Moines Is Victor After Great Finish," *Des Moines Evening Tribune*.

46 "Des Moines Is Victor After Great Finish," *Des Moines Evening Tribune*.

47 "Love Feat For Joyous Fans," *Des Moines Evening Tribune*, September 29, 1909: 7.

48 "Love Feat For Joyous Fans," *Des Moines Evening Tribune*.

49 "Love Feat For Joyous Fans," *Des Moines Evening Tribune*.

50 "Love Feat For Joyous Fans," *Des Moines Evening Tribune*.

51 "How Sioux City Feels," *Des Moines Evening Tribune*, September 30, 1909: 6.

52 "How Sioux City Feels," *Des Moines Evening Tribune*.

53 "Des Moines Is Victor After Great Finish," *Des Moines Evening Tribune*.

CHAPTER 3

1 "Charles M. Sherman Dies," *Des Moines Register and Leader*, September 2, 1911: 2.

2 Norman Coder, "Fairweather Still Sees Sunny Side After 42 Years in O.B.," *Des Moines News*, 1949.

3 Coder, "Fairweather Still Sees Sunny Side After 42 Years in O.B."

4 "Mirrors of Iowa," *Des Moines News*, January 20, 1919.

5 "Tom Fairweather Deserts Politics for Dairy Farming," *Des Moines Register*, July 10, 1933, 12.

6 "Dwyer To Lincoln," *The Sporting News*, February 15, 1912: 5.

7 "Dwyer To Lincoln," *The Sporting News*.

8 "Dwyer To Lincoln," *The Sporting News*.

9 "Dwyer To Lincoln," *The Sporting News*.

10 "Des Moines' Opportunity," *Des Moines Tribune*, August 5, 1915: 6.

11 "Des Moines' Opportunity," *Des Moines Tribune*.

12 Ralph Christian, "Wilkie: James Leslie Wilkinson and the Iowa Years," *Iowa Heritage Illustrated*, Spring 2006, 41.

13 Christian, "Wilkie: James Leslie Wilkinson and the Iowa Years."

____

14 "Union Giants Whip All-Nations Club," *Des Moines Register and Leader*, September 20, 1915: 6.

15 Sec Taylor, "Musser To Oppose Former Teammate," *Des Moines Register*, May 1, 1917: 8.

16 Taylor, "Musser To Oppose Former Teammate."

17 Sec Taylor, "Some Of Boosters Who Open Local Baseball Season Today," *Des Moines Register*, May 1, 1917: 8.

18 Sec Taylor, "Boosters Open Local Season With Brilliant 13 Inning Victory," *Des Moines Register*, May 2, 1917: 6.

19 Taylor, "Boosters Open Local Season With Brilliant 13 Inning Victory."

20 "Would Modify Blue Law," *Des Moines Register*, April 13, 1917: 4.

21 "Blue Laws Will Remain Unchanged," *Des Moines Register*, April 17, 1917: 4.

22 "Western League Season To Open Tomorrow Afternoon," *Des Moines Tribune*, April 17, 1917: 10.

23 "Western League Season To Open Tomorrow Afternoon," *Des Moines Tribune*.

24 "Better Go Slow," *Des Moines Tribune*, April 26, 1917: 6.

25 "Better Go Slow," *Des Moines Tribune*.

26 "Better Go Slow," *Des Moines Tribune*.

27 "Sunday Lid Put On At Midnight," *Des Moines Register*, May 13, 1917: 11.

28 "Sunday Lid Put On At Midnight," *Des Moines Register*.

29 "Blue Law Lid To Go Down All Over Iowa Next Sunday," *Des Moines Register*, May 18, 1917: 1.

30 "Blue Law Lid To Go Down All Over Iowa Next Sunday," *Des Moines Register*.

31 "Blue Law Lid To Go Down All Over Iowa Next Sunday," *Des Moines Register*.

32 "Here's What You May and May Not Do on Sunday, a la Havner," *Des Moines Tribune*, May 23, 1917: 3.

33 "Druggists Return To Safe Side," *Des Moines Register*, May 20, 1917: 1.

34 "Boosters End Home Stay By Taking Tenth Straight Game, 10 To 8," *Des Moines Register*, May 21, 1917: 6.

35 "Havner Not Told of Meyer Decision," *Des Moines Register*, May 23, 1917: 3.

CHAPTER 4

1 Sec Taylor, "King of Swat Has Busy Day on Visit Here," *Des Moines Register*, October 28, 1926: 15.

2 Jack North, "Ruth Thrills Fans With Three Long Home Runs," *Des Moines Tribune*, October 28, 1926: 23.

3 North, "Ruth Thrills Fans With Three Long Home Runs."

4 Ruth compiled a 94-46 record and a 2.28 earned run average in ten seasons pitching for the Boston Red Sox and New York Yankees. In 1916, he was 23-12 for

Boston with a 1.75 earned run average. In 1917, he finished 24-13 with a 2.01 earned run average for the Red Sox.

[5] North, "Ruth Thrills Fans With Three Long Home Runs."

[6] Taylor, "King of Swat Has Busy Day on Visit Here."

[7] Des Moines Demons, www.baseball-reference.com/bullpen/Des_Moines_Demons, accessed May 31, 2023.

[8] Harlan Miller, "Bush Hurlers Get My Goat," *Des Moines Tribune*, October 1, 1927: 1.

[9] Sec Taylor, "Ruth, Gehrig Fail To Hit Homers," *Des Moines Register*, October 18, 1927: 7.

[10] Miller, "Bush Hurlers Get My Goat."

CHAPTER 5

[1] Bob Rives, "Good Night," *A Review of Baseball History*, 1998, 22.

[2] Mark Metcalf, "Organized Baseball's Night Birth," *Fall 2016 Baseball Research Journal* (Phoenix, Arizona: Society for American Baseball Research, 2016).

[3] Metcalf, "Organized Baseball's Night Birth."

[4] "Night Baseball To Make Debut at League Park," *Des Moines Tribune*, May 2, 1930: 41.

[5] "Night Baseball To Make Debut at League Park, *Des Moines Tribune*.

[6] Bert McGrane, "Keyser the Pioneer As Night Baseball Becomes Reality in Des Moines," *Des Moines Register*, May 1, 1930: 15.

[7] McGrane, "Keyser the Pioneer As Night Baseball Becomes Reality in Des Moines."

[8] McGrane, "Keyser the Pioneer As Night Baseball Becomes Reality in Des Moines."

[9] "Will Baseball Bugs Become Night Hawks?" *The Literary Digest*, May 31, 1930.

[10] Sec Taylor, "Tinning Will Pitch Opener," *Des Moines Register*, May 1, 1930: 15.

[11] Sec Taylor, "Tinning Will Pitch Opener."

[12] "D.M. Is Sport Center Today," *Des Moines Register*, May 2, 1930.

[13] Mike Wellman, "Long before Iowa Cubs baseball, Des Moines Demons hosted first professional game under permanent lights," *Des Moines Register*, April 30, 2015.

[14] Gayle Hayes, "Demons Pound Out 13-6 Triumph In Night Contest," *Des Moines Tribune*, May 3, 1930: 8.

[15] Hayes, "Demons Pound Out 13-6 Triumph In Night Contest."

[16] "Managers, Umpires and Players Approve Contest," *Des Moines Register*, May 3, 1930: 8.

[17] Keyes played minor-league baseball for seventeen years from 1924 to 1940 when he was forty years old. He also played for Des Moines in 1936 when he hit .287 with twenty home runs and eighty-one RBIs at age thirty-six. He finished his

career with a .324 batting average, 2,652 hits, 510 doubles, 200 triples, 344 home runs, and 4,594 total bases. Baseball-reference.com, accessed May 3, 2023.

18 "Managers, Umpires and Players Approve Contest," *Des Moines Register*:

19 "Managers, Umpires and Players Approve Contest," *Des Moines Register*:

20 "Managers, Umpires and Players Approve Contest," *Des Moines Register*: 7.

21 "Managers, Umpires and Players Approve Contest," *Des Moines Register*.

22 Hayes, "Demons Pound Out 13-6 Triumph In Night Contest."

23 UPI, "Night Baseball Thrills Fans," *Wichita Beacon*, May 3, 1930.

24 Roy Sourbeer, "Trailing the Game," *Wichita Beacon*, May 3, 1930.

25 Bert McGrane, "Officials All Pleased With Night Contest," *Des Moines Register*, May 3, 1930: 7-8.

26 McGrane, "Officials All Pleased With Night Contest."

27 "Will Baseball Bugs Become Night Hawks?" *The Literary Digest.*

28 John Liepa, "Cy Slapnicka," *2015 Iowa Cubs Yearbook*, 46. Slapnicka's other signings for Cleveland included Earl Averill, Bobby Avila, Lou Boudreau, Gordy Coleman, Mel Harder, Jim Hegan, Ken Keltner, Roger Maris, Herb Score, and Dick Stigman.

29 "Will Baseball Bugs Become Night Hawks?" *The Literary Digest.*

30 Bert McGrane, "Officials All Pleased With Night Contest."

31 McGrane, "Officials All Pleased With Night Contest," 7.

32 McGrane, "Officials All Pleased With Night Contest," 8.

33 McGrane, "Officials All Pleased With Night Contest," 8.

34 McGrane, "Officials All Pleased With Night Contest," 8.

35 McGrane, "Officials All Pleased With Night Contest," 8.

36 McGrane, "Officials All Pleased With Night Contest," 8.

37 "3,311 Autos At Ballpark," *Des Moines Register*, May 3, 1930: 1.

38 "Wichita Loses Second Ball Game Played Under Flood Lights," *Wichita Eagle*, May 4, 1930: 12.

39 Associated Press, "16 Killed in Midwest Storms," *Des Moines Register*, May 2, 1930: 1.

40 Second-place Rock Island, Illinois, played thirty-one of its sixty-three home games under the lights and drew 43,404, up 23,266. Waterloo played forty-seven out of sixty-three home games at night and drew 41,630 fans, up 15,851. Moline, Illinois, played thirty-one home games under the lights and attracted 34,292 fans, up 15,126. Keokuk had only twenty-one home night games and drew about 34,000, up about 3,772. Davenport, the 1929 attendance leader, played no home games during the day and slipped to 30,622, down 11,571. Burlington played twenty-nine home games under the lights and drew 29,207, up 1,970. League-champion Cedar Rapids, which played all day home games, totaled 27,650 fans, up 5,077. Dubuque garnered 24,104 fans, down 1,021. Attendance overall totaled 264,909 compared to 212,439 in 1929. "Night Baseball in Mississippi Valley Loop Seems Permanent Fixture," *Des Moines Register*, September 13, 1930: 8.

41 Mike Wellman, "Long before Iowa Cubs baseball, Des Moines Demons hosted first professional game under permanent lights," desmoinesregister.com, accessed May 3, 2023.

42 "Death Claims W.P. Chase, 64," *Des Moines Register*, June 20, 1934: 18.

43 Sec Taylor, "Sittin' In With the Athletes," *Des Moines Register*, October 5, 1936: 5.

44 Leighton Housh, "Feller Stars In Exhibition Game, " *Des Moines Register,* October 8, 1936: 15.

45 Associated Press, "Landis Rules Feller Indian Property Club Must Pay Des Moines $7,500 Keyser Says Decision Wise and Just," *Des Moines Tribune*, December 10, 1936: 27.

46 Associated Press, "Landis Rules Feller Indian Property Club Must Pay Des Moines $7,500 Keyser Says Decision Wise and Just."

47 Associated Press, "Landis Rules Feller Indian Property Club Must Pay Des Moines $7,500 Keyser Says Decision Wise and Just."

48 Associated Press, "Landis Rules Feller Indian Property Club Must Pay Des Moines $7,500 Keyser Says Decision Wise and Just."

49 I.N.S., "Bob Indignant," *Des Moines Tribune*, December 10, 1936: 27.

50 Associated Press, "Keyser Not Entitled to $7,500, Says Feller's Dad," *Des Moines Tribune*, December 10, 1936: 27.

51 Paul Mickelson, "Moguls Place Big Fortune On Feller's Head," *Des Moines Register*, October 8, 1936: 15.

52 Associated Press, "Landis Rules Feller Indian Property Club Must Pay Des Moines $7,500 Keyser Says Decision Wise and Just."

53 Bob Feller with Burton Rocks, *Bob Feller's Little Black Book of Baseball Wisdom* (Lincolnwood, Illinois: Contemporary Books, 2001), 16-17.

54 Feller with Rocks, *Bob Feller's Little Black Book of Baseball Wisdom,* 17.

55 Feller with Rocks, *Bob Feller's Little Black Book of Baseball Wisdom,* 60.

56 "1937," *Encyclopedia of Minor League Baseball (Durham, North Carolina, Baseball America, Inc., 2007)*, 355.

57 Sec Taylor, "Sittin' In With the Athletes," *Des Moines Register*, May 18, 1937: 7.

58 Taylor, "Sittin' In With the Athletes."

59 Kevin Warneke and John Shorey, "Major League Baseball in Iowa: Iowa's History of Hosting Negro League Contests," *The National Pastime: Heart of the Midwest*, Society for American Baseball Research, 2023. sabr.org, accessed July 29, 2023.

60 Warneke and Shorey, "Major League Baseball in Iowa: Iowa's History of Hosting Negro League Contests."

61 Warneke and Shorey, "Major League Baseball in Iowa: Iowa's History of Hosting Negro League Contests."

62 Warneke and Shorey, "Major League Baseball in Iowa: Iowa's History of Hosting Negro League Contests."

63 Cincinnati Tigers, retroseasons.com/team/cincinnati-tigers/, accessed July 29, 2023.

64 "Strong Negro Nines to Play," *Des Moines Register*, July 28, 1938: 9.

65 "Brown's Bat Lets Monarch Club Win, 11-2," *Des Moines Register*, May 27, 1939: 7.

66 "Brown's Bat Lets Monarch Club Win, 11-2," *Des Moines Register*.

67 "Brown's Bat Lets Monarch Club Win, 11-2," *Des Moines Register*.

68 "Brown's Bat Lets Monarch Club Win, 11-2," *Des Moines Register*.

69 "Negroes Clash Friday at Park," *Des Moines Register*, July 6, 1939: 8.

70 "Kansas City's Negro Team Beats Chicago," *Des Moines Register*, July 29, 1939: 9.

CHAPTER 6

1 Brad Wilson, "Monarchs Beat Giants, 7-3," *Des Moines Register*, June 11, 1940: 14.

2 Sec Taylor, "Sittin' In With the Athletes," *Des Moines Register*, June 10, 1940: 7.

3 Taylor, "Sittin' In With the Athletes."

4 "Grandstand Brings $2,200 At School District Auction," *Des Moines Register*, April 27, 1945: 9.

5 "Grandstand Brings $2,200 At School District Auction," *Des Moines Register*.

6 "Grandstand Brings $2,200 At School District Auction," *Des Moines Register*.

7 Sec Taylor, "Bruins Bonness tops Lincoln on 3 hits," *Des Moines Register*, June 21, 1947: 8.

8 Michael Gartner, "Welcome to Principal Park. We're glad you're here!" *2014 Iowa Cubs Yearbook*, 11.

9 Gartner, "Welcome to Principal Park. We're glad you're here!"

10 Gartner, "Welcome to Principal Park. We're glad you're here!"

11 "Monarchs Meet Memphis Here," *Des Moines Register*, June 24, 1948: 14.

12 Bill Bryson, "Stabelfeld pitches no-hitter, 7-0," *Des Moines Register*, August 17, 1949: 13.

13 Bryson, "Stabelfeld pitches no-hitter, 7-0."

14 Sec Taylor, "Sittin' In With the Athletes," *Des Moines Register*, September 8, 1949: 13.

15 Taylor, "Sittin' In With the Athletes."

16 Bill Bryson, "D.M. Gains Playoffs, Beats Cubs," *Des Moines Register*, September 7, 1949: 13.

17 Taylor, "Sittin' In With the Athletes."

18 Bryson, "D.M. Gains Playoffs, Beats Cubs."

19 Bryson, "D.M. Gains Playoffs, Beats Cubs."

20 Taylor, "Sittin' In With the Athletes."

CHAPTER 7

1 Baker finished his second season in professional baseball by hitting .280 in 100 games for triple-A Los Angeles in the Pacific Coast League. Three years later, he formed the first Black double play combination in MLB history with shortstop Ernie Banks.

2 Bill Bryson, "Baker's Zip on Bases Dazzles Root," *Des Moines Tribune*, May 17, 1950: 31.

3 Bryson, "Baker's Zip on Bases Dazzles Root."

4 Bryson, "Baker's Zip on Bases Dazzles Root."

5 Bryson, "Baker's Zip on Bases Dazzles Root."

6 Bill Bryson, "Cubs Complete Deal for Baker," *Des Moines Tribune*, May 23, 1950: 18.

7 "Bruins To Get A Negro Short," *Des Moines Register*, May 16, 1950: 15.

8 "Fairweather Is Dead at 71," *Des Moines Tribune*, January 25, 1951: 1.

9 *Des Moines Tribune*, January 26, 1951: 16.

10 Tony Cordaro, "Minors to Hold Beauty Contest," *Des Moines Tribune*, January 27, 1951: 7.

11 Sec Taylor, "Sittin' In With the Athletes," *Des Moines Register*, February 9, 1951: 13.

12 Taylor, "Sittin' In With the Athletes."

13 Taylor, "Sittin' In With the Athletes."

14 Taylor, "Sittin' In With the Athletes."

15 In the National League the number of farm clubs per major league team were: Brooklyn, nineteen; St. Louis, sixteen; New York, fifteen; Chicago and Pittsburgh, fourteen each; Philadelphia, twelve; Boston, ten; and Cincinnati, five. In the American League, New York had fourteen; Cleveland, twelve; St. Louis, eleven; Philadelphia, nine; Boston, Chicago, and Detroit, eight each; and Washington, seven.

16 Taylor, "Sittin' In With the Athletes."

17 Tony Cordaro, "Hermanski and Ump Argue – Golf!" *Des Moines Tribune*, June 26, 1951:16 .

18 Bill Bryson, "Cubs Top Bruins, 9-0, Before 5,398," *Des Moines Register*, June 26, 1951: 13.

19 Bryson, "Cubs Top Bruins, 9-0, Before 5,398."

20 Bryson, "Cubs Top Bruins, 9-0, Before 5,398."

21 Cordaro, "Hermanski and Ump Argue – Golf!"

22 Cordaro, "Hermanski and Ump Argue – Golf!"

23 Bill Bryson, "Feller Takes It Easy, Bows to Stars, 8-5," *Des Moines Register*, October 15, 1951.

24 Bryson, "Feller Takes It Easy, Bows to Stars, 8-5."

25 Bill Bryson, "Kuncl Beats Cubs On 2-Hitter, 2-0," *Des Moines Register*, July 9, 1952: 13.

26 Maury White, "Garagiola Has Good Time Here," *Des Moines Tribune*, August 18, 1953: 18.

27 White, "Garagiola Has Good Time Here."

28 Sec Taylor, "Sittin' In With the Athletes," *Des Moines Register*, August 18, 1953: 9.

29 Tony Cordaro, "Cohen's Concern: Get It Over," *Des Moines Tribune*, July 13, 1954: 30.

30 "Clowns Win In 10th, 6-3," *Des Moines Register*, August 12, 1954.

31 "Clowns Win In 10th, 6-3," *Des Moines Register*.

32 Tony Cordaro, "Bruins Pass 100,000 Mark at Gate," *Des Moines Tribune*, September 6, 1954: 14.

33 Bill Bryson, "Bruins' 'Gashouse' Era Begins," *Des Moines Register*, July 9, 1955: 10.

34 Bill Bryson, "W.L. Attendance Up," *Des Moines Register*, September 23, 1955: 18.

35 Leighton Housh, "2,747 Watch Bruins Win, 8-3," *Des Moines Register*, August 12, 1956: 29.

36 Housh, "2,747 Watch Bruins Win, 8-3."

37 Housh, "2,747 Watch Bruins Win, 8-3."

38 Bill Bryson, "Wives-Bruins Tilt Saturday," *Des Moines Tribune*, August 6, 1956: 16.

39 Dick Stuart had a league-leading sixty-six home runs and 158 runs-batted-in for second-place Lincoln in 1956. Johnson and Wolff, *Encyclopedia of Minor League Baseball*, 488.

40 "Sec Taylor: Always 'Sittin' In With the Athletes," www.milb.com.

41 "Sec Taylor: Always 'Sittin' In With the Athletes," www.milb.com.

42 "Garner W. 'Sec' Taylor," *Des Moines Register*, January 16, 2022: 2G.

CHAPTER 8

1 "Sec Taylor Dies in Florida," *Des Moines Register*, February 26, 1965: 1.

2 "Garner W. (Sec) Taylor," *Des Moines Register*, February 28, 1965: 100.

3 "Garner W. (Sec) Taylor," *Des Moines Register*.

4 "Garner W. (Sec) Taylor," *Des Moines Register*.

5 "Sec Taylor Dies in Florida," *Des Moines Register*.

6 Bill Bryson, "Texan Would Take Gamble on D.M. Baseball," *Des Moines Tribune*, November 19, 1968: 19.

7 Bryson, "Texan Would Take Gamble on D.M. Baseball."

8 Bryson, "Texan Would Take Gamble on D.M. Baseball."

9 "Hope for Baseball In Des Moines," *Des Moines Tribune*, November 20, 1968: 28.

10 "Hope for Baseball In Des Moines," *Des Moines Tribune*.

11 Bill Bryson, "Begins Groundwork Today For Baseball Club Here," *Des Moines Register*, December 5, 1968: 23.

12 On December 4, 1968, the PCL did not back down on its demand of $1.1 million for the Seattle and San Diego territories.

13 Bryson, "Begins Groundwork Today For Baseball Club Here."

CHAPTER 9

1 Bill Bryson, "Oaks' Blue Fans 14 In Debut," *Des Moines Register*, April 30, 1970: 23.

2 Bill Bryson, "Blue's Deuces Not Wild," *Des Moines Tribune*, April 30, 1970: 30.

3 Bryson, "Blue's Deuces Not Wild."

4 Bryson, "Blue's Deuces Not Wild."

5 Bryson, "Blue's Deuces Not Wild."

6 Bryson, "Oaks' Blue Fans 14 In Debut, 7-1."

7 Ron Maly, "Blue's 3-Hitter Lifts Oaks, 4-0," *Des Moines Register*, May 7, 1970: 23.

8 Bill Bryson, "Carried Away With Oaks' Blue," *Des Moines Tribune*, June 26, 1970: 20.

9 Bryson, "Carried Away With Oaks' Blue."

10 Bryson, "Carried Away With Oaks' Blue."

11 Bill Fluty, "Oak Bats Alive for Sweep," *Des Moines Tribune*, August 28, 1970: 19.

12 Fluty, "Oak Bats Alive for Sweep."

13 Fluty, "Oak Bats Alive for Sweep."

14 Bill Bryson, "Oaks' Blue Yearns to Be Quarterback," *Des Moines Register*, April 16, 1970: 25.

15 Judy Borwick, interviewed by Steve Dunn, Des Moines Public Library, May 16, 2023.

16 Borwick, interview, May 16, 2023.

17 Borwick, interview, May 16, 2023.

18 Borwick, interview, May 16, 2023.

19 Borwick, interview, May 16, 2023.

20 The seven former Oaks on the Oakland A's roster in 1972 were pitchers Vida Blue and Dave Hamilton, catcher Gene Tenace, infielder Ron Clark, and outfielders Joe Rudi, George Hendrick, and Angel Mangual. Bill Bryson, "Bill Bryson," *Des Moines Tribune*, June 8, 1972: 36.

21 Howard Kluender, "7,277 See A's Trip Oaks in 10th," *Des Moines Register*, August 4, 1972: 23.

22 Maury White, "Homecoming for Locker," *Des Moines Register*, August 4, 1972: 23.

23 Bill Bryson, "Astros Drub Oaks, 10-2," *Des Moines Register*, August 22, 1975: 24.

24 Bryson, "Astros Drub Oaks, 10-2."

25 Phil Maly, "Sox-Oaks Show Goes On Despite Bad Weather," *Des Moines Tribune*, May 13, 1976: 25.

26 "White Sox's pitching puzzle still unsolved," *Des Moines Register*, May 13, 1976: 28.

27 Maly, "Sox-Oaks Show Goes On Despite Bad Weather."

28 Bill Bryson, "Wood Sharp As Sox Trim Oaks, 12-5," *Des Moines Register*, May 17, 1977: 23.

29 Ron Maly, "Smalley chip off old block – plays shortstop for D.M," *Des Moines Register*, May 24, 1977: 27.

30 Maly, "Smalley chip off old block – plays shortstop for D.M."

31 Wayne Grett, "Carew's bat comes alive, but Twins let Oaks win," *Des Moines Tribune*, May 24, 1977: 12.

32 Grett, "Carew's bat comes alive, but Twins let Oaks win."

33 Gene Raffensperger, "Oaks Kucek hurls no-hitter," *Des Moines Register*, May 27, 1978: 1S.

34 Raffensperger, "Oaks Kucek hurls no-hitter."

35 Raffensperger, "Oaks Kucek hurls no-hitter."

CHAPTER 10

1 David Westphal, "Oaks stay on D.M., group's deal," *Des Moines Tribune*, December 3, 1981: 21.

2 Westphal, "Oaks stay on D.M., group's deal."

3 Cindy Grandquist, interviewed by Steve Dunn, Des Moines Public Library, July 13, 2023.

4 Grandquist, interview, July 13, 2023.

5 Walter Shotwell, "Sports fan Grandquist going all out to keep Oaks in D. M.," *Des Moines Tribune*, December 1, 1981: 3.

6 Shotwell, "Sports fan Grandquist going all out to keep Oaks in D. M."

7 Marc Hansen, "Ray Johnston has done his part," *Des Moines Tribune*, November 18, 1981: 21.

8 Hansen, "Ray Johnston has done his part."

9 Hansen, "Ray Johnston has done his part."

10 Hansen, "Ray Johnston has done his part."

11 Hansen, "Ray Johnston has done his part."

12 "The Oaks will stay," *Des Moines Tribune*, December 4, 1981: 16.

13 "The Oaks will stay," *Des Moines Tribune*.

14 Grandquist, interview, July 13, 2023.

15 Grandquist, interview, July 13, 2023.

16 Gene Raffensperger, "Cubs Slate Exhibition In D.M.," *Des Moines Register*, January 13, 1981: 26.

17 Raffensperger, "Cubs Slate Exhibition In D.M."

18 Wayne Grett, "Hundley wants to run," *Des Moines Tribune*, January 13, 1981: 13.

19 Grett, "Hundley wants to run."

20 Gene Raffensperger, "Oaks hand Cubs another loss, 6-5," *Des Moines Register*, May 19, 1981: 13.

21 Mark Hansen, "It's only Cubs, but victory still gives Oaks lift," *Des Moines Tribune*, May 19, 1981: 11.

22 Raffensperger, "Oaks hand Cubs another loss, 6-5."

23 Hansen, "It's only Cubs, but victory still gives Oaks lift," 11-12.

24 David Westphal, "I-Cubs pound 'big brothers,' 7-2," *Des Moines Register*, June 4, 1982: 17.

25 Marc Hansen, "Fun time for 6,228 at old ballyard," *Des Moines Tribune*, June 4, 1982: 17.

26 Hansen, "Fun time for 6,228 at old ballyard."

27 Gary Heinlein, "'Cadillac Cubs' are on the move," *Des Moines Tribune*, July 17, 1982: 44.

28 Heinlein, "'Cadillac Cubs' are on the move."

29 Heinlein, "'Cadillac Cubs' are on the move."

30 Heinlein, "'Cadillac Cubs' are on the move."

31 David Westphal, "Cubs appear likely to remain in Iowa," *Des Moines Register*, September 4, 1982.

32 Eliot Nusbaum, "Triple-A rating for Cubs' Sec Taylor Stadium," *Des Moines Register*, April 14, 1983.

33 Bob Dyer, "Buckner's key hits lift Chicago over Iowa," *Des Moines Register*, May 15, 1984: 19.

34 Bob Dyer, "Patterson pitches no-hitter as I-Cubs edge Omaha, 2-0," *Des Moines Register*, August 22, 1984: 1S.

35 Dyer, "Patterson pitches no-hitter as I-Cubs edge Omaha, 2-0."

36 Dyer, "Patterson pitches no-hitter as I-Cubs edge Omaha, 2-0."

37 Wayne Grett, "Record crowd sees Chicago beat I-Cubs," *Des Moines Register*, May 31, 1985: 27.

38 Marc Hansen, "Dunston resigned to season in minors," *Des Moines Register*, May 31, 1985: 27.

39 Marc Hansen, "Big crowd watches I-Cubs beat parent club, 5-1," *Des Moines Register*, May 16, 1986: 26.

40 Hansen, "Big crowd watches I-Cubs beat parent club, 5-1."

41 Hansen, "Big crowd watches I-Cubs beat parent club, 5-1."

42 Fred Mitchell, "Sanderson says he's ready, proves it against Iowa," *Chicago Tribune*, April 21, 1987: 47.

43 Don Muret, "Homecoming," *Iowa City Press-Citizen*, April 19, 1988: 9.

44 Randy Peterson, "8,115 watch I-Cubs win lackluster exhibition," *Des Moines Register*, May 26, 1989: 24.

45 Peterson, "8,115 watch I-Cubs win lackluster exhibition," 10.

CHAPTER 11

1 Perry Beeman and Tom Witosky, "D.M. voters tell I-Cubs: Play Ball!" *Des Moines Register*, August 8, 1990: 1A, 4A.

2 Beeman and Witosky, "D.M. voters tell I-Cubs: Play Ball!"

3 Randy Peterson, "Fate of I-Cubs in voters' hands," *Des Moines Register*, August 1, 1990: 1S.

4 Beeman and Witosky, "D.M. voters tell I-Cubs: Play Ball!"

5 Randy Peterson, "Record 10,749 watch I-Cubs win," *Des Moines Register*, April 17, 1992: 26.

6 Peterson, "Record 10,749 watch I-Cubs win."

7 Peterson, "Record 10,749 watch I-Cubs win": 28.

8 Peterson, "Record 10,749 watch I-Cubs win."

9 Mark Hansen, "Game steals show – almost," *Des Moines Register*, April 17, 1992: 26.

¹⁰ Hansen, "Game steals show – almost": 28.

¹¹ Hansen, "Game steals show – almost": 26.

¹² Randy Peterson, "Look who's sitting in the stadium's new skyboxes," *Des Moines Register*, April 12, 1992: 25.

¹³ Randy Peterson, "I-Cubs Champs!" *Des Moines Register*, September 16, 1993.

¹⁴ Mark Hansen, "I-Cubs Win! I-Cubs Win!" *Des Moines Register*, September 16, 1993.

¹⁵ Hansen, "I-Cubs Win! I-Cubs Win!"

¹⁶ Randy Peterson, "While some hit it out, Iowa Cubs pull it off," *Des Moines Register*, July 10, 1997.

¹⁷ Mark Hansen, "Show is key with Triple-A All-Stars, not outcome," *Des Moines Register*, July 10, 1997.

¹⁸ Dan McCool, "Robinson urges fans to be hero, like her dad," *Des Moines Register*, July 10, 1997.

¹⁹ Randy Peterson, "Lasorda to visit Des Moines for All-Star game," *Des Moines Register*, July 6, 1997.

²⁰ Randy Peterson, "Sosa socks one in Des Moines," *Des Moines Register*, August 14, 1998: 27.

²¹ Peterson, "Sosa socks one in Des Moines."

²² Randy Peterson, "The boys are back in town," *Des Moines Register*, April 7, 1998: 17.

CHAPTER 12

¹ Sean Keeler, "Prior's debut on the Mark, out of sight," *Des Moines Register*, May 8, 2002: 23.

² Keeler, "Prior's debut on the Mark, out of sight."

³ Keeler, "Prior's debut on the Mark, out of sight."

⁴ Keeler, "Prior's debut on the Mark, out of sight."

⁵ Randy Peterson, "Bang-Bang Start," *Des Moines Register*, May 8, 2002: 23.

⁶ Randy Peterson, "Sec Taylor to become Principal Park," *Des Moines Register*, August 5, 2004.

⁷ Peterson, "Sec Taylor to become Principal Park."

⁸ Randy Peterson, "Record crowd watches Wood get fired up," *Des Moines Register*, June 25, 2005.

⁹ "2005 High School Tournament," *2006 Iowa Cubs Yearbook*, 63.

¹⁰ "A Milestone Season," *2006 Iowa Cubs Yearbook*, 65.

¹¹ A Milestone Season," *2006 Iowa Cubs Yearbook*, 11.

¹² Randy Peterson, "I-Cubs beat Sounds in an empty Principal Park," *Des Moines Register*, June 15, 2008: 3C.

¹³ Sam Bernabe, interviewed by Steve Dunn, Principal Park, Des Moines, February 9, 2016.

¹⁴ Randy Peterson, "Principal Park given back to flood-weary I-Cub fans," *Des Moines Register*, June 16, 2008: 3C.

¹⁵ Sean Keeler, "I-Cubs take over Wrigley," *Des Moines Register*, August 10, 2009: 11.

¹⁶ Keeler, "I-Cubs take over Wrigley": 12.

¹⁷ Keeler, "I-Cubs take over Wrigley": 12.

¹⁸ Keeler, "I-Cubs take over Wrigley": 12.

¹⁹ Sophia Ahmad, "Dave Matthews Band draws big cheers at the ballpark," *Des Moines Register*, September 26, 2009: 2B.

²⁰ Ahmad, "Dave Matthews Band draws big cheers at the ballpark."

²¹ Bernabe, interview, February 9, 2016.

CHAPTER 13

¹ "Iowa Cubs Manager Ryne Sandburg," *2010 Iowa Cubs Yearbook*, 16.

² "Iowa Cubs Manager Ryne Sandburg," *2010 Iowa Cubs Yearbook*, 17.

³ "Iowa Cubs Manager Ryne Sandburg," *2010 Iowa Cubs Yearbook*, 17.

⁴ "Iowa Cubs Manager Ryne Sandburg," *2010 Iowa Cubs Yearbook*, 17.

⁵ "Our Story," Iowa Sports Turf Management website, https://iowasportsturf.com, accessed June 14, 2023.

⁶ "Number, please," *2013 Iowa Cubs Yearbook*, 12.

⁷ "Sam Bernabe Named Baseball America MiLB Exec of Year," www.milb.com/news/gcs-102979426, accessed June 20, 2023.

⁸ Bernabe, interview, February 9, 2016.

⁹ Michael Gartner, "Welcome to Principal Park," *2015 Iowa Cubs Yearbook*, 11.

¹⁰ Gartner, "Welcome to Principal Park."

¹¹ "I-Cubs announce new fan safety measures," www.milb.com, December 31, 2015.

¹² Michael Gartner, "Welcome to Principal Park," *2016 Iowa Cubs Yearbook*, 11.

¹³ Michael Gartner, "Welcome to Principal Park," *2017 Iowa Cubs Yearbook*, 11.

¹⁴ Tommy Birch, "Marty Pevey sets Iowa Cubs managerial wins record," *Des Moines Register*, April 13, 2018: C2.

¹⁵ Tommy Birch, "Iowa Cubs plan to extend netting for 2020 season," https://www.desmoinesregister.com/story/sports/baseball/iowa-cubs/2019/05/31/iowa-cubs-extend-netting-foul-poles-albert-almora/1297861001, accessed May 24, 2020.

¹⁶ Tommy Birch, "Iowa Cubs reach PCL playoffs for 1st time since 2008. What's next?" *Des Moines Register*, September 1, 2019: C2.

¹⁷ Tommy Birch, "Iowa Cubs' season ends in PCL playoffs," *Des Moines Register*, September 9, 1919.

¹⁸ Birch, "Iowa Cubs' season ends in PCL playoffs."

CHAPTER 14

[1] Tommy Birch, "Iowa Cubs Broadcaster Alex Cohen is the subject of a new 'House Hunters' episode," *Des Moines Register*, March 29, 2021.

[2] Tommy Birch, "The Wait Is Over: Iowa Cubs Are Back," *Des Moines Register*, April 30, 2021: A1.

[3] "Provisional Mortality Data – United States, 2020," Centers for Disease Control and Prevention, https://www.cdc.gov/mmwr/volumes/70/wr/mm7014e1.htm, accessed August 7, 2023.

[4] Tommy Birch, "MiLB Finally Returns to Principal Park," *Des Moines Register*, May 6, 2021: B1.

[5] David Morrow, "Iowa Cubs see Marquee Network as tool to reach new fans," *Des Moines Register*, May 18, 2021: B1.

[6] Morrow, "Iowa Cubs see Marquee Network as tool to reach new fans."

[7] "Diamond Baseball Holdings will support the Iowa Cubs in every aspect of the fan experience, community involvement and partnership opportunities," www.milb.com, accessed March 8, 2022.

[8] "Diamond Baseball Holdings will support the Iowa Cubs in every aspect of the fan experience, community involvement and partnership opportunities," www.milb.com.

[9] "A letter to the Fans from Michael Gartner," www.milb.com, accessed March 8, 2022.

[10] "A letter to the Fans from Michael Gartner," www.milb.com.

[11] "D.M. leaders will have to look out for I-Cubs' future," *Des Moines Register*, December 19, 2021: 4OP.

[12] Tommy Birch, "Michael Gartner gave Iowa Cubs employees $600,000 from the team's sale. Here's how it went down," *Des Moines Register*, January 3, 2022, desmoinesregister.com, accessed July 1, 2023.

[13] Birch, "Michael Gartner gave Iowa Cubs employees $600,000 from the team's sale. Here's how it went down."

[14] Birch, "Michael Gartner gave Iowa Cubs employees $600,000 from the team's sale. Here's how it went down."

[15] Birch, "Michael Gartner gave Iowa Cubs employees $600,000 from the team's sale. Here's how it went down."

[16] Birch, "Michael Gartner gave Iowa Cubs employees $600,000 from the team's sale. Here's how it went down."

[17] Birch, "Michael Gartner gave Iowa Cubs employees $600,000 from the team's sale. Here's how it went down."

[18] Todd Magel, "Principal Park changes to block view of Capitol from batters," kcci.com, accessed April 20, 2022.

[19] Magel, "Principal Park changes to block view of Capitol from batters."

[20] Tyler Jett, "Iowa Cubs sold as Endeavor unloads minor league clubs after less than a year of ownership,"

https://www.desmoinesregister.com/story/money/business/2022/08/09/endeavor-sells-iowa-cubs-silver-lake-partners-amid-mlb-pressure/10281970002/, accessed July 20, 2023.

[21] Jett, "Iowa Cubs sold as Endeavor unloads minor league clubs after less than a year of ownership."

[22] Jett, "Iowa Cubs sold as Endeavor unloads minor league clubs after less than a year of ownership."

[23] Principal Park Master Plan, December 10, 2021: 3.

[24] Principal Park Master Plan, December 10, 2021.

[25] Principal Park Master Plan.

[26] Principal Park Master Plan.

[27] Principal Park Master Plan, 4.

[28] Principal Park Master Plan.

[29] "Perlaza Walks-Off Redbirds in Comeback Win," MiLB.com, accessed June 24, 2023.

Acknowledgments

This book would have not been possible without the help of several people. My brother, Jeff Dunn, an author of fiction and poetry in his own right, shared his knowledge of the book publishing industry.

Former Iowa Oaks employees Judy Borwick and Cindy Grandquist, the daughter of a former owner, graciously accepted my requests for interviews at the Des Moines Public Library.

The Reference Department staff at the Des Moines Public Library led me to biographies of notable Des Moines residents, city directories, and photos. The staff at the State Historical Society Research Center in Des Moines allowed me to look at and copy an issue of a Des Moines publication from 1887 that featured information and pictures of that season's ballclub.

Iowa Cubs president and general manager Sam Bernabe took time out from his busy schedule to write a forward for the book. Scott Sailor of the Iowa Cubs provided some photos of former Des Moines players. Noted Iowa baseball historian John Liepa contributed images of former Des Moines players and teams from his vast collection of Iowa baseball memorabilia and lent his third edition of the *Encyclopedia of Minor League Baseball*. I used a Des Moines baseball timeline compiled by Ralph Christian for the local Society for American Baseball Research chapter in 2002 as a guide.

Finally, thanks to Lynne Feldman for editing and proofreading the manuscript and Amazon Books Publishers for publishing and marketing the book. It truly takes a village to publish a book.

About the Author

Author Steve Dunn had four decades of newspaper experience before he retired in early 2014 and moved to Des Moines, Iowa. He worked as a reporter, sportswriter, and managing editor for daily and weekly newspapers in three states, including the last fifteen and a half years as managing editor of the *Daily Gate City* in Keokuk, Iowa.

He has written eleven bios and eleven game stories for the Society for American Baseball Research. Last year, he self-published a book about the history of professional baseball at the confluence of the Des Moines and Raccoon Rivers in Des Moines, *Principal Park: A Diamond in the Rough*. He and former state senator Pat Deluhery have published a book about the latter's political career called *Engaged: Pat Deluhery and the Golden Age of Democratic Party Activism*.

He and his wife, Cindy, have two daughters, two sons-in-law, and four grandchildren. His hobbies include bike riding, playing pickleball, volunteering at Capitol View Elementary School in Des Moines, participating in Des Moines Golden K Kiwanis Club activities, and playing his clarinet in the Greater Des Moines Community Band.